Practice Papers for SQA Exams

Higher

English

001/20032015

10 9 8 7 6 5 4 3 2 1

ISBN 9780007590988

Published by
Leckie & Leckie Ltd
An imprint of HarperCollins*Publishers*
Westerhill Road, Bishopbriggs, Glasgow, G64 2QT
T: 0844 576 8126 F: 0844 576 8131
leckieandleckie@harpercollins.co.uk
www.leckieandleckie.co.uk

Publisher: Fiona Burns
Project manager: Craig Balfour

Special thanks to
Roda Morrison (copy edit)
Louise Robb (proofread)
Jennifer Richards (proofread)
QBS (layout)
Ink Tank (cover)

Printed in Italy by Grafica Veneta S.P.A.

A CIP Catalogue record for this book is available from the British Library.

Acknowledgements

Extract from 'Aging' by Paulina Porizkova on pages 8–9, published in The Huffington Post and reproduced by permission of Paulina Porizkova; extract from 'Sorry, Rosie Huntington-Whiteley, but I don't buy into this idea of a female shelf life' by Barbara Ellen on pages 10–11, published in the Observer and reproduced by permission of Guardian News & Media Ltd; extract from 'Now's the Moment for Mindfulness' by Judith Woods on pages 52–53 published in the Telegraph and reproduced by permission of Telegraph Media Group Limited 2014; extract from 'The Art of Being Mindful' by Kate Pickert on pages 54–55 and extract from 'The Virtual Genius of Oculus Rift' by Lev Grossman on pages 96–97 © Time Inc. All rights reserved. Reprinted/Translated from TIME and published with permission of Time Inc. Reproduction in any manner in any language in whole or in part without written permission is prohibited; extract from 'Facebook's virtual reality gamble is (again) about data mining' by Joshua Kopstein on pages 98–99 published on Aljazeera America and reproduced by permission of Joshua Kopstein; extracts from *The Slab Boys* by John Byrne reproduced by permission of Casarotto Ramsay & Associates Ltd; Extracts from *The Cheviot, the Stag and the Black, Black Oil* by John McGrath reproduced by permission of Bloomsbury Methuen Drama, an imprint of Bloomsbury Publishing Plc; extracts from *Men Should Weep* by Ena Lamont Stewart reproduced by permission of Alan Brodie Representation; Extracts from 'Mother and Son', 'The Crater' and 'The Painter' by Iain Crichton Smith reproduced by permission of Birlinn Ltd; extracts from 'The Eye of the Hurricane', 'The Whaler's Return' and 'The Wireless Set' by George Mackay Brown reproduced by permission of Jenny Brown Associates; extracts from *The Trick is To Keep Breathing* by Janice Galloway published by Vintage and reprinted by permission of The Random House Group Limited; extracts from *The Cone-Gatherers* by Robin Jenkins reproduced by permission of Canongate Books Ltd; 'Anne Hathaway', 'Mrs Midas' and 'Valentine' by Carol Ann Duffy reproduced by permission of Pan MacMillan and author c/o Rogers Coleridge & White Ltd; 'Last Supper', 'The Bargain' and 'My Rival's House' by Liz Lochhead reproduced by permission of Birlinn Ltd; 'Aunt Julia', 'Basking Shark' and 'Visiting Hour' by Norman MacCaig reproduced by permission of Birlinn Ltd; 'An Autumn Day', 'Hallaig' and 'XIX I Gave You Immortality' by Sorely MacLean reproduced by permission of Birlinn Ltd; 'Nil Nil', 'The Thread' and 'Two Trees' by Don Paterson reproduced by permission of Rogers, Coleridge and White and Faber & Faber.

Whilst every effort has been made to trace the copyright holders, in cases where this has been unsuccessful, or if any have inadvertently been overlooked, the Publishers would gladly receive any information enabling them to rectify any error or omission at the first opportunity.

Introduction

This book contains three brand new and complete question papers for Higher English, which are in line with the new SQA Higher English exam in question style, level, layout and appearance. It will be a valuable tool in your exam preparation; you will not only become familiar with the style of exam paper you are going to sit, but you will also develop your understanding of the texts through exam practice and applying the detailed, thoughtful marking schemes in this book to your own answers.

In the marking schemes there is not only guidance on the allocation of marks, but also fully worked answers to each question. The marking schemes are designed to make it clear to you what the answer is and how it has been derived.

In addition to this, there are useful hints and tips that remind you of correct exam technique in order to maximise your success.

To derive the most benefit from these practice papers, you might:

- Revise specific sections of the exam such as the Scottish set texts. Make sure you use the answer scheme AFTER you have attempted the questions. Make a note of any points you have missed and include these in your future revision of the text.
- Revise specific question types in the Reading for Understanding, Analysis and Evaluation paper by selecting your chosen focus and completing these questions in full before using the marking scheme. Again, note areas for development and focus on these in future revision.
- Attempt the full paper in the time allocated. This is best done close to the exam and will show you how prepared you are and also how best to manage your time effectively.

The external assessment of Higher English is divided into Part 1: Reading for Understanding, Analysis and Evaluation and Part 2: Critical Reading. Critical Reading is further divided into Section 1: Scottish texts and Section 2: Critical essay.

Part 1: Reading for Understanding, Analysis and Evaluation

You will have one and a half hours to complete this exam. There are 30 marks available.

This is the paper which in Intermediate and the previous Higher was known as Close Reading. You will be required to read two non-fiction passages, answering questions on Passage 1 and comparing and/or contrasting Passage 1 with Passage 2 in a final 5 mark question.

The questions will cover these three areas:

- Showing your understanding of the passage by putting things in your own words, summarising and selecting key areas.
- Analysing the way the writer conveys these ideas through techniques such as word choice, imagery, sentence structure and tone.
- Evaluating how effectively the writer conveys these ideas, giving your opinion about the writer's use of language.

Part 2: Critical Reading

One and a half hours is allocated for the Scottish texts and critical essay question. It is up to you to divide your time appropriately. (45 minutes for each section is a good guide.)

Section 1: Scottish texts

Here you will have approximately 45 minutes to answer questions on a text you have studied in class. In total, 20 marks are available. In this part of the exam you will be given an extract from the text or texts you have studied. You will answer questions on this extract and then, in a final 10 mark question, compare the extract to the rest of the text/the other set texts by the same writer.

This part of the paper asks you to consider:

1. Why is the extract important? What ideas does it present? How is language used?

2. How does this extract fit into the whole text or set of texts? For example, what themes or ideas in the extract relate to other stories or poems by the same writer?

Section 2: Critical essay

Here you will have approximately 45 minutes, depending on your time management, to answer a question on a text you have studied in class. 20 marks are available for this part of the paper. There will be a choice of questions in different genres: drama, prose, poetry, film and television drama or language study. You will be asked to focus on aspects of your chosen text. To be able to write a well-structured, detailed answer to the question, you will need to know the text fully, and demonstrate this with textual reference. Remembering quotations is not what you're being assessed on – it is what you do with the quotations and the comments you make about them that count. In terms of length, 1000 words is a good target; you need to show breadth and depth in your answer which is difficult to do in shorter responses.

You should make sure that you leave sufficient time to write a strong conclusion, regardless of whether you have developed all the points in your plan or not. Remember, you need to focus on the question throughout the essay and particularly in the conclusion. Look at the SQA supplementary marking grid to understand the standards and evaluate your own work. Set yourself targets for improvement in critical essay writing and work on them in your next essay.

There is lots of advice on writing successful critical essays on pages 262–264 of this book.

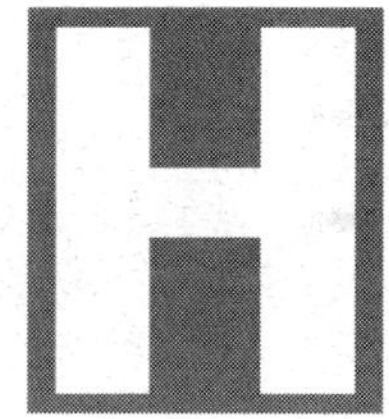

CfE Higher English

Practice Papers for SQA Exams

Exam A

Reading for Understanding, Analysis and Evaluation

Duration – 1 hour 30 minutes

Total marks – 30

Attempt ALL questions.

Passage 1

In the first passage Paulina Porizkova, writing for the Huffington Post, reflects on her own attitude towards beauty and ageing.

Old age is the revenge of the ugly ones is a French proverb; one that I first heard at the very advanced age of 15 upon my arrival in Paris. I had spent five years in the ugly bin at school in Sweden, and had only recently been upgraded to beautiful. My ego was still fragile and my mind still pumped full of highbrow arty self-education and nerdy jokes, which is how one gets by when one is ugly. Which of course, I promptly realised, is exactly what will pay off as one ages: beauty fades, but a mind constantly energised will shine even brighter with age. I immediately took the proverb as my own personal motto and patted myself on the back with satisfaction. I will continue to be intelligent, I vowed, no matter how beautiful I become. And then at, like, the old age of 35, I'll be an incredibly smart and kinda attractive old lady.

In interviews I gave at the wise age of 17 and 18, I pontificated about the beauty of age and wisdom, and blabbered on about how I looked forward to my first wrinkle. What an idiot I was.

My first recognition of age setting in occurred on my 36th birthday. I have no idea why, on this day of all days, I looked in the mirror and realised my face no longer looked young. I didn't look bad; only, the freshness had somehow disappeared. I immediately became hyper-conscious of my looks and went out and bought the most expensive cream on the market (for your information, it did nothing). And I began the battle of acceptance, something I have to do now almost every time I face a mirror.

Like everything else in life, there is always payback and it's a bitch. Beauty, unlike the rest of the gifts handed out at birth, does not require dedication, patience and hard work to pay off. But it's also the only gift that does NOT keep on giving. It usually blossoms at an age where you're least equipped to handle its benefits and rewards and instead take it all for granted, and by the time you start understanding the value of it, it slowly trickles away. How's that for revenge of the ugly ones?

To me, to let yourself age means that you're comfortable with who you are. Yes, sorry, I do believe that all the little shots here and there, and the pulling of skin here and there, and the removal of fat here and there, means you still have something to prove; you're still not comfortable in your skin. The beauty of age was supposed to be about the wisdom acquired, and with it an acceptance and celebration of who you are. Now all we want for people to see is that we have not yet attained that wisdom. Aging has become something to fight, not something to accept. Aging is a matter of control and control of matter.

I recently saw a comment posted on to one of the blogs I had written by a woman who stated that my problem is that I'm obviously jealous of these women I criticise, because they are not only beautiful but successful; something I'm clearly not. That gave me pause. Am I just jealous? Is my entire creative output completely reliant on this baser of emotions? It's true I'm trying to find a new place in the world that would rather I had just shut up and stayed beautiful (dying young is a terrific way to achieve this, by the way), which makes me a tad resentful. It's also true I'm still very insecure and want attention and universal love and have not a friggin' clue on how to achieve it. And likewise, it is true that I am jealous, and envious, and covetous of things I don't have. Which are, or is, rather – surprise, surprise – not an unlined forehead or puffy lips, nor a hot career, but confidence. True confidence: the kind that should come with age and that I keep glimpsing off in the distance, the kind I tell myself I would have developed already had I relied on wit rather than looks.

I keep a list of my "heroines," the women who have dared to age, and I'm always stupidly grateful to see these women highlighted in the media. I just found out that Jamie Lee Curtis, one of the women on my list, and Madonna are the same age. Looking at photos of them side by side is a revelation. One looks no older than 30, hard-edged, determined and hungry. The other looks like she's old enough to be her mother, but radiant, confident and content.

I already know I'm too vain and too insecure to follow her footsteps. This is what and whom I'm jealous of.

But even as I struggle with the choices – age, age a little, age not at all – I realise I'm blessed to even be in the position to age. To age is a privilege, not a birthright, even though most of us in the civilised world seem to forget this. This choice of "not-aging" is actually reserved for well-off women with lots of time and money. I've met a lot of these women at parties and social gatherings, and they were all lovely, gracious, generous and often way smarter than me. So when I asked them all who they would elect as their symbol of graceful aging, the overwhelmingly popular choice, Madonna, was disheartening. With all the choices we have, with all those beautiful and strong and powerful women in their 40 and 50s (Oprah? Arianna Huffington? Kathryn Bigelow? Christiane Amanpour? And although I hate to include her, Sarah Palin?), the choice was the one woman who has elected to NOT age. Of course, the kicker is: artificial youth takes a lot maintenance. Maintenance takes a lot of time.

So, the more time you chase – the more time you waste.

Passage 2

In the second passage Barbara Ellen, writing in the Observer, responds to comments made by Rosie Huntington-Whiteley on beauty and ageing.

Rosie Huntington-Whiteley, the model, has been pondering that her career is limited, saying: "Looks go, and you fade." Well, good for Rosie – a canny young woman, looking for ways to maximise her earning potential, not feeling ashamed or anxious about the future, but instead thinking ahead, getting organised. Saying that, it would be a shame if the mantra "Looks go, and you fade" becomes one size fits all, even for Rosie.

Who has ultimate control over the shelf life of female beauty? After all, "Looks go, and you fade" is really only applicable to model employability. It should never apply to non-models, but still in a weird way it does. This feeling, this pressure, that there is an ever-shortening shelf life for female looks, and, by association, psychosexual appeal.

Real lives played out against the sparkly but sinister sand of an egg timer, constantly falling: signifying, on the one hand, not just biology, but also judgment, gloating, sometimes even hate – on the other, dread and powerlessness. A pressure that taps into female vulnerability, making them feel that their very viability is determined by shadowy outside forces, and out of their control.

Of course Huntington-Whiteley was referring to her own profession – a tiny enclave mainly comprised of very pretty thin young people, who do indeed usually have short shelf lives (though not all of them, as evidenced by the still-strutting Kate Moss, et al). Complaints about the fashion industry, and the toxic messages it sends out, rage on, and it's good and healthy they do. However, right now, in this flawed reality, sobbing over the short shelf lives of models seems as illogical as becoming upset that most sportspeople retire while still relatively youthful.

In this way, for the model, "Looks go, and you fade", is a practical career self-appraisal, akin to a footballer ruefully observing that he missed a goal because he's not as fast as he used to be. The difference being that men would respond to this, probably by yelling: "Too right, you useless overpaid prat!" You'd never get hordes of men wailing: "No, footballer, don't put yourself down, you're just displaying a different more mature, kind of footballing speed, and anyone who says otherwise is ageist and sexist – and sport needs to change!"

This just wouldn't happen, and that's partly because women have vastly more to put up with on myriad levels, and thus are far more likely to support each other. But also because men would never feel that a footballer's legs directly relate to them – not in terms of getting older, or anything else.

They wouldn't say: "Oh no, that reminds me, my legs are ageing too!" Odd then that a model's, or any other famous female's comment, about her looks fading, so often automatically becomes framed as an anguished lament applicable to all womankind – not just by paranoid women, but by those particular men who seek to keep them paranoid.

In truth, outside professional modelling, "You lose your looks, and you fade" is not a reasonable or logical mantra, rather, it's self-defeating and self-hating. This also applies to Huntington-Whiteley – who, even once she's left modelling would doubtless be turning heads, nowhere near "fading", for years to come.

For a non-model, it should be even simpler. All a woman has to do is look around and notice that she's being suckered – that men also don't stay in the same physical shape as in their youth, and they don't seem too bothered. So, isn't it about time the specious concept of a shelf life specifically for female beauty was similarly marginalised? This is what the smart females have known all along: that in all the important ways, female ageing is really not that different from the male variety. Not only that, perception is completely in women's own power, and always has been.

Passage 1 questions

1. Re-read lines 1–11.

(a) Explain what the writer's attitude was towards 'beauty' at the age of 15. **2**

(b) Analyse how the writer's use of language in lines 2–11 reveals the wavering self-confidence she felt as a young woman. You should refer to such features as word choice, imagery, tone … **4**

2. 'What an idiot I was.'
Re-read lines 10–11. Analyse how the writer's use of language introduces this idea. **2**

3. Re-read **paragraph 3**.
Explain fully how the writer reacts to ageing. **2**

4. Re-read lines 18–22.
Explain fully what the writer means by the 'payback' of beauty. **3**

5. Re-read lines 23–29.
By referring to at least one example, analyse the writer's use of sentence structure to develop her argument. **2**

6. By referring to at least two features of language in lines 30–40, analyse how the writer creates tone in this section. **4**

7. Re-read lines 41–47.

(a) In your own words, explain the contrast between Madonna and Jamie Lee Curtis. **2**

(b) Identify what the writer is jealous of. **2**

8. What is ironic about the choice of Madonna as a symbol of graceful ageing? **2**

Passage 2 question

9. Both writers express their views about ageing. Identify key areas on which they agree and/or disagree. In your answer you should refer to both passages. **5**

CfE Higher English

Practice Papers for SQA Exams

Exam A
Critical Reading

Duration – 1 hour 30 minutes

Total marks – 40

SECTION 1 – Scottish text – 20 marks

Read an extract from a Scottish text you have previously studied and attempt the questions.

Choose ONE text from either

Part A – Drama

or

Part B – Prose

or

Part C – Poetry

Attempt ALL the questions for your chosen text.

SECTION 2 – critical essay – 20 marks

Attempt ONE question from the following genres – Drama, Prose, Poetry, Film and Television Drama, or Language.

Your answer must be on a different genre from that chosen in Section 1.

You should spend approximately 45 minutes on each section.

Section 1 – Scottish text – 20 marks

Choose one text from Drama, Prose or Poetry.

Read the text extract carefully and then attempt ALL the questions for your chosen text.

You should spend about 45 minutes on this section.

Text 1: Drama

If you choose this text you may not attempt a question on drama in Section 2.

Read the extract below and then attempt the following questions.

***The Slab Boys* by John Byrne**

Phil:	Hey, Spanks.
Spanky:	What?
Phil:	D'you think going off your head's catching?
Spanky:	Eh? You mean like crabs or Jack's plooks?
Phil:	No, I'm serious … d'you think it is?
Spanky:	How … who do you know that's off their head apart from everybody in … 's not your maw again, is it?
Phil:	Yeh … they took her away last night.
Spanky:	Christ …
Phil:	She wasn't all that bad either … not for her, that is. All she done was run up the street with her hair on fire and dive through the Co-operative windows.
Spanky:	Thought that was normal down your way?
Phil:	Yeh … but that's mostly the drink.
Spanky:	How long'll she be in this time?
Phil:	Usual six weeks, I expect. First week tied to a rubber mattress, next five wired up to a generator.
Spanky:	That's shocking.
Phil:	That's when we get in to see her. Never knew us the last time. Kept looking at my old man and saying, 'Bless me, Father, for I have sinned.' Course, he's hopeless … thinks it's like diphtheria or something. 'The doctors is doing their best, Annie … you'll be home soon. You taking that medicine they give you?' Medicine? Forty bennies crushed up in their cornflakes before they frogmarch them down to the 'Relaxation Classes', then it's back up to Cell Block Eleven for a kitbagful of capsules that gets them bleary-eyed enough for a chat with the consultant psychiatrist.
Spanky:	Not much of a holiday, is it?

Phil: Did I ever tell you about that convalescent home my maw and me went to? At the seaside ... West Kilbride ...

Spanky: Don't think so.

Phil: I was about eleven at the time. Got took out of school to go with her ... on the train. Some holiday. Place was chock-a-block with invalids ... headcases soaking up the Clyde breeze before getting pitched back into the burly-burly of everyday life ... Old-age pensioners, their skulls full of mush ... single guys in their forties in too-short trousers and intellects to match ... Middle-aged women in ankle socks roaming about looking for a letterbox to stick their postcards through. Abject bloody misery, it was. Dark-brown waxcloth you could see your face in ... bathroom mirrors you couldn't. Lights out at half seven ... no wireless, no comics, no nothing. Compulsory hymn-singing for everybody including the bedridden. Towels that tore the skin off your bum when you had a bath. Steamed fish on Sundays for a special treat ...

Spanky: Bleagh ...

Phil: The one highlight was a doll of about nineteen or twenty ... There we all were sitting in our deckchairs in the sun lounge ... curtains drawn ... listening for the starch wearing out on the Matron's top lip ... when this doll appears at the door, takes a coupla hops into the room, then turns this cartwheel right down the middle of the two rows of deckchairs ... lands on her pins ... daraaaaa! Brilliant! I started to laugh and got a skelp on the nut. The Matron was heeling ...

Spanky: About the skelp?

Phil: About the doll's cartwheel, stupid. Two old dears had to get carried up to their rooms with palpitations and a guy with a lavvy-brush moustache wet himself. It was the high spot of the holiday.

Spanky: What was it got into her?

Phil: Who knows? Maybe she woke up that morning and seen her face in the waxcloth ... remembered something ... 'Christ, I'm alive!' Everybody hated her after that.

Spanky: Did you have much bother when they took your maw away last night?

Phil: No ... they gave her a jag to knock her out.

Spanky: Eh?

Phil: So they could sign her in as a 'Voluntary Patient'.

Questions

1. By referring to two examples, explain how the dialogue in lines 1–17 creates black humour. **4**

2. By referring to lines 18–24, analyse how Byrne's use of language creates an effective portrayal of Phil's father. **4**

3. Explain fully how irony is created in lines 54–56. **2**

4. Discuss this scene's importance to the development of Phil's character. You should refer to this extract and, in more detail, to the play as a whole. **10**

Text 2: Drama

If you choose this text you may not attempt a question on drama in Section 2.

Read the extract below and then attempt the following questions.

***The Cheviot, the Stag and the Black, Black Oil* by John McGrath**

Enter PATRICK SELLAR and JAMES LOCH, looking very grand. SELLAR sniffs the bucket, ignores the women, who are huddled under their shawls.

SELLAR (*with a Lowland Scots accent*): Macdonald has told me, Mr Loch, there are three hundred illegal stills in Strathnaver at this very moment. They claim they have no money for rent – clearly they have enough to purchase the barley. The whole thing smacks of a terrible degeneracy in the character of these aboriginals …

LOCH: The Marquis is not unaware of the responsibility his wealth places upon him, Mr Sellar. The future and lasting interest and honour of his family, as well as their immediate income, must be kept in view.

They freeze. A phrase on the fiddle. Two SPEAKERS intervene between them, speak quickly to the audience.

SPEAKER 1: Their immediate income was over £120,000 per annum. In those days that was quite a lot of money.

SPEAKER 2: George Granville, Second Marquis of Stafford, inherited a huge estate in Yorkshire; he inherited another at Trentham in the Potteries; and he inherited a third at Lilleshall in Shropshire, that had coal-mines on it.

SPEAKER 1: He also inherited the Bridgewater Canal. And, on Loch's advice, he bought a large slice of the Liverpool-Manchester Railway.

SPEAKER 2: From his wife, Elizabeth Gordon, Countess of Sutherland, he acquired three-quarters of a million acres of Sutherland – in which he wanted to invest some capital.

Another phrase on the fiddle: they slip away. SELLAR and LOCH re-animate.

SELLAR: The common people of Sutherland are a parcel of beggars with no stock, but cunning and lazy.

LOCH: They are living in a form of slavery to their own indolence. Nothing could be more at variance with the general interests of society and the individual happiness of the people themselves, than the present state of Highland manners and customs. To be happy, the people must be productive.

SELLAR: They require to be thoroughly brought to the coast, where industry will pay, and to be convinced that they must worship industry or starve. The present enchantment which keeps them down must be broken.

LOCH: The coast of Sutherland abounds with many different kinds of fish. (*LOCH takes off his hat, and speaks directly to the audience.*) Believe it or not, Loch and Sellar actually used these words. (*Puts hat on again.*) Not only white fish, but herring too. With this in mind, His Lordship is considering several sites for new villages on the East Coast – Culgower, Helmsdale, Golspie, Brora, Skelbo and Knockglass – Helmsdale in particular is a perfect natural harbour for a fishing station. And there is said to be coal at Brora.

SELLAR: You will really not find this estate pleasant or profitable until by draining to your coast-line or by emigration you have got your mildewed districts cleared. They are just in that state of society for a savage country, such as the woods of Upper Canada – His Lordship should consider seriously the possibility of subsidising their departures. They might even be inclined to carry a swarm of dependants with them.

LOCH: I gather you yourself Mr Sellar, have a scheme for a sheep-walk in this area.

SELLAR: The highlands of Scotland may sell £200,000 worth of lean cattle this year. The same ground, under the Cheviot, may produce as much as £900,000 worth of fine wool. The effects of such arrangements in advancing this estate in wealth, civilisation, comfort, industry, virtue and happiness are palpable.

Fiddle in – Tune, 'Bonnie Dundee', *quietly behind.*

LOCH: Your offer for this area, Mr. Sellar, falls a little short of what I had hoped.

SELLAR: The present rents, when they can be collected, amount to no more than £142 per annum.

LOCH: Nevertheless, Mr Sellar, His Lordship will have to remove these people at considerable expense.

SELLAR: To restock the land with sheep will cost considerably more.

LOCH: A reasonable rent would be £400 per annum.

SELLAR: There is the danger of disturbances to be taken into account. £300.

LOCH: You can depend on the Reverend David Mackenzie to deal with that. £375.

SELLAR: Mackenzie is a Highlander. £325.

LOCH: He has just been rewarded with the parish of Farr – £365.

SELLAR: I shall have to pay decent wages to my plain, honest, industrious South-country shepherds – £350.

LOCH: You're a hard man, Mr Sellar.

SELLAR: Cash.

LOCH: Done.

Questions

5. From the outset it is suggested that the men of the upper classes scorned the Highlanders. With reference to the stage directions and dialogue, analyse how this is revealed. **3**

6. The action is paused so that the two speakers can reveal important information to the audience. With reference to at least two examples, explain how these details are relevant to a theme of the play. **3**

7. Both Sellar and Loch appear very confident and certain in their view of the best course of action for those living in the North. With reference to one example of the dialogue between them, explain what is revealed about their proposals for the Highlands. **2**

8. With close reference to the text, explain how McGrath highlights the ruthless approach taken by the upper classes at this time. **2**

9. Throughout this play, McGrath allows the flow of events to be broken and interrupted through such features as sudden shifts in time or location, and songs or music. With reference to this extract and elsewhere in the play, discuss how this is used to develop theme. **10**

Text 3: Drama

If you choose this text you may not attempt a question on drama in Section 2.

Read the extract below and then attempt the following questions.

***Men Should Weep* by Ena Lamont Stewart**

In this extract from Act I, Scene 1, Lily and Maggie are in the kitchen, talking. Edie has just told them that a classmate has nits.

Edie drifts around.

EDIE: Ma, I canna find the flannel.

MAGGIE: Noo, whaur did I lay it doon? I did Christopher before he went oat ta-tas …

LILY: How you ever find onythin in this midden beats me.

MAGGIE: Oh, here it is. It beats me tae sometimes. Edie, bend ower the sink till I scart some o this dirt aff ye.

LILY: D'ye no tak aff her dress tae wash her neck?

MAGGIE: Awa for Goad's sake! It's no Setterday nicht.

LILY: She's old enough tae dae it hersel. The way you rin efter they weans is the bloomin limit. Nae wunner y're hauf-deid.

MAGGIE: I'm no hauf-deid!

LILY: Well, ye look it.

MAGGIE: I canna help ma looks any mair than you can help yours.

LILY: The difference is, I try. Heve ye looked in the mirror since ye rose the morn?

MAGGIE: I havena time tae look in nae mirrors and neither would you if ye'd a hoose an a man an five weans.

LILY: Yin o they days your lovin Johnnie' s gonna tak a look at whit he married and it'll be ta-ta Maggie.

MAGGIE: My lovin Johnnie's still ma loving Johnnie, whitever I look like. *(Finishing off Edie)* Comb yer hair noo, Edie … I wonder whaur it's gottae?

They both look for the comb.

EDIE: I canna find it Ma. Auntie Lily, could you lend us yours?

LILY: (*starting to look in her bag, then thinking better of it*) I didna bring it the night.

EDIE: I've nae beasts, Auntie Lily.

LILY: Jist the same, I didnae bring it. Scram aff tae yer bed.

MAGGIE: Aye, Edie, get aff afore yer feyther comes in frae the library.

LILY: Oh, is that whaur he is?

Edie takes down from wall key to the outside WC and goes off.

MAGGIE: Whaur else wad he be? He disna go tae the pubs noo.

LILY: Oh aye! I'd forgot he'd went TT.

MAGGIE: Ye ken fine he's TT; but ye jist canna resist a dig at him. He hasna been inside a pub since Marina was born.

LILY: That's whit he tells you, onywey.

MAGGIE: My the tongue you have on you, Lily; it's a pity ye had yon disappointment; ye might hev been real happy wi the right man and a couple weans.

Lily holds out her sleeve and laughs up it.

LILY: Dae you think you're happy?

MAGGIE: Aye! I'm happy!

LILY: In this midden?

MAGGIE: Ye canna help havin a midden o a hoose when there's kids under yer feet a day. I dae the best I can.

LILY: I ken ye do. I'd gie it up as hopeless. Nae hot water. Nae place tae dry the weans' clothes, nae money. If John wad gie hissel a shake …

MAGGIE: You leave John alane! He does his best for us.

LILY: No much o a best. OK. OK. Keep yer wig on! Ye're that touchy ye'd think ye wis jist new merriet. I believe ye still love him!

MAGGIE: Aye. I still love John. And whit's more, he loves me.

LILY: Ye ought tae get yer photies took and send them tae the Sunday papers! 'Twenty-five years merriet and I still love ma husband. Is this a record?'

MAGGIE: I'm sorry for you, Lily. I'm right sorry for you.

LILY: We're quits then.

MAGGIE: Servin dirty hulkin brutes o men in a Coocaddens pub.

LILY: Livin in a slum and slavin efter a useless man an his greetin weans.

MAGGIE: They're my weans! I'm workin for ma ain.

LILY: I'm paid for ma work.

MAGGIE: So'm I! No in wages – I'm paid wi love. (*Pause*) And when did you last have a man's airms roon ye?

LILY: Men! I'm wantin nae man's airms roon me. They're a dirty beasts.

MAGGIE: Lily, yer mind's twisted. You canna see a man as a man. Ye've got them a lumped thegether. You're daft!

LILY: You're saft! You think yer man's wonderful and yer weans is a angels.

Questions

10. Referring closely to the extract, explain why Lily is frustrated with Maggie in lines 1–27. **2**

11. By referring closely to this extract, explain what Maggie's responses show about her character and/or her feelings about her life. **4**

12. Referring closely to this extract, analyse Lily's attitudes to men and/or love. **4**

13. Lamont Stewart uses the relationship between the sisters Maggie and Lily to develop both characters. Referring to this extract and the play as a whole, discuss how the relationship between Maggie and Lily adds to your appreciation of the play. You should refer to **both** Maggie and Lily in your answer. **10**

Text 1: Prose

If you choose this text you may not attempt a question on prose in Section 2.

Read the extract below and then attempt the following questions.

***Mother and Son* by Iain Crichton Smith**

His mind now seemed gradually to be clearing up, and he was beginning to judge his own actions and hers. Everything was clearing up: it was one of his moments. He turned round on his chair from a sudden impulse and looked at her intensely. He had done this very often before, had tried to cow her into submission: but she had always laughed at him. Now however he was looking at her as if he had never seen her before. Her mouth was open and there were little crumbs upon her lower lip. Her face had sharpened itself into a birdlike quickness: she seemed to be pecking at the bread with a sharp beak in the same way as she pecked cruelly at his defences. He found himself considering her as if she were some kind of animal. Detachedly he thought: how can this thing make my life a hell for me? What is she anyway? She's been ill for ten years: that doesn't excuse her. She's breaking me up so that even if she dies I won't be any good for anyone. But what if she's pretending? What if there is nothing wrong with her? At this a rage shook him so great that he flung his half-consumed cigarette in the direction of the fire in an abrupt, savage gesture. Out of the silence he heard a bus roaring past the window, splashing over the puddles. That would be the boys going to the town to enjoy themselves. He shivered inside his loneliness and then rage took hold of him again. How he hated her! This time his gaze concentrated itself on her scraggy neck, rising like a hen's out of her plain white nightgown. He watched her chin wagging up and down: it was stained with jam and flecked with one or two crumbs. His sense of loneliness closed round him, so that he felt as if he were on a boat on the limitless ocean, just as his house was on a limitless moorland. There was a calm, unspeaking silence, while the rain beat like a benediction on the roof. He walked over to the bed, took the tray from her as she held it out to him. He had gone in answer to words which he hadn't heard, so hedged was he in his own thoughts.

'Remember to clean the tray tomorrow,' she said. He walked back with the tray fighting back the anger that swept over him carrying the rubbish and debris of his mind in its wake. He turned back to the bed. His mind was in a turmoil of hate, so that he wanted to smash the cup, smash the furniture, smash the house. He kept his hands clenched, he the puny and unimaginative. He would show her, avenge her insults with his unintelligent hands. There was the bed, there was his mother. He walked over.

She was asleep, curled up in the warmth with the bitter, bitter smile upon her face. He stood there for a long moment while an equally bitter smile curled up the edge of his lips. Then he walked to the door, opened it, and stood listening to the rain.

Questions

14. At the beginning of the extract John, the main character, has a revelation. Explain what the revelation is and analyse how it is conveyed through the writer's use of language. **4**

15. By referring closely to lines 11–25, analyse how the writer's use of language is effective in making the reader aware of John's attitude towards his mother. **4**

16. Evaluate the effectiveness of lines 25–30 as a conclusion to the story. Your answer should deal with ideas and/or language. **2**

17. The repression of the individual is a common theme in Iain Crichton Smith's short stories. By referring to this and at least one other short story by Crichton Smith, discuss how he develops this theme. **10**

Text 2: Prose

If you choose this text you may not attempt a question on prose in Section 2.

Read the extract below and then attempt the following questions.

The Eye of the Hurricane by George Mackay Brown

Chapter Five got wedged in some deep rut of my mind. I sat most of a morning with my black biro poised over the writing pad. The phrases and sentences that presented themselves were dull, flaccid, affected. I looked blankly at the crucifix on the wall, but the Word that spanned all history with meaning was only a tortured image. The words I offered to the Word were added insults, a few more random thorns for the crown. I scored out everything I had written since breakfast-time.

It flatters us writers to think of ourselves as explorers, probing into seas that have never been mapped, or charted with only a few broken lines. But the spacious days of 'Here be Whales', cherubs puffing gales from the four quarters, mid-ocean mermaids, are gone for ever. There is nothing new to find; every headland has been rounded, every smallest ocean current observed, the deepest seas plumbed. Chaucer, Cervantes, Tolstoy, Proust charted human nature so well that really little is left for a novelist like myself to do. For the most part we voyage along old trade routes, in rusty bottoms; and though we carry cargoes of small interest to anyone – coal or wheat – we should be glad that hungry cupboards here and there are stored with bread and there are fires burning in cold snow villages of the north.

Miriam came in without knocking. 'The captain's had a terrible night, the poor man,' she said. 'There's six broken cups in the sideboard. The rug's saturated. He was trying to make himself a pot of tea, and his hands all spasms. He never so much as closed an eye.' She had her coat on to go home for, as I said, she only works in the house mornings.

'He wanted me to get him more rum,' I said, 'two bottles, but I wouldn't do it.'

'You were right,' said Miriam.

'He's going to put me out on the road,' I said.

'Don't worry about that,' said Miriam. 'That was the devil talking, not the poor captain at all. Once he's better he won't know a thing he's said this past day or two.'

'I'm glad,' I said, 'because I like it here.'

'It must be lonely for you,' said Miriam. 'You should come to our Joy Hour some Thursday evening. There's choruses and readings from the Good Book, and O, everybody's so happy!' Her eyes drifted uneasily over the crucifix and the Virgin.

I said nothing.

'I'm pleased with you,' said Miriam, 'for saying No to him. He'll suffer, but his bout'll be over all the sooner. Tomorrow, or the day after, he'll be his old self again.'

There came a violent double thump on the ceiling. 'Get off, you bitch!' roared Captain Stevens. 'What are you talking to that pansy for? This is my house. Away home with you!'

Miriam lowered her voice. 'Be firm for one day more,' she whispered. 'He'll try to wheedle you in the afternoon for sure. I know him. Just keep saying No.'

'I will,' I said.

'If only Robert Jansen and Stony Hackland keep away,' whispered Miriam. 'You mustn't let them in. If they come to the door, just send them packing. Be very firm.'

'Who are they?' I said.

'Seamen who used to sail in his ships,' she whispered. 'They carry the drink in to him whenever he has a bout.'

'They won't get in,' I said. When she smiled her plain little face shone for a moment like one of Botticelli's angels.

If she had been born in a Breton village, I thought, she would be a devout Catholic girl, and rosary and image and candle – that she shied away from with such horror – would be the gateway to her dearest treasures and delights. As it was, she merely touched the hem of Christ's garment in passing.

Questions

18. By referring closely to two examples from lines 1–5, analyse how Mackay Brown conveys Barclay's feelings about his writing. **4**

19. Mackay Brown uses the metaphor of the writer as sailor in lines 7–15. By referring closely to the extract, explain what he means by his comparison of:

(i) The writer as explorer

(ii) The writer as voyager of 'old trade routes'. **4**

20. By referring closely to one example of Mackay Brown's description of Miriam explain how he conveys her religious conviction. **2**

21. Alcohol and its effects is a frequent theme in George Mackay Brown's writing. With reference to this story and to at least one other by George Mackay Brown, discuss how this theme is developed. **10**

Text 3: Prose

If you choose this text you may not attempt a question on prose in Section 2.

Read the extract below and then attempt the following questions.

The Trick Is To Keep Breathing **by Janice Galloway**

In this extract, Joy recollects her first serious relationship.

I lived with a man for the better part of seven years. We met at school: fifth form romance. Our first date was in a cafe when we should have been in French. We ate salad rolls and doughnuts that tasted like sacred wafer because we were out of school and we both liked the same things: doughnuts and salad rolls. Once we went late into school eating opposite ends of an eclair, giggling, faces too close, smeared with chocolate icing and cream. Half way across the playground, a stray teacher caught sight of us. He shouted SEPARATE YOURSELVES and sliced the air between us with the flat of his hand. We separated. He said we were a terrible example.

I wiped the cream off my nose as defiantly as I could and said I couldn't see why. He stopped short.

Pardon? he said.

Look, I said. You're holding a cigarette. That's a worse example to impressionable young minds than anything we're doing. I knew it wouldn't make things any better but I couldn't stop. Paul kept his mouth shut and looked apologetic. We got hell. Paul never ate eclairs in the playground with me again. He always did have a better instinct for keeping out of trouble.

We had bad times and we had good times on and off over the seven years. I learned to cook good meals and run a house. The fridge was always well stocked and the cupboards interesting. I cleaned the floors and the rings round the bath that showed where we had been but I knew there was something missing. I felt we were growing apart. We were. It was called growing up but I didn't know that at the time. I tried to talk to him because the magazines I was reading said communication was important. He was reading different magazines: his magazines told him different things altogether. I thought the answer was soul-searching and he thought it was split-crotch knickers. Stalemate. We were unhappy. He punished me for his unhappiness by refusing to touch me. Night after night. I punished him for my unhappiness by not speaking but I hadn't the same willpower. His willpower lasted out for months. A year. More. Practice was making him perfect and me desperate for kisses. I had an affair. I couldn't see it wasn't the sex I missed so much as someone to care whether I missed it or not. The affair didn't help. Paul found out because he read my letters when I wasn't in and knew everything I was doing. I didn't know he was doing that and thought he had xray vision. I thought I was going crazy. I started writing my diary in code. I started thinking in code because I thought he could tap my brain. I became afraid to leave the flat in case he could tell things by feeling the walls when I was out or maybe through supervision. I thought he was Superman. I couldn't live with Superman without thinking

(a) Superman's weaknesses are my fault (like Kryptonite) and

(b) I was vastly inferior in every respect.

He talked to me even less and I talked to myself more and more. He still ate my meals and let me make the beds, do his washing and attend to the Superflat but it wasn't the same. Now there was no talk at all, only the sound of two people suffocating into different pillows. We were killing each other. There was nobody to ask for help because I was too proud and too ashamed I wasn't fit to live with. My mother was dying and it wasn't right to speak to her about this kind of thing. That was a romantic idea. Even if she had been well, I wouldn't have said anyway. Besides, I needed his car to supervise my mother's dying. They always build hospitals a million miles away from people. The day of the funeral, he shook my hand in line with everybody else waiting outside the crematorium. I looked at his face and couldn't think who he was for a minute. It didn't feel better when I remembered. It felt worse. But still I stayed in his flat, where there was nothing of mine, nothing of me. I got more and more guilty about sapping his Superpowers and thought I couldn't cope. I knew I had to leave and I had to get help. I found a shoulder to cry on. The shoulder thought I might be more comfortable crying in bed. Paul found out about this too. He wanted to hurt me so he told me he was screwing everything in skirts within a fifteen-mile radius. I told him it was a source of comfort to know I hadn't inflicted permanent damage on his erectile tissue. That was when he played his ace.

Questions

22. Look closely at lines 1–14. By close reference to the text, analyse how two aspects of Joy's personality are revealed. **2**

23. What does Joy mean when she says her relationship with Paul has reached a 'stalemate'? With close reference to lines 19–24, explain the reasons why Joy and Paul's relationship has reached this point. **4**

24. Examine how, in this extract, Galloway highlights the breakdown in Joy and Paul's relationship. **4**

25. In this novel, Joy's relationships with men play a central role in developing our understanding of her. With reference to this extract and elsewhere in the novel, discuss how Galloway uses these relationships to develop our understanding of Joy and her situation. **10**

Text 4: Prose

If you choose this text you may not attempt a question on prose in Section 2.

Read the extract below and then attempt the following questions.

***Sunset Song* by Lewis Grassic Gibbon**

In this extract, which is from Part III (Seed-Time), Chris sets out to rescue her horses from lightning.

It was then, in a lull of the swishing, she heard the great crack of thunder that opened the worst storm that had struck the Howe in years. It was far up, she thought, and yet so close Blawearie's stones seemed falling about her ears, she half-scrambled erect. Outside the night flashed, flashed and flashed, she saw Kinraddie lighted up and fearful, then it was dark again, but not quiet. In the sky outside a great beast moved and purred and scrabbled, and then suddenly it opened its mouth again and again there was the roar, and the flash of its claws, tearing at the earth, it seemed neither house nor hall could escape. The rain had died away, it was listening—quiet in the next lull, and then Chris heard her Auntie crying to her *Are you all right, Chrissie?* and cried back she was fine. Funny Uncle Tam had cried never a word, maybe he was still in the sulks, he'd plumped head-first in when he'd heard of the old woman that Semple was sending to help keep house in Blawearie. They were off to Auchterless the morn, and oh! she'd be glad to see them go, she'd enough to do and to think without fighting relations.

The thunder clamoured again, and then she suddenly sat shivering, remembering something—Clyde and old Bob and Bess, all three of them were out in the ley field there, they weren't taken in till late in the year. Round the ley field was barbed wire, almost new, that father had put up in the Spring, folk said it was awful for drawing the lightning, maybe it had drawn it already.

She was out of bed in the next flash, it was a ground flash, it hung and it seemed to wait, sizzling, outside the window as she pulled on stockings and vest and knickers and ran to the door and cried up *Uncle Tam, Uncle Tam, we must take in the horses!* He didn't hear, she waited, the house shook and dirled in another great flash, then Auntie was crying something, Chris stood as if she couldn't believe her own ears. Uncle Tam was feared at the lightning, he wouldn't go out, she herself had best go back to her bed and wait for the morning.

She didn't wait to hear more than that, but ran to the kitchen and groped about for the box of matches and lighted the little lamp, it with the glass bowl, and then found the littlest lantern and lighted that, though her fingers shook and she almost dropped the funnel. Then she found old shoes and a raincoat, it had been father's and came near to her ankles, and she caught up the lamp and opened the kitchen door and closed it quick behind her just as the sky banged again and a flare of sheet lightning came flowing down the hill-side, frothing like the incoming tide at Dunnottar. It dried up, leaving her blinded, her eyes ached and she almost dropped the lantern again.

In the byre the kye were lowing fit to raise the roof, even the stirks were up and stamping about in their stalls. But they were safe enough unless the biggings were struck, it was the horses she'd to think of.

Right athwart her vision the haystacks shone up like great pointed pyramids a blinding moment, vanished, darkness complete and heavy flowed back on her again, the lantern-light seeking to pierce it like the bore of a drill. Still the rain held off as she stumbled and cried down the sodden fields. Then she saw that the barbed wire was alive, the lightning ran and glowed along it, a living thing, a tremulous, vibrant serpent that spat and glowed and hid its head and quivered again to sight. If the horses stood anywhere near to that they were finished, she cried to them again and stopped and listened, it was deathly still in the night between the bursts of the thunder, so still that she heard the grass she had pressed underfoot crawl and quiver erect again a step behind her. Then, as the thunder moved away—it seemed to break and roar down the rightward hill, above the Manse and Kinraddie Mains,—something tripped her, she fell and the lantern-flame flared up and seemed almost to vanish; but she righted it, almost sick though she was because of the wet, warm thing that her body and face lay upon.

Questions

26. By referring to at least one example from lines 17–30, explain how the writer's sentence structure conveys Chris' panic. **2**

27. Referring closely to the extract, analyse one example of the imagery used in lines 1–12 to convey the ferocity of the storm. **2**

28. Referring closely to the extract, explain Chris' opinion of Uncle Tam. Give at least two examples to support your answer. **2**

29. By referring closely to lines 31–45, analyse how Grassic Gibbon conveys the danger of the situation Chris is in. **4**

30. Chris is both independent and practical. By referring to this extract and elsewhere in the novel, discuss how Grassic Gibbon conveys these aspects of Chris' personality. **10**

Text 5: Prose

If you choose this text you may not attempt a question on prose in Section 2.

Read the extract below and then attempt the following questions.

The Cone-Gatherers by Robin Jenkins

In this extract, from the opening scene of the novel, Neil and Calum are returning to their hut after a day of cone gathering.

'This wood,' said Neil, 'it's to be cut down in the spring.'

'I ken that,' whimpered Calum.

'There's no sense in being sorry for trees,' said his brother, 'when there are more men than trees being struck down. You can make use of a tree, but what use is a dead man? Trees can be replaced in time. Aren't we ourselves picking the cones for seed? Can you replace dead men?'

He knew that the answer was: yes, the dead men would be replaced. After a war the population of the world increased. But none would be replaced by him. To look after his brother, he had never got married, though once he had come very near it: that memory often revived to turn his heart melancholy.

'We'd better get down,' he muttered. 'You lead the way, Calum, as usual.'

'Sure, I'll lead the way, Neil.'

Delighted to be out of this bondage of talk, Calum set his bag of cones firmly round his shoulders, and with consummate confidence and grace began the descent through the inner night of the great tree. Not once, all the long way down, was he at a loss. He seemed to find holds by instinct, and patiently guided his brother's feet on to them. Alone, Neil would have been in trouble; he was as dependent on his brother as if he was blind; and Calum made no attempt to make his superiority as climber compensate for his inferiority as talker. Every time he caught his brother's foot and set it on a safe branch it was an act of love. Once, when Neil slid down quicker than he meant and stamped on Calum's fingers, the latter uttered no complaint but smiled in the dark and sucked the bruise.

It was different as soon as they were on the ground. Neil immediately strode out, and Calum, hurrying to keep close behind, often stumbled. Gone were the balance and sureness he had shown in the tree. If there was a hollow or a stone or a stick, he would trip over it. He never grumbled at such mishaps, but scrambled up at once, anxious only not to be a hindrance to his brother.

When they reached the beginning of the ride that divided a cluster of Norway spruces, Neil threw over his shoulder the usual warning: to leave the snares alone, whether there were rabbits in them half throttled or hungry or frantic; and Calum gave the usual sad guilty promise.

During their very first day in the wood they had got into trouble with the gamekeeper. Calum had released two rabbits from snares. Neil had been angry and had prophesied trouble. It had come next evening when Duror, the big keeper, had been waiting for them outside their hut. His rage had been quiet but intimidating. Neil had said little in reply, but had faced up to the gun raised once or twice to emphasise threats. Calum, demoralised as always by hatred, had cowered against the hut, hiding his face.

Duror had sworn that he would seize the first chance to hound them out of the wood; they were in it, he said, sore against his wish. Neil therefore had made Calum swear by an oath which he didn't understand but which to Neil was the most sacred on earth: by their dead mother, he had to swear never again to interfere with the snares. He could not remember his mother, who had died soon after he was born.

Now this evening, as he trotted down the ride, he prayed by a bright star above that there would be no rabbits squealing in pain. If there were, he could not help them; he would have to rush past, tears in his eyes, fingers in his ears.

Several rabbits were caught, all dead except one; it pounded on the grass and made choking noises. Neil had passed it without noticing. Calum moaned in dismay at this dilemma of either displeasing his brother or forsaking a hurt creature. He remembered his solemn promise; he remembered too the cold hatred of the gamekeeper; he knew that the penalty for interfering might be expulsion from this wood where he loved to work; but above all he shared the suffering of the rabbit.

Questions

31. Explain how Neil's speech and actions reveal the hierarchy between the two brothers. **3**

32. 'Delighted to be out of this bondage of talk'.
Explain fully what the writer means by this. **2**

33. By referring closely to lines 12–23, analyse how the writer's use of language highlights the contrast between Calum in the tree and on the ground. **3**

34. By referring closely to at least one example from lines 41–45, explain how the writer's use of language reveals Calum's inner turmoil. **2**

35. *The Cone-Gatherers* is set during the Second World War. With reference to such features as setting, characterisation and narrative in this extract and elsewhere in the novel, explain the impact of war. **10**

Text 1: Poetry

If you choose this text you may not attempt a question on poetry in Section 2.

Read the extract below and then attempt the following questions.

A Poet's Welcome To His Love-Begotten Daughter **by Robert Burns**

Thou's welcome, wean; mishanter fa' me,
If thoughts o' thee, or yet thy mamie,
Shall ever daunton me or awe me,
My bonie lady,
Or if I blush when thou shalt ca' me
Tyta or daddie.

Tho' now they ca' me fornicator,
An' tease my name in kintry clatter,
The mair they talk, I'm kent the better,
E'en let them clash;
An auld wife's tongue's a feckless matter
To gie ane fash.

Welcome! my bonie, sweet, wee dochter,
Tho' ye come here a wee unsought for,
And tho' your comin' I hae fought for,
Baith kirk and queir;
Yet, by my faith, ye're no unwrought for,
That I shall swear!

Wee image o' my bonie Betty,
As fatherly I kiss and daut thee,
As dear, and near my heart I set thee
Wi' as gude will

As a' the priests had seen me get thee
That's out o' hell.

Sweet fruit o' mony a merry dint,
My funny toil is now a' tint,
Sin' thou came to the warl' asklent,
Which fools may scoff at;
In my last plack thy part's be in't
The better ha'f o't.

Tho' I should be the waur bestead,
Thou's be as braw and bienly clad,
And thy young years as nicely bred
Wi' education,
As ony brat o' wedlock's bed,
In a' thy station.

Lord grant that thou may aye inherit
Thy mither's person, grace, an' merit,
An' thy poor, worthless daddy's spirit,
Without his failins,
'Twill please me mair to see thee heir it,
Than stockit mailens.

For if thou be what I wad hae thee,
And tak the counsel I shall gie thee,
I'll never rue my trouble wi' thee,
The cost nor shame o't,
But be a loving father to thee,
And brag the name o't.

Questions

36. With reference to two examples, explain Burns' attitude to his daughter in lines 1–6. **4**

37. How does the attitude of the community contrast with Burns' own attitude? Refer to at least one example from lines 1–24 to support your answer. **2**

38. Burns is open in his writing about sexual matters. With reference to two examples, explain how he does this and what this reveals about his attitude to sexual liaisons. **4**

39. Burns was outspoken in his criticism of repressive religion – Calvinism in particular. With reference to this and one other poem by Burns, discuss how he presents religion and demonstrates this criticism. **10**

Text 2: Poetry

If you choose this text you may not attempt a question on poetry in Section 2.

Read the extract below and then attempt the following questions.

***Anne Hathaway* by Carol Ann Duffy**

'Item I gyve unto my wife my second best bed … '
(from Shakespeare's will)

The bed we loved in was a spinning world
of forests, castles, torchlight, clifftops, seas
where we would dive for pearls. My lover's words
were shooting stars which fell to earth as kisses
on these lips; my body now a softer rhyme
to his, now echo, assonance; his touch
a verb dancing in the centre of a noun.
Some nights, I dreamed he'd written me, the bed
a page beneath his writer's hands. Romance
and drama played by touch, by scent, by taste.
In the other bed, the best, our guests dozed on,
dribbling their prose. My living laughing love –
I hold him in the casket of my widow's head
as he held me upon that next best bed.

Questions

40. Look closely at lines 3–7. Analyse how Duffy conveys the intensity of the relationship between the speaker and her husband. **4**

41. By referring closely to lines 7–12, analyse the use of poetic technique to emphasise the closeness between husband and wife. **4**

42. With reference to lines 8–14, analyse how Duffy highlights the difference between the relationship of the guests and that of the speaker. **2**

43. Discuss how Duffy uses symbolism in this poem and at least one other of her poems to develop theme. **10**

Text 3: Poetry

If you choose this text you may not attempt a question on poetry in Section 2.

Read the extract below and then attempt the following questions.

Last Supper **by Liz Lochhead**

She is getting good and ready to renounce
his sweet flesh.
Not just for lent. (For
Ever)
But meanwhile she is assembling the ingredients
for their last treat, the proper
feast (after all
didn't they always
eat together
rather more than rather well?)
So here she is tearing foliage, scrambling
the salad, maybe lighting candles even, anyway
stepping back to admire the effect of
the table she's made (and oh yes now
will have to lie on) the silverware,
the nicely al-
dente vegetables, the cooked goose.
He could be depended on to bring the bottle
plus betrayal with a kiss.

Already she was imagining it done with, this feast, and
exactly
what kind of leftover hash she'd make of it
among friends, when it was just

The Girls, when those three met again.
What very good soup
she could render from the bones,
then something substantial, something extra
tasty if not elegant.

Yes, there they'd be cackling around the cauldron,
spitting out the gristlier bits
of his giblets;
gnawing on the knucklebone of some
intricate irony;
getting grave and dainty at the
petit-gout mouthfuls of reported speech.

'That's rich!' they'd splutter,
munching the lies, fat and sizzling as sausages.
Then they'd sink back
gorged on truth
and their own savage integrity,
sleek on it all, preening
like corbies, their bright eyes blinking
satisfied
till somebody would get hungry
and go hunting again.

Questions

44. In stanza one, we are introduced to the narrator who is preparing for the 'last supper' with her lover. With close reference to this stanza, analyse how Lochhead conveys the conflict of emotions felt. **4**

45. Look closely at stanza two. Examine the use of poetic techniques in clarifying the writer's meaning. **2**

46. Evaluate the effectiveness of Lochhead's use of extended metaphor in the final stanza of the poem. **4**

47. In many of Lochhead's poems she examines the position and role held by women. With reference to this poem and at least one other work by Lochhead, discuss how this theme is explored in her work. **10**

Text 4: Poetry

If you choose this text you may not attempt a question on poetry in Section 2.

Read the extract below and then attempt the following questions.

***Aunt Julia* by Norman MacCaig**

Aunt Julia spoke Gaelic
very loud and very fast.
I could not answer her —
I could not understand her.

She wore men's boots
when she wore any.
— I can see her strong foot,
stained with peat,
paddling with the treadle of the spinningwheel
while her right hand drew yarn
marvellously out of the air.

Hers was the only house
where I've lain at night
in the absolute darkness
of a box bed, listening to
crickets being friendly.

She was buckets
and water flouncing into them.
She was winds pouring wetly
round house-ends.
She was brown eggs, black skirts
and a keeper of threepennybits
in a teapot.

Aunt Julia spoke Gaelic
very loud and very fast.
By the time I had learned
a little, she lay
silenced in the absolute black
of a sandy grave
at Luskentyre. But I hear her still, welcoming me
with a seagull's voice
across a hundred yards
of peatscrapes and lazybeds
and getting angry, getting angry
with so many questions
unanswered.

Questions

48. By referring closely to lines 1–11, analyse MacCaig's use of content and poetic techniques to create a sense of character. **3**

49. Look at lines 12–16. Explain how the poet conveys the uniqueness of staying at his aunt's house. **3**

50. One of the key themes in the poem is MacCaig's frustration in his inability to communicate with his aunt. By referring to at least two examples, analyse the effectiveness of the final stanza in conveying this theme. **4**

51. By referring to this poem and at least one other poem by MacCaig, discuss the importance of the theme of loss in his work. **10**

Text 5: Poetry

If you choose this text you may not attempt a question on poetry in Section 2.

Read the extract below and then attempt the following questions.

***An Autumn Day* by Sorley MacLean**

On that slope
on an autumn day,
the shells soughing about my ears
and six dead men at my shoulder,
dead and stiff – and frozen were it not for the heat –
as if they were waiting for a message.

When the screech came
out of the sun,
out of an invisible throbbing,
the flame leaped and the smoke climbed
and surged every way:
blinding of eyes, splitting of hearing.

And after it, the six men dead
the whole day:
among the shells snoring
in the morning,
and again at midday and in the evening.

In the sun, which was so indifferent,
so white and painful;
on the sand which was so comfortable,
easy and kindly;
and under the stars of Africa,
jewelled and beautiful.

One Election took them
and did not take me,
without asking us
which was better or worse:
it seemed as devilishly indifferent
as the shells.

Six men dead at my shoulder on an Autumn day.

Questions

52. What is MacLean describing in lines 7–12? Explain your answer with reference to the text. **2**

53. Comment, with reference to the text, on how MacLean's language and structure in lines 24–29 reflect the injustice of war and life in general. **4**

54. Comment on the effectiveness of the final line as a conclusion to the poem. **4**

55. Time is very important in Sorley MacLean's poetry. With close reference to this poem and to another poem or poems by MacLean, discuss how he develops this theme. **10**

Section 2 – Critical essay – 20 marks

Attempt ONE question from the following genres — Drama, Prose, Poetry, Film and Television Drama, or Language.

You may use a Scottish text but NOT the one used in Section 1.

Your answer must be on a different genre from that chosen in Section 1.

You should spend approximately 45 minutes on this section.

DRAMA

Answers to questions on **drama** should refer to the text and to such relevant features as characterisation, key scene(s), structure, climax, theme, plot, conflict, setting …

1. Choose a play in which a central character feels uncertain about their position in their family/society/workplace.

Briefly explain the reasons for their uncertainty and discuss how the dramatist's presentation of this feature enhances your understanding of the play as a whole.

2. Choose a play in which the opening scene(s) effectively introduce the central concerns of the play.

By referring in detail to the opening scene(s), discuss in what ways it is important for your understanding of the play as a whole.

3. Choose a play in which the setting is an important feature.

Briefly explain how the dramatist establishes the importance of this setting and discuss how this feature enhances your understanding of the play as a whole.

PROSE — FICTION

Answers to questions on **prose fiction** should refer to the text and to such relevant features as characterisation, setting, language, key incident(s), climax, turning point, plot, structure, narrative technique, theme, ideas, description …

4. Choose a novel which carries a strong message that may have a powerful impression on the reader.

Briefly outline what this message is and discuss why the novel or short story has such an impact on the reader.

5. Choose a novel or short story which reaches a climax that is dramatic, disturbing or moving.

Briefly explain how the writer achieves this effect and how this enhances your appreciation of the text as a whole.

6. Choose a novel or short story in which there is a character you admire.

Explain briefly why you admire this character and then, in detail, discuss how the writer achieves this.

PROSE — NON-FICTION

Answers to questions on **prose non-fiction** should refer to the text and to such relevant features as ideas, use of evidence, stance, style, selection of material, narrative voice …

7. Choose a piece of non-fiction writing in which the writer's presentation of an experience triggers an emotional response from you.

Give a brief description of the experience and then, in more detail, discuss how the writer's presentation of this description evokes this strong emotional response.

8. Choose a non-fiction text which explores a significant aspect of political or cultural life.

Discuss how the writer's presentation enhances your understanding of the chosen aspect of political or cultural life and how this impacts on your appreciation of the text as a whole.

9. Choose an example of biography or autobiography which gives you a detailed insight into a person's life.

Explain how the writer's presentation made you think deeply about the person and his or her life, enhancing your overall appreciation of the text.

POETRY

Answers to questions on **poetry** should refer to the text and to such relevant features as word choice, tone, imagery, structure, content, rhythm, rhyme, theme, sound, ideas …

10. Choose two poems which deal with an important issue such as crime or poverty.

Discuss which you find more effective in deepening your understanding of the issue.

11. Choose a poem in which form (such as a ballad, ode, sonnet, monologue …) plays a significant role.

Show how the poet uses the distinctive features of the form to enhance your appreciation of the poem.

12. Choose a poem which deals with the theme of loss **or** death **or** the end of a relationship.

Show how the content and poetic techniques used increase your understanding of the theme.

FILM AND TELEVISION DRAMA

Answers to questions on **film and television drama*** should refer to the text and to such relevant features as use of camera, key sequence, characterisation, mise en scène, editing, setting, music/sound, special effects, plot, dialogue ...

13. Choose a film or television drama* in which the main character could be described as an antihero.

Explain how the character is introduced and then developed throughout the film or television drama.

14. Choose a film or television drama* in which setting is used to create mood and/or atmosphere.

Explain how the film or programme makers' use of this setting creates mood and/or atmosphere and go on to show how the mood and/or atmosphere is important to the effectiveness of the film or television drama as a whole.

15. Choose a film or television drama* which has an unexpected ending.

By referring to key features (such as setting, characterisation, narrative ...) and techniques used by the film or programme maker, explain how the ending is unexpected.

***"television drama" includes a single play, a series or a serial.**

LANGUAGE

Answers to questions on **language** should refer to the text and to such relevant features as register, accent, dialect, slang, jargon, vocabulary, tone, abbreviation ...

16. Consider the use of the Scots language today.

Identify examples of its use and discuss to what extent these examples promote the language.

17. Choose at least one example of a new form of social networking.

Identify some of the distinctive features of the language used and discuss to what extent these features contribute to effective communication.

18. Choose a speech which makes use of persuasive language.

By referring to specific features of language in this speech, discuss to what extent you feel the speech is successful in achieving its purpose of persuasion.

[END OF SECTION 2]

CfE Higher English

Practice Papers for SQA Exams

Exam B
Reading for Understanding, Analysis and Evaluation

Duration – 1 hour 30 minutes

Total marks – 30

Attempt ALL questions.

Passage 1

Journalist Judith Woods writing about mindfulness for The Telegraph newspaper.

Mindfulness. If you're not yet au fait with the concept, it might be a good idea to familiarise yourself with it now, because you'll be hearing a lot more about it; from business leaders, academics, politicians and – of course – educationalists.

In other words: mindfulness may well be coming to a classroom near you.

But don't, whatever you do, call it a buzzword, for it's the very opposite. By definition, mindfulness aims to shut out the buzz; it is a brain-training technique based on using your breath to achieve mental clarity.

It has been discussed in Parliament as a therapy in relation to both unemployment and depression. But it isn't about zoning out. If anything, it's about zooming in; paying attention to the present and decluttering the brain to make room for creativity – and in business that means boosting the bottom line.

To that end, mindfulness training has been embraced by organisations as diverse as Google, Transport for London, PricewaterhouseCoopers and the Home Office, by way of an antidote to the relentless pressure and information overload common in many workplaces.

Many of us have so much on our minds at any given time that we function quite regularly on autopilot. It's not uncommon to set off in your car and arrive at your destination only to realise you remember nothing about the journey, or walk into a room to accomplish a task only to forget instantly what it was you wanted to do.

Mindfulness teaches individuals to be present in the moment rather than being distracted about the past or projecting into the future. It doesn't stop you feeling emotions per se, but it does allow you to deal with them more dispassionately.

The technique draws on the breathing exercises commonly used in meditation and yoga, but there the comparison ends. The aim is to become more aware of thoughts and feelings, in a non-judgmental way, so that instead of being overwhelmed by them, we can manage them better. It may sound deceptively airy-fairy, but make no mistake, this isn't about chanting and there's no cross-legged spirituality involved.

The US military (hardly a bastion of hippiedom) offers marines mindfulness training before they are deployed, in recognition that it is an effective form of mental discipline.

The principles and practice of "mindful leadership" are taught at Harvard, while Oxford University's dedicated Mindfulness Centre is carrying out research into its clinical and general health benefits.

"Advances in neuroscience and psychology in relation to depression over the past 15 years have coincided with the current economic situation, which has made the condition more prevalent, and mindfulness is a solution that is emerging at just the right time," says Mark Leonard, who helped establish the Oxford centre and also runs an offshoot, the Mindfulness Exchange, which provides training. "As a culture, we are so prone to overthinking and ruminating that we need to develop a way of stilling our minds."

The World Health Organisation recently stated that by 2030, mental health issues will form the biggest burden on health care resources including heart conditions and cancer.

"Mindfulness has been shown to help those suffering from depression to manage their emotions better and dwell less on negative memories and feelings," says Leonard. "It's remarkable to see someone transformed in five weeks from an unhappy, withdrawn person who feels overburdened to someone who is receptive and upbeat and can experience pleasure in the moment."

Mindfulness-based cognitive therapy (MBCT) is recommended by the National Institute for Clinical Excellence (Nice) for preventing relapse in patients with recurrent depression, and is successful in half of all cases. Such findings have been backed up by neuroscience. When people feel stressed, the part of the brain associated with "fight or flight" – the amygdala – fires up, reducing the brain's ability to cope.

Modern crises such as a deluge of work-related emails or a clash of personalities are complex and require flexibility and emotional intelligence, but in its primitive state of high alert, the brain fixates on the immediate problem rather than thinking strategically.

The practice of mindfulness has been shown to calm the body down, reduce levels of the stress hormone cortisol and even reduce the size of grey matter in the amygdala. By contrast, the amount of grey matter in those areas of the brain associated with attention, memory and empathy appears to have increased in those who have practised mindfulness exercises.

It's not just beneficial to adults; when applied in schools, mindfulness increases both children's self-esteem and performance in class.

"I used to teach at a highly academic independent girls' school, and I found that by introducing mindfulness into lessons, it had a profound effect on the students' anxiety levels, their confidence and their concentration," says Claire Kelly, a mindfulness practitioner who is now involved with the Mindfulness in Schools Project (MiSP), a not-for-profit body that runs an eight-week programme in schools.

"Teaching mindfulness to young people gives them crucial tools to deal with the pressures of life. It's empowering, and once they know how to do it, they can draw on it whenever they need to."

Tonbridge School in Kent and Hampton School in Middlesex were the first British schools to include mindfulness in the curriculum for all 13- and 14-year-olds in 2010. Since then, more schools here and abroad have become involved. "I think mindfulness training should be made available to every child," says Kelly. "Once you've seen the tangible effect it has on behaviour and performance, it makes complete sense to incorporate it into school life and beyond."

So if you would like to embrace enhanced emotional equilibrium, a greater sense of perspective and a feeling that you can cope with the challenges the year will bring, mindfulness could well be the way forward. You have nothing to lose but your stress.

Passage 2

From the pages of

Kate Pickert, writing for TIME magazine, explores the effects of mindfulness.

The Art of Being Mindful

Mindfulness is rooted in Eastern philosophy, specifically Buddhism. But two factors set it apart and give it a practical veneer that is helping project it into the mainstream.

One might be thought of as smart marketing. Kabat-Zinn and other proponents are careful to avoid any talk of spiritualism when espousing mindfulness. Instead, they advocate a common sense approach: think of your attention as a muscle. As with any muscle, it makes sense to exercise it (in this case, with meditation), and like any muscle, it will strengthen from that exercise.

A related and potentially more powerful factor in winning over skeptics is what science is learning about our brains' ability to adapt and rewire. This phenomenon, known as neuroplasticity, suggests there are concrete and provable benefits to exercising the brain. The science – particularly as it applies to mindfulness – is far from conclusive. But it's another reason it's difficult to dismiss mindfulness as fleeting or contrived.

For Stuart Silverman, mindfulness has become a way to deal with the 24/7 pace of his job consulting with financial advisors. Silverman receives hundreds of phone calls and emails each day. "I'm nuts about being in touch," he says. Anxiety in the financial industry reached a high mark in the 2008 meltdown, but even after the crisis began to abate, Silverman found that the high stress level remained. So in 2011, he took a group of his clients on a mindfulness retreat. The group left their smartphones behind and spent four days at a resort in the Catskills in upstate New York, meditating, participating in group discussions, sitting in silence, practising yoga and eating meals quietly and mindfully. "For just about everybody there, it was a life-changing experience," says Silverman.

Researchers have found that multitasking leads to lower overall productivity. Students and workers who constantly and rapidly switch between tasks have less ability to filter out irrelevant information, and they make more mistakes. And many corporate workers today find it impossible to take breaks. According to a recent survey, more than half of employed American adults check work messages on the weekend and 4 in 10 do so while on vacation. "It's hard to unwind when your boss or employees know you're just a smartphone away," says Marturano, a former vice president at General Mills: "The technology has gone beyond what we are capable of handling."

In the years since, scientists have been able to prove that meditation and rigorous mindfulness training can lower cortisol levels and blood pressure, increase immune response and possibly even effect gene expression. Scientific study is also showing that meditation can have an impact on the structure of the brain itself. Building on the discovery that brains can change based on experiences and are not, as previously believed, static masses that are set by the time a person reaches adulthood, a growing field of neuroscientists are now studying whether meditation – and the mindfulness that results from it – can counteract what happens to our minds because of stress, trauma and constant distraction. The research has fuelled the rapid growth of MBSR and other mindfulness programs inside corporations and public institutions.

Educators are turning to mindfulness with increasing frequency – perhaps a good thing, considering how digital technology is splitting kids' attention spans too. (The average teen sends and receives more than 3,000 text messages a month.) A Bay Area-based program called Mindful Schools offers online mindfulness training to teachers, instructing them in how to equip children with concentration in classrooms and deal with stress. Launched in 2010, the group has reached more than 300,000 pupils, and educators in 43 countries and 48 states have taken its courses online.

"It was always my intention that mindfulness move into the mainstream," says Kabat-Zinn, whose MBSR bible, *Full Catastrophe Living*, first published in 1990, was just reissued. Lately, the professor has also been spreading the gospel abroad. On a November trip to Beijing, he helped lead a mindfulness retreat for about 250 Chinese students, monks and scientists.

"This is something that people are now finding compelling in many countries and many cultures, and the reason is the science," he says.

Passage 1 questions

1. Re-read lines 1–7.

(a) Explain fully what mindfulness is. **2**

(b) Analyse how the writer's use of language highlights the significance of mindfulness. **2**

2. Re-read lines 8–14.

Give two reasons why people are interested in mindfulness. **2**

3. Re-read lines 12–30.

(a) What does the writer mean when she says we 'function quite regularly on autopilot' and what two examples does she provide to support this? **3**

(b) Re-read lines 22–30. Analyse how two examples of the writer's language suggest that mindfulness is to be taken seriously. **4**

4. Re-read lines 29–36.

(a) Explain fully why depression is becoming more widely recognised. **2**

(b) Why does Mark Leonard believe we need mindfulness? **2**

5. Re-read lines 37–68.

(a) By referring to at least two features of language, analyse how Woods and/or Leonard and/or Kelly emphasise the potential of mindfulness. **4**

(b) With reference to lines 48–68, summarise the benefits of mindfulness. **4**

Passage 2 question

6. Both writers discuss the concept of mindfulness. Identify key areas on which they agree. In your answer you should refer to both passages. **5**

CfE Higher English

Practice Papers for SQA Exams

Exam B
Critical Reading

Duration – 1 hour 30 minutes

Total marks – 40

SECTION 1 – Scottish text – 20 marks

Read an extract from a Scottish text you have previously studied and attempt the questions.

Choose ONE text from either

Part A – Drama

or

Part B – Prose

or

Part C – Poetry

Attempt ALL the questions for your chosen text.

SECTION 2 – critical essay – 20 marks

Attempt ONE question from the following genres – Drama, Prose, Poetry, Film and Television Drama or Language.

Your answer must be on a different genre from that chosen in Section 1.

You should spend approximately 45 minutes on each section.

Section 1 – Scottish text – 20 marks

Choose one text from Drama, Prose or Poetry.

Read the text extract carefully and then attempt ALL the questions for your chosen text.

You should spend about 45 minutes on this section.

Text 1: Drama

If you choose this text you may not attempt a question on drama in Section 2.

Read the extract below and then attempt the following questions.

***The Slab Boys* by John Byrne**

(Exeunt. Hector's pleas fade off down the corridor. Spanky stands for a moment ... then starts going over the list of colours in his head.)

Spanky: Crimson lake, magenta, olive, cobalt blue, persian red, raw sienna, cadmium yellow, rose pink, french ultramarine, violet, and Hooker's green ... *(Starts working quickly and methodically.)*

(Pause.)

Jack: *(Off)* Sorry about that bum steer, Alan ... thought I had him pinned down for sure that time ... trouble is that nobody else knows as much about the bloody biz as he does ...

(He and Alan enter.)

Jack: Aha ... all on your ownio, Georgie? What ... nobody pulling the strings? Thought Alan here might come back and do another spot in the Slab ...

Spanky: The floor's just been mopped.

Jack: I'll leave you to it, Alan. Don't take any snash from these guys. (*To Spanky*) Look, why don't you go through the entire process from the top, Farrell?

Spanky: I'm busy, Jack.

Jack: Source materials ... pigmentation ... texture ... density ... all that sort of guff ... fugitive colours ... wrist technique. See the way he's handling that knife, Alan? Strain some gum ... that's always gripping. (*To Alan*) I'd love to show you myself but the Boss has just hit me with a half-drop for Holland. Any problems give me a shout ... OK? OK, Farrell? Ciao. (*Exit.*)

(*Spanky works on. Alan watches. Silence.*)

Spanky: OK, OK ... you get the stuff, pap it on the slab, water, gum, bingo ... you grind away till you feel like a smoke.

Alan: And that's it?

Spanky: That is it.

Alan: Fugitive colours … all that stuff?

Spanky: Listen, kiddo, the only fugitive colours we've ever had in here was Coronation Year … 1953. Six drums of red, white, and blue went missing. There … you can use Phil's slab …

Alan: What about texture? Density?

Spanky: Texture … seldom varies. Rough … that goes for the lot. Smoothest colour we ever had delivered was a poke of mahogany lake … lumps the size of Jacky boy's plooks. Hughie Maxwell broke a wrist grinding a pot this big for Bobby Sinclair … him and his wife were going to the Baptists' Christmas Ball as Amos 'n' Andy.

Alan: Density?

Spanky: Doesn't matter a bugger as long as it doesn't run off the paper on to their cavalry twills. Best to err this side of the concrete scale. Fling us up that daud of muslin … I'll strain some more gum.

(*Alan works away while Spanky prepares the gum …*)

Alan: Phew … goes for the wrists …

Spanky: Don't worry, kiddo … by the time five o'clock comes you'll have arms like Popeye. No, no … too high up the shank. (*Adjusts Alan's grip*) That's better.

Alan: Yeh. How long have you been in here?

Spanky: Too long, kiddo. Be three years this Christmas.

Alan: That's quite normal, is it?

Spanky: Nothing's normal in this joint, son. If you mean is that average? (*Shrugs.*) Jack Hogg was four … Gavin Dyer, two … Hughie Maxwell, six months … who knows? Depends if they take to your features … how many desks are free … how the Boss is feeling … what the Berlin situation's like …

Alan: How long's your pal done?

Spanky: Phil? Year and a bit. Stayed on at school … to get his Highers …

Alan: And did he?

Spanky: No … jacked it in. Got sent down for smacking the French teacher in the mouth with a German biscuit.

Alan: What'd he do that for?

Spanky: What does Phil do anything for? Laughs of course.

Alan: You mean he's nuts …

Spanky: We're all nuts, kiddo.

Alan: Look, going to cut calling me 'kiddo'? It gets really annoying …

Spanky: Sure, sure … anything you say … kiddo.

Alan: Is this about ready to dish, d'you think?

Spanky: What d'you think?

Alan: I'm asking you ...

Spanky: That's one thing you'll learn in here, Archie ... don't ask nobody nothing. It's up to you.

Alan: I think I'll dish it ... or maybe I'll give it a bit more ... no, I'll dish it, I reckon. (*Does so.*)

Spanky: (*Waiting till he's finished*) Enough gum in it?

Alan: Gum? Oh, Christ ... (*Pours it back on to slab. Accepts dish of gum from Spanky ... keeps an eye on Spanky as he adds it to paint.*) ... I thought you might be able to add it once it was dished ...

Spanky: You can.

Questions

1. By referring closely to lines 11–35, analyse how the writer's use of language conveys the contrasting views to work held by Spanky and Jack. **4**

2. By referring to at least two examples, analyse how the writer's use of language reveals Spanky's attitude towards Alan. **4**

3. By referring to any one example, explain how the stage direction reveals Spanky's competence as a slab boy. **2**

4. The importance of education is a significant issue in this play. By referring to this extract and elsewhere in the play, discuss how this theme is developed. **10**

Text 2: Drama

If you choose this text you may not attempt a question on drama in Section 2.

Read the extract below and then attempt the following questions.

***The Cheviot, the Stag and the Black, Black Oil* by John McGrath**

Enter outrageous FRENCH NORTHWEST TRADER. He signals the INDIANS to leave. They do, tugging forelocks. He taps Sturdy Highlander (S.H.). S.H. collapses thinking it's the tomahawks. His WIFE and GRANNY rush on and watch with suspicion.

N.W.T.: I am Nor-west Tra-der! Oo are you?

S.H.: I'm fine, hoo's yersel'?

N.W.T.: No no, *what* are you?

S.H.: I am a sturdy Highlander and this is my Granny. And this is wee Calum.

He indicates the baby she is carrying still.

N.W.T. (*Patting the baby's head*): Thank heaven for little Gaels! I have a très bonne idée!

S.H.: What?

N.W.T.: A very good idea – why don't you go back home!

S.H.: Because we have no home to go back to, this is our home now.

WIFE and GRANNY nod.

N.W.T.: That is where you are very wrong my friend, we have ways of making you leave! Où sont mes peaux rouges – (*To audience.*) Anyone who says walla walla wooskie or the waving of the palms will (*He makes throat cutting gesture.*) Tonto!

RED INDIAN 1 (*Leaps on*): Pronto!

N.W.T.: Hawkeye!

RED INDIAN 2 (*Leaps on*): Och aye!

The INDIANS come on and stand menacing the group one on each side.

N.W.T.: These are my little friends. They give me furs, beaver skins, Davy Crockett hats and all the little necessities of life. I give them beads, baubles, V.D., diphtheria, influenza, cholera, fire water and all the benefits of civilisation. These – are my mountains, and you're going home.

S.H. (*Clinging to his womenfolk*): I'll have to speak to Lord Selkirk about that.

Exit N.W.T. with hollow laugh.

The INDIANS remain where they are.

The group huddle and freeze.

LORD SELKIRK: Things are not going well in the Red River Valley.

S.H. (*Turning his head*): You can say that again!

LORD SELKIRK: Things are not going well in the Red River Valley. The Governor of the Province seems to have no control over the hooligans of the Northwest Company and their half-breed servants. I have complained to the Colonial Secretary. Unfortunately the Northwest Company denies our allegations and the Governor will not provide troops to protect the settlers. However – the highlanders are a sturdy breed and accustomed to the hazards of life in the wild so I am sending out another three boatloads.

He exits pleased. The lights change to fire on the encampment. The INDIANS dance round the family, with scalping gestures while they sink down with wails to the ground.

WIFE and GRANNY remain and hum the song, 'Take me Back to the Red River Valley', while S.H. rises, crosses to the microphone and narrates.

STURDY HIGHLANDER (*Out of character*): But we came, more and more of us, from all over Europe, in the interests of a trade war between two lots of shareholders, and in time, the Red Indians were reduced to the same state as our fathers after Culloden – defeated, hunted, treated like the scum of the earth, their culture polluted and torn out with slow deliberation and their land no longer their own.

The humming dies away and the mouth-organ takes over quietly.

But still we came. From all over Europe. The highland exploitation chain-reacted around the world; in Australia the aborigines were hunted like animals; in Tasmania not one aborigine was left alive; all over Africa, black men were massacred and brought to heel. In America the plains were emptied of men and buffalo, and the seeds of the next century's imperialist power were firmly planted. And at home, the word went round that over there, things were getting better.

Questions

5. Examine the use of humour at the start of this section. You should comment on at least one piece of evidence. **3**

6. Explain the irony of the Northwest Trader's remarks regarding the relationship with his 'little friends'. **2**

7. What impression are we given of Lord Selkirk from his remarks? You should comment on at least one piece of evidence. **2**

8. With reference to the Sturdy Highlander's closing remarks, analyse what is revealed about his attitude towards the activities in the colonies. **3**

9. Throughout this play, McGrath utilises a surprisingly large number of voices and characters in one 'scene'. With reference to this extract and elsewhere in the play, discuss how this is used to develop theme. **10**

Text 3: Drama

If you choose this text you may not attempt a question on drama in Section 2.

Read the extract below and then attempt the following questions.

Men Should Weep **by Ena Lamont Stewart**

This extract is from Act II, Scene 2.

The same. A month later. Afternoon.

Alec and Isa are quarrelling in the bedroom: their raised voices are heard off.

Isa comes out in a soiled, tawdry negligee with her hair about her shoulders, a cigarette hanging from her lip.

ISA: Aw shut up! I'm sick o yer jawin.

Alec appears behind her, half dressed.

ALEC: I'm tellin ye, Isa, I'll no staun much mair! I'm jist warnin ye. That's a.

ISA: An I'm warnin you! If you think I'm gaun on like this a ma life, ye've anither think comin. You're no the only pebble on ma beach, no by a lang chalk. If you want tae keep me, it's time ye wis makin a bit o dough again. I canna live on air.

ALEC: (*Placating*) Come an we'll go tae the dugs the night, Isa; mebbe we'll hae a bit o luck.

ISA: Aye. Mebbe.

ALEC: Mind the last time I won –

ISA: Aye, an I mind the last hauf dizzen times ye lost … Whit did ye dae wi yon bag?

ALEC: I flung it ower a wa.

ISA: Ye stupid fool! I'm needin a bag.

ALEC: It's no safe, Isa – ye've got tae get rid o the evidence – the Polis …

ISA: Three quid and a handfu o coppers! A fat lot o use that is tae me. Why the Hell did ye no pick on a toff! We wis in the right district.

ALEC: She looked like a toff; honest, Isa! She'd on a fur coat …

ISA: Whit kind o fur? Rabbit? You're that dumb ye wouldnae ken. Next time, I'm no jookin up a lane, I'm stayin wi ye.

ALEC: No ye're no! It's no safe. Ye've got tae be able tae rin fast.

ISA: Rin! That's a you're guid for. Rinnin. It's aboot time I wis daein the rinnin. I' m sick fed up wi you. If I'd went wi Peter Robb I'd hae a fur coat an it wouldna be rabbit. An he's got a caur …

ALEC: You say Peter Robb tae me again an I'll kill ye! I wull! I'll kill ye!

He gets hold of her by the throat: she makes strangling noises. He panics and drops her.

ISA: (*Frightened first, then angry*) You … ! Ma Goad! (*Rubbing her throat*) You'll pey for that!

ALEC: Isa! Did I hurt ye? I didnae mean tae hurt ye – I lost ma heid.

ISA: Get oot! Clear aff oot o ma sight!

ALEC: Isa, I'm sorry. I jist see red when ye talk aboot Peter Robb. I canna see naethin but him an you taegether an the way ye wis last night, cairryin oan wi him.

ISA: Aye! Ye can use yer hauns a right on a wumman; but if ye wis hauf a man, ye'd have kicked his teeth in last night.

ALEC: He's bigger nor me – he'd have hauf-killed me!

ISA: Fancy me mairryin a rat like you. The joke wis on me a right.

ALEC: Isa, I'll hae plenty again, you'll see … I've a coupla pals that's got ideas … wait on, Isa! I'll get ye onythin ye want … a fur coat an crockydile shoes – ye said ye wanted crockydile shoes – I proamise, Isa! I proamise! If ye'll stay wi me … I love ye, Isa; honest, I dae. I love ye.

ISA: Love! Hee-haw! There's nae sich a thing. There's wantin tae get intae bed wi someone ye fancy … or wantin someone'll let ye lie in yer bed an no have tae work; but there's nae love. No roon aboot here, onyway. Don't kid yersel.

ALEC: (*Trying to take her in his arms*) That's no true! I love ye. I'm no fit for onythin when ye're oot o ma sight. I'm … lost waitin on ye comin back. I get tae thinkin … an wonderin whaur ye are … and if –

ISA: If I'm behavin masel? Well, hauf the time, I'm no.

ALEC: Isa!

ISA: Aw shut up! (*She pushes him away*) Ye're aye wantin tae slobber ower me. If ye wis onythin decent tae look at it wouldna be sae bad, but ye're like somethin that's been left oot a night in the rain. G'on blow! I canna staun yer fumblin aboot – unless I'm canned. Get oot ma way. I'm gonnae get dressed.

She slams the bedroom door in his face.

He stands looking at it.

Questions

10. What do the stage directions at the beginning of this extract reveal about the character of Isa? **2**

11. Alec desperately wants Isa to stay with him. Referring closely to the extract, analyse how Alec tries to persuade Isa and what this reveals about his character. **4**

12. This scene would have been shocking to a contemporary audience. Referring closely to the extract, explain why this would be the case. **4**

13. Referring closely to this extract, and the play as a whole, discuss the dramatic importance of Alec and Isa's relationship. **10**

Text 1: Prose

If you choose this text you may not attempt a question on prose in Section 2.

Read the extract below and then attempt the following questions.

***The Crater* by Iain Crichton Smith**

In this extract, Lieutenant Mackinnon decides to go back for the missing soldier.

Once more he heard it. It sounded like someone crying 'Help'.

He stopped. 'All right,' he said. 'We're going for him. Come on.'

And he stood up. There was no reason for crawling any more. The night was clear. And they would have to hurry. And the other two stood up as well when they saw him doing so. He couldn't leave a man to die in the pit of green slime. 'We'll run,' he said. And they ran to the first one and listened. They cried fiercely, 'Are you there?' But there was no answer. Then they seemed to hear it from the next one and they were at that one soon too, peering down into the green slime, illuminated by moonlight. But there was no answer. There was one left and they made for that one. They screamed again, in the sound of the shells, and they seemed to hear an answer. They heard what seemed to be a bubbling. 'Are you there?' said Robert, bending down and listening. 'Can you get over here?' They could hear splashing and deep below them breathing, frantic breathing as if someone was frightened to death. 'It's all right,' he said, 'if you come over here, I'll send my rifle down. You two hang on to me,' he said to the others. He was terrified. That depth, that green depth. Was it Morrison down there, after all? He hadn't spoken. The splashings came closer. The voice was like an animal's repeating endlessly a mixture of curses and prayers. Robert hung over the edge of the crater. 'For Christ's sake don't let me go,' he said to the other two. It wasn't right that a man should die in green slime. He hung over the rim holding his rifle down. He felt it being caught, as if there was a great fish at the end of a line. He felt it moving. And the others hung at his heels, like a chain. The moon shone suddenly out between two clouds and in that moment he saw it, a body covered with greenish slime, an obscene mermaid, hanging on to his rifle while the two eyes, white in the green face, shone upward and the mouth, gritted, tried not to let the blood through. It was a monster of the deep, it was a sight so terrible that he nearly fell. He was about to say, 'It's no good, he's dying,' but something prevented him from saying it, if he said it then he would never forget it. He knew that. The hands clung to the rifle below in the slime. The others pulled behind him. 'For Christ's sake hang on to the rifle,' he said to the monster below. 'Don't let go.' And it seemed to be emerging from the deep, setting its feet against the side of the crater, all green, all mottled, like a disease. It climbed as if up a mountainside in the stench. It hung there against the wall. 'Hold on,' he said. 'Hold on.' His whole body was concentrated. This man must not fall down again into that lake. The death would be too terrible. The face was coming over the side of the crater, the teeth gritted, blood at the mouth. It hung there for a long moment and then the three of them had got him over the side. He felt like cheering, standing up in the light of No Man's Land and cheering. Sergeant Smith was kneeling down beside the body, his ear to the heart. It was like a body which might have come from space, green and illuminated and slimy. And over it poured the merciless moonlight.

'Come on,' he said to the other two. And at that moment Sergeant Smith said, 'He's dead.'

Questions

14. By referring closely to lines 1–23, explain how any two aspects of Lieutenant Robert Mackinnon's character are revealed. **4**

15. By referring to at least two examples from lines 14–34, analyse how the writer conveys the degradation and dehumanisation of war. **4**

16. '"Come on," he said to the other two. And at that moment Sergeant Smith said, "He's dead."'
Explain how the use of anti-climax develops a key message about war. **2**

17. Discuss Iain Crichton Smith's use of contrasting characters in his short stories.
You should refer to this and at least one other story by Crichton Smith. **10**

Text 2: Prose

If you choose this text you may not attempt a question on prose in Section 2.

Read the extract below and then attempt the following questions.

***The Whaler's Return* by George Mackay Brown**

He woke in a ditch below Fadoon, in broad daylight, a mile and more from the tinkers' quarry. Painfully he got to his feet. His bones creaked. Water ran out of his sleeve. His tongue lay in his mouth like a filthy rag.

His first thought was for his money. His fingers groped under his shirt. There were two sovereigns left in his belt. Out of his pocket he brought twelve shillings in silver and a few coppers. A surge of relief went through him. He would at least be able to pay the first half year's rent for Breck, two guineas.

He walked between two fields to Fadoon. The last green was gone from the oats now; the harvest burnish was on every blade. There was a curl of smoke from the roof and the door stood open. He bowed his head under the lintel and went in. Peterina was sitting at her spinning wheel.

'Peace to this place,' said Flaws.

'You're back from the whales, Andrew Flaws,' said Peterina.

'Yes,' he said.

'You're in better shape than I expected,' said Peterina. 'There are thirty-four ale-houses in the town of Hamnavoe and sixteen ale-houses on the road between Hamnavoe and Birsay. Some men from the ships are a long time getting home.'

'I have the rent for the croft of Breck,' said Flaws, 'and a shilling or two besides.'

'We move in in November,' said Peterina. She went over to the cupboard and brought out a jug and a bannock. 'Bring over your chair to the table,' she said. 'Here's some bread and ale.' While Flaws was eating, Peterina said, 'There's little news in the parish. My father was killed by a horse in the month of June. God forgive me for speaking ill of the dead, but it's been a quiet house since then. A quiet house but a bare house. I've had to live on the parochial poor fund since the funeral. With the shame of that, I don't show my face in the public. I wasn't able to pay any of the death money, neither the shrouding fee nor the fee for the digging of the grave nor the minister's fee.'

'I saw to all that on my way home,' said Flaws. 'Everything is paid.'

'That was a good thing you did, Andrew Flaws,' said Peterina.

'And the wedding fee is paid too,' said Flaws.

'That will be in the last week of September,' said Peterina. 'I will try to be a good wife to you, Andrew Flaws. Before that time I must make a blanket for the bed, and a christening shawl for the first bairn, and two shrouds, one for you and one for me, for no man can tell the day or the hour, and we must be ready at all times.' The wheel went round and the new grey wool slid between her fingers.

'I tarred the boat down at the beach,' said Peterina. 'You'll fish until such time as we reap our first harvest at Breck.'

'Yes,' said Flaws.

'There was a wedding last night at the tinkers' camp in the quarry,' said Peterina. 'It was a wild celebration. I heard fiddles at three o'clock in the morning.'

'Yes,' said Flaws. He drank the last of the ale. It was the sweetest drink he had ever tasted. 'I think I'll sleep for an hour or two,' he said, 'then I'll maybe catch a few haddocks, before sunset. The laird will be wanting harvesters tomorrow or the day after.'

Questions

18. By referring closely to the extract, analyse how Mackay Brown conveys how Flaws feels on waking. You may refer to ideas and/or language. **2**

19. Referring closely to the extract, analyse how Mackay Brown conveys Peterina's practical nature. **4**

20. Lines 38–40 conclude the short story as well as the extract. Referring closely to the extract, evaluate the effectiveness of lines 38–40 as a conclusion to the **extract** as a whole. **4**

21. George Mackay Brown's writing often shows a deep awareness of the cyclical nature of life, both in nature and human relationships. With close reference to this story, and to at least one other by Mackay Brown, discuss how he conveys this awareness. **10**

Text 3: Prose

If you choose this text you may not attempt a question on prose in Section 2.

Read the extract below and then attempt the following questions.

***The Trick Is To Keep Breathing* by Janice Galloway**

Look
all I wanted to be was civilised and polite. I wanted to be no trouble. I wanted to be brave and discreet. This had to be the final stage of the endurance test and all I had to do was last out. I thought I was Bunyan's Pilgrim and Dorothy in the Wizard of Oz. But the lasting out was terrible. I made appointments with the doctor and he gave me pills to tide me over when I got anxious. I got anxious when they didn't tide me over into anything different. He gave me more pills. I kept going to work. I was no nearer Kansas or the Celestial City. Then

I started smelling Michael's aftershave in the middle of the night. I would go to bed and there it was, in a cloud all round my head. I thought if I could smell his aftershave he must be around somewhere. I saw him in cars, across the street, in buses, roaring past on strange motorbikes, drifting by the glass panel of my classroom door. I read his horoscope. How could he be having a difficult phase with money if he was dead? Of course he wasn't *dead*: just hiding. At night I sunk my face into his clothes and howled at the cloth. A magazine article said it was fairly common and not as unhealthy as you'd think. Then I would go to bed and wait for the slow seep of aftershave through the ether. I knew he wasn't just a carcass liquefying in a wooden box but an invisible presence hovering in a cloud of Aramis above my bed. I also suspected I was lying. When I found the bottle, tipped on its side and leaking along the rim I knew for sure. I had put it there myself ages ago so I could reach for it and smell his neck when I wanted to feel like hell in the middle of the night. Then I must have knocked it over and been too wilful to admit to what it was later. My own duplicity shocked me. I held onto the bottle for a week or so then threw it out.

My mother was right. I have no common sense. I don't know a damn thing worth knowing.

THE CHURCH	THE MARRIED
THE LAW	WHAT'S WHAT

I haven't a clue.

The clock ticks too loud while I lie still, shrinking.

Please god make boulders crash through the roof. In three or four days when the Health Visitor comes she will find only mashed remains, marrowbone jelly oozing between the shards like bitumen. *Well, she'll say, We're not doing so well today, are we?* It's too cold. The hairs on my legs are stiff. I shiver and wish the phone would ring.

Needing people yet being afraid of them is wearing me out. I struggle with the paradox all the time and can't resolve it. When people visit I am distraught trying to look as if I can cope. At work I never speak but I want to be spoken to. If anyone does I get anxious and stammer. I'm scared of the phone yet I want it to ring.

Questions

27. With close reference to the extract, explain what Chris means by 'that troubled thinking' (line 13). **4**

28. The oppressive heat and the impending storm are used to mirror Chris' feelings and to foreshadow the death of Jean Guthrie. With close reference to two examples from the extract, analyse the effectiveness of this device. **4**

29. Comment on the presentation of Dod and Alec in this extract. **2**

30. A central theme in the novel is that of change. By referring to this extract, and elsewhere in the novel, discuss how Grassic Gibbon conveys the notion of change in *Sunset Song*. **10**

Text 5: Prose

If you choose this text you may not attempt a question on prose in Section 2.

Read the extract below and then attempt the following questions.

***The Cone-Gatherers* by Robin Jenkins**

In this extract, Duror is returning home to his wife, Peggy, and mother-in-law Mrs Lochie.

'Is that you, John?' called his mother-in-law sharply from the living room.

'Aye, it's me,' he answered, and went in.

She was seated knitting beside the wireless set. The door to Peggy's bedroom was wide open to let her too listen to the cheerful music.

Mrs Lochie was a stout white haired woman, with an expression of dour resoluteness that she wore always, whether peeling potatoes or feeding hens or as at present knitting a white bed jacket. It was her intimation that never would she allow her daughter's misfortune to conquer her, but that also never would she forgive whoever was responsible for that misfortune. Even in sleep her features did not relax, as if God too was a suspect, not to be trusted.

'You're late,' she said, as she rose and put down her knitting. It was an accusation. 'She's been anxious about you. I'll set out your tea.'

'Thanks,' he said, and stood still.

'Aren't you going in?' she asked. 'That's her shouting for you.' She came close to him and whispered. 'Do you think I don't ken what an effort it is for you?'

There was no pity in her question, only condemnation; and his very glance towards the bedroom where his wife, with plaintive giggles, kept calling his name proved her right.

'It's a pity, isn't it,' whispered Mrs Lochie, with a smile, 'she doesn't die and leave you in peace?'

He did not deny her insinuation, nor did he try to explain to her that love itself perhaps could become paralysed.

'Take care, though,' she muttered, as she went away, 'you don't let her see it.'

With a shudder he walked over and stood in the doorway of the bedroom.

Peggy was propped up on pillows, and was busy chewing.

The sweetness of her youth still haunting amidst the great wobbling masses of pallid fat that composed her face added to her grotesqueness a pathos that often had visitors bursting into unexpected tears. She loved children but they were terrified by her; she would for hours dandle a pillow as if it was a baby. Her hair was still wonderfully black and glossy, so that she insisted on wearing it down about her shoulders, bound with red ribbons. White though was her favourite colour. Her nightdresses, with lace at neck and sleeves, were always white and fresh and carefully ironed. When she had been well, in the first two years of their marriage, she had loved to race with him hand-in-hand over moor and field, through whins and briers, up knolls and hills to the clouds: any old skirt and jumper had done then.

Though not capable of conveying it well, either by word or expression, she was pleased and relieved to see him home. Her voice was squeaky with an inveterate petulance, although sometimes, disconcerting everybody who heard it, her old gay laughter could suddenly burst forth, followed by tears of wonder and regret.

He stood by the door.

'Am I to get a kiss?' she asked.

'I've still to wash, Peggy. I've been in the wood, handling rabbits.'

'I don't care. Amn't I a gamekeeper's wife? I used to like the smell of rabbits. I want a kiss.'

Her wheedling voice reminded him of the hunchback's.

There wouldn't, he thought, be room in the hut for so large a bed. Here too everything was white and immaculate, whereas yonder everything was dull, soiled, and scummy. Yet he could see, almost as plainly as he saw his wife in heart-rending coquettish silly tears, the hunchback carving happily at his wooden squirrel.

'It was another fine afternoon,' he said.

'Fine for some folk,' she whimpered.

'Didn't you manage to get out into the garden?'

'You know it's too much for my mother to manage by herself. I just had to lie here and watch the tops of the trees.' Then her voice brightened. 'Do you know what I was thinking about, John?'

'No, Peggy.'

'I was thinking of a day at Fyneside long ago. It was autumn then too. I think autumn's the bonniest season. You put rowan berries in my hair.'

'The rowans are just about past,' he said.

'For me they're past forever,' she cried. 'I used to love the time when the berries were ripe and red.'

He saw the appeal in her streaming eyes, but he could not respond to it; once it had sent him away with his own eyes wet. 'Red as blood,' she sobbed.

Questions

31. By referring closely to lines 1–21, analyse how the writer conveys the tension between Duror and Mrs Lochie. **3**

32. Analyse how the writer's use of language in lines 23–31 creates an unpleasant depiction of Peggy. **2**

33. By referring closely to lines 32–56, analyse how the interaction between Duror and his wife adds to our understanding of Peggy's character. **3**

34. In the scene, Peggy reminds Duror of Calum. Explain fully why Duror chooses to compare his home to Calum's hut at this point. **2**

35. By referring to this scene and elsewhere in the novel, analyse the impact female characters have on Duror's downfall. **10**

Text 1: Poetry

If you choose this text you may not attempt a question on poetry in Section 2.

Read the extract below and then attempt the following questions.

An extract from *Tam o'Shanter* by Robert Burns

This extract begins at stanza 11.

Inspiring bold John Barleycorn!
What dangers thou canst make us scorn!
Wi' tippenny, we fear nae evil;
Wi' usquabae, we'll face the devil!
The swats sae ream'd in Tammie's noddle,
Fair play, he car'd na deils a boddle,
But Maggie stood, right sair astonish'd,
Till, by the heel and hand admonish'd,
She ventur'd forward on the light;
And, wow! Tam saw an unco sight!

Warlocks and witches in a dance:
Nae cotillon, brent new frae France,
But hornpipes, jigs, strathspeys, and reels,
Put life and mettle in their heels.
A winnock-bunker in the east,
There sat auld Nick, in shape o' beast;
A towzie tyke, black, grim, and large,
To gie them music was his charge:
He screw'd the pipes and gart them skirl,
Till roof and rafters a' did dirl. –
Coffins stood round, like open presses,
That shaw'd the Dead in their last dresses;
And (by some devilish cantraip sleight)

Each in its cauld hand held a light.
By which heroic Tam was able
To note upon the haly table,
A murderer's banes, in gibbet-airns;
Twa span-lang, wee, unchristened bairns;
A thief, new-cutted frae a rape,
Wi' his last gasp his gab did gape;
Five tomahawks, wi' blude red-rusted:
Five scimitars, wi' murder crusted;
A garter which a babe had strangled:
A knife, a father's throat had mangled.
Whom his ain son of life bereft,
The grey-hairs yet stack to the heft;
Wi' mair of horrible and awfu',
Which even to name wad be unlawfu'.
Three lawyers tongues, turned inside oot,
Wi' lies, seamed like a beggars clout,
Three priests hearts, rotten, black as muck,
Lay stinkin, vile in every neuk.

Questions

36. Burns talks of drink in stanza 11 (lines 1–10). With reference to one example from the extract in support, identify the tone he uses here. **2**

37. With reference to the extract, explain how the structure of stanza 12 (lines 11–42) adds to its effect. **4**

38. Burns presents a vigorous, yet terrifying vision in stanza 12 (lines 11–42). With reference to at least two examples, analyse how he does this. **4**

39. Burns is often referred to as the 'ploughman poet' and saw himself as the voice of the common man. From your reading of this poem and at least one other poem by Burns, discuss how he presents the life of the common man and how he might champion it. **10**

Text 2: Poetry

If you choose this text you may not attempt a question on poetry in Section 2.

Read the extract below and then attempt the following questions.

An extract from *Mrs Midas* by Carol Ann Duffy

Separate beds. In fact, I put a chair against my door,
near petrified. He was below, turning the spare room
into the tomb of Tutankhamun. You see, we were passionate then,
in those halcyon days; unwrapping each other, rapidly,
like presents, fast food. But now I feared his honeyed embrace,
the kiss that would turn my lips to a work of art.

And who, when it comes to the crunch, can live
with a heart of gold? That night, I dreamt I bore
his child, its perfect ore limbs, its little tongue
like a precious latch, its amber eyes
holding their pupils like flies. My dream-milk
burned in my breasts. I woke to the streaming sun.

So he had to move out. We'd a caravan
in the wilds, in a glade of its own. I drove him up
under cover of dark. He sat in the back.
And then I came home, the woman who married the fool
who wished for gold. At first I visited, odd times,
parking the car a good way off, then walking.

You knew you were getting close. Golden trout
on the grass. One day, a hare hung from a larch,
a beautiful lemon mistake. And then his footprints,
glistening next to the river's path. He was thin,

delirious; hearing, he said, the music of Pan
from the woods. Listen. That was the last straw.

What gets me now is not the idiocy or greed
but lack of thought for me. Pure selfishness. I sold
the contents of the house and came down here.
I think of him in certain lights, dawn, late afternoon,
and once a bowl of apples stopped me dead. I miss most,
even now, his hands, his warm hands on my skin, his touch.

Questions

40. With reference to the first stanza in this extract, analyse how Duffy highlights the dramatic change in the relationship between Mr and Mrs Midas. **2**

41. Examine how Duffy reveals both the desire and fear the speaker feels when dreaming of having Midas' child. You should refer to two pieces of evidence. **4**

42. In line 23, we discover the state of Midas after the couple's separation. Explain why it is fitting that he should be 'hearing … the music of pan'. **2**

43. Look carefully at the closing two lines. Evaluate their effectiveness as a conclusion to the poem. **2**

44. In many of Duffy's poems, the personality of the speaker is central to the poem's message. With reference to this poem and another poem or poems by Duffy, discuss how Duffy uses this feature to explore theme. **10**

Text 3: Poetry

If you choose this text you may not attempt a question on poetry in Section 2.

Read the extract below and then attempt the following questions.

An extract from *The Bargain* by Liz Lochhead

The river in January is fast and high.
You and I
are off to the Barrows.
Gathering police-horses twitch and fret
at the Tron end of London Road and Gallowgate.
The early kick-off we forgot
has us, three thirty, rubbing the wrong way
against all the ugly losers
getting ready to let fly
where the two rivers meet.

January, and we're
looking back, looking forward,
don't know which way

but the boy
with three beautiful Bakelite
Bush radios for sale in Meadow's Minimarket is
buttonpopping stationhopping he
doesn't miss a beat   sings along   it's easy
to every changing tune

Yes today we're in love aren't we?
with the whole splintering city
its big quick river   wintry bridges
its brazen black Victorian heart.

So what if every other tenement
wears its hearth on its gable end?
All I want
is my glad eye to catch
a glint in your flinty Northern face again
just once. Oh I know it's cold
and coming down
and no we never lingered long among
the Shipbank traders.
Paddy's Market   underneath the arches
Stank too much today
the usual wetdog reek rising
from piles of old damp clothes

Questions

45. By referring to **two** examples from stanza one, analyse the use of poetic technique in establishing atmosphere. **2**

46. Look closely at stanza two. What is the narrator trying to suggest about her relationship? **2**

47. In the third stanza there is a marked shift in mood. Choose **two** poetic techniques and analyse how they help to convey this change. **3**

48. In stanza four we are given an even stronger sense of the relationship between the narrator and her partner.
With reference to **two** examples from this stanza, explain what is suggested about this couple. **3**

49. In many of Lochhead's poems, she highlights the significance of a single moment. By referring to this poem and at least one other work by Lochhead, discuss how this is used to explore theme in her work. **10**

Text 4: Poetry

If you choose this text you may not attempt a question on poetry in Section 2.

Read the extract below and then attempt the following questions.

***Basking Shark* by Norman MacCaig**

To stub an oar on a rock where none should be,
To have it rise with a slounge out of the sea
Is a thing that happened once (too often) to me.

But not too often – though enough. I count as gain
That once I met, on a sea tin-tacked with rain,
That roomsized monster with a matchbox brain.

He displaced more than water. He shoggled me
Centuries back – this decadent townee
Shook on a wrong branch of his family tree.

Swish up the dirt and, when it settles, a spring
Is all the clearer. I saw me, in one fling,
Emerging from the slime of everything.

So who's the monster? The thought made me grow pale
For twenty seconds while, sail after sail,
The tall fin slid away and then the tail.

Questions

50. With reference to the text, explain fully MacCaig's contradictory feelings about his encounter with the basking shark in **stanzas 1** and **2**. **2**

51. By referring to lines 1–6, analyse how MacCaig's use of poetic technique conveys an effective depiction of the basking shark. **3**

52. Look at **stanza 3**.
'He displaced more than water.'
Explain fully what the poet means by this. **2**

53. Evaluate the effectiveness of **stanza 5** as a conclusion to the poem. Your answer should deal with ideas and/or language. **3**

54. By referring to this poem and at least one other by Norman MacCaig, discuss his use of nature and the natural world to develop theme in his work. **10**

Text 5: Poetry

If you choose this text you may not attempt a question on poetry in Section 2.

Read the extract below and then attempt the following questions.

An extract from *Hallaig* by Sorley MacLean

I will wait for the birches to move,
The wood to come up past the cairn
Until it has veiled the mountain
Down from Beinn na Lice in shade.

If it doesn't, I'll go to Hallaig,
To the Sabbath of the dead,
Down to where each departed
Generation has gathered.

Hallaig is where they survive,
All the MacLeans and MacLeods
Who were there in the time of Mac Gille Chaluim:
The dead have been seen alive,

The men at their length on the grass
At the gable of every house,
The girls a wood of birch trees
Standing tall, with their heads bowed.

Between The Leac and Fearns
The road is plush with moss
And the girls in a noiseless procession
Going to Clachan as always

And coming back from Clachan
And Suisnish, their land of the living,
Still lightsome and unheartbroken,
Their stories only beginning.

From Fearns Burn to the raised beach
Showing clear in the shrouded hills
There are only girls congregating,
Endlessly walking along

Back through the gloaming to Hallaig
Through the vivid speechless air,
Pouring down the steep slopes,
Their laughter misting my ear

And their beauty a glaze on my heart.
Then as the kyles go dim
And the sun sets behind Dun Cana
Love's loaded gun will take aim.

It will bring down the lightheaded deer
As he sniffs the grass round the wallsteads
And his eye will freeze: while I live,
His blood won't be traced in the woods.

Questions

55. With close reference to lines 1–12, why is Hallaig important to the poet? **4**

56. How does MacLean show Hallaig is deserted in lines 5–28? **2**

57. Referring closely to the poem, analyse MacLean's use of imagery in lines 36–40, explaining its significance. **4**

58. Sorley MacLean often uses the landscape as a symbol to represent his ideas. Referring closely to this poem and to another poem or poems by MacLean, discuss how effectively the poet uses this device. **10**

Text 6: Poetry

If you choose this text you may not attempt a question on poetry in Section 2.

Read the extract below and then attempt the following questions.

***The Thread* by Don Paterson**

Jamie made his landing in the world
so hard he ploughed straight back into the earth.
They caught him by the head of his one breath
and pulled him up. They don't know how it held.
And so today I thank what higher will
brought us to here, to you and me and Russ,
the great twin-engined swaying wingspan of us
roaring down the back of Kirrie Hill

and your two-year-old lungs somehow out-revving
every engine in the universe.
All that trouble just to turn up dead
was all I thought that long week. Now the thread
is holding all of us: look at our tiny house,
son, the white dot of your mother waving

Questions

59. By referring closely to lines 1–4, analyse how the writer's use of poetic techniques is effective in conveying the difficulties of Paterson's son's birth. **4**

60. With reference to poetic technique, analyse how lines 5–10 act as a contrast to the opening lines of the poem. **4**

61. Look at **stanza 2**.
'Now the thread is holding all of us'
Comment on the effectiveness of this use of imagery. **2**

62. The miraculous and mysterious nature of life is a common theme in Don Paterson's poems. By referring to this and at least one other poem by Paterson, discuss how he develops this theme. **10**

[END OF SECTION 1]

Section 2 – Critical essay – 20 marks

Attempt ONE question from the following genres — Drama, Prose, Poetry, Film and Television Drama, or Language.

You may use a Scottish text but NOT the one used in Section 1.

Your answer must be on a different genre from that chosen in Section 1.

You should spend approximately 45 minutes on this section.

DRAMA

Answers to questions on **drama** should refer to the text and to such relevant features as characterisation, key scene(s), structure, climax, theme, plot, conflict, setting …

1. Choose a play in which a character makes a vital error.

Briefly explain the reasons for their error and discuss how the dramatist's presentation of this feature enhances your understanding of the play as a whole.

2. Choose a play in which a scene acts as a clear turning point.

By referring in detail to the turning point, discuss in what ways it is important for your understanding of the play as a whole.

3. Choose a play in which tension exists between two characters.

Briefly explain the root of this tension and discuss how the dramatist's presentation of this feature enhances your understanding of the play as a whole.

PROSE — FICTION

Answers to questions on **prose fiction** should refer to the text and to such relevant features as characterisation, setting, language, key incident(s), climax, turning point, plot, structure, narrative technique, theme, ideas, description …

4. Choose a novel or short story in which the fate of a main character is important in conveying the writer's theme.

Explain what you consider the theme to be and discuss how effectively the fate of the character conveys it.

5. Choose a novel or short story which explores the dark side of human nature or human society.

Discuss how the writer explores this theme and discuss how this theme is used to enhance your appreciation of the text as a whole.

6. Choose a novel or short story in which the narrator's voice is an important feature in your appreciation of the text.

Discuss how the writer uses this technique in an effective way.

PROSE — NON-FICTION

Answers to questions on **prose non-fiction** should refer to the text and to such relevant features as ideas, use of evidence, stance, style, selection of material, narrative voice ...

7. Choose a non-fiction text which is set in a society that is different to the one in which we live.

Briefly explain what is significantly different and discuss how the writer made you aware of this.

8. Choose a non-fiction text in which the writer's ability to evoke a sense of place is very important to the success of the text.

Show how the writer's presentation of the location(s) enhanced your appreciation of the text.

9. Choose a non-fiction text in which the writer presents a strong point of view on a particular subject.

Briefly explain what the writer's view is and discuss in detail how this view is presented convincingly.

POETRY

Answers to questions on **poetry** should refer to the text and to such relevant features as word choice, tone, imagery, structure, content, rhythm, rhyme, theme, sound, ideas ...

10. Choose a poem in which the opening or closing lines are effective in revealing the central concern(s) of the text.

Show how the content and the poetic techniques used are effective in revealing the central concern(s) of the text.

11. Choose a poem in which a place or scene or person is portrayed vividly.

Show how the poet captures the place or scene or person vividly and go on to discuss how the poet exploits the place or scene or person to explore an important theme.

12. Choose two poems in which the portrayal of nature is important in conveying the central concern(s).

Discuss which poem you find more effective in deepening your understanding of the central concern(s) through the portrayal of nature.

FILM AND TELEVISION DRAMA

Answers to questions on **film and television drama*** should refer to the text and to such relevant features as use of camera, key sequence, characterisation, mise en scène, editing, setting, music/sound, special effects, plot, dialogue …

13. Choose a film or television drama* in which a main character faces a moral dilemma.

Explain the moral dilemma faced by the character, and then discuss how the film or programme makers' presentation of the character's moral dilemma deepens your understanding of the central concern(s) of the text.

14. Choose a film or television drama* which evokes a particular period of history to convey a message about modern life.

By referring to selected sequences and the text as a whole, show how the film or programme makers evoke the period and go on to explore how this period is used to convey a message about modern life.

15. Choose a film or television drama* in which there is a key scene which is important to the text as a whole.

Discuss how the techniques used by the film or programme makers emphasise the significance of the scene and go on to show its importance to the text as a whole.

***"television drama" includes a single play, a series or a serial.**

LANGUAGE

Answers to questions on **language** should refer to the text and to such relevant features as register, accent, dialect, slang, jargon, vocabulary, tone, abbreviation …

16. Choose at least one example of travel journalism.

Identify the key features of the language used in this particular journalistic area and discuss that area's contribution to effective reporting.

17. Choose at least one example of promotional writing such as advertising leaflets or posters, campaign leaflets, television advertisements.

Identify some of the distinctive features of the language used and discuss to what extent these features contribute to effective communication.

18. Choose at least one example of comedy such as stand-up, sit-com, sketches.

By referring to specific features of language, discuss to what extent you feel the speech is successful in achieving its purpose.

[END OF SECTION 2]

The following two passages discuss the arrival of a new virtual reality headset, Oculus Rift, and its purchase by Mark Zuckerberg (owner/creator of Facebook).

Passage 1

From the pages of

In the first passage Lev Grossman, writing in TIME magazine, recalls his first experience of Oculus Rift and discusses reactions to the Facebook buyout.

The Virtual Genius of Oculus Rift

On March 26, Facebook announced that it was purchasing Oculus VR in a deal worth $2 billion. The social-networking giant, Mark Zuckerberg, is getting top-flight engineering expertise as well as the technology behind the company's flagship and only product, a virtual-reality headset. "Mobile is the platform of today, and now we're also getting ready for the platforms of tomorrow," Zuckerberg said in a press conference. "Oculus has the chance to create the most social platform ever and change the way we work, play and communicate."

Two billion dollars is a lot of money – a head-snapping amount – for a social network to pay for a two-year-old hardware company with an ultra-nerdy name that has yet to ship a consumer-ready product and whose founder is still only 21. But what's really surprising is that Zuckerberg is putting down a massive bet on virtual reality, which until very recently was considered not just a failure but a punch line.

The Oculus Rift – the dorky name is a point of nerd pride – doesn't look particularly futuristic. It looks like a pair of chunky ski goggles with opaque black plastic where the lenses should be. Time will tell whether it's a gateway to a new virtual frontier, but one thing is clear already: you look weird wearing it.

But put it on anyway – it embraces your head slightly more forcefully than would be ideally comfortable – because you'll get the rare sensation of experiencing a technology that is genuinely new. Google Glass feels like what it looks like: you put it on and think, *Yup, it's a pair of glasses with a tiny screen in one lens.* Oculus Rift is different. It's not what you expect.

The first time I tried the Rift (which seems to be winning out over Oculus as the shorthand of choice) it showed a simulation of a craggy, rocky mountainside. I turned my head experimentally, and the view changed, with no discernible lag, just as it would have in reality. Instinctively my brain started looking for the edge of the image – but it didn't come. I kept turning until I was looking all the way behind me. There was nothing but mountain back there.

Then I looked up and watched snowflakes sift down out of a grey sky straight into my face. That's when my brain admitted defeat. It surrendered to the illusion that it was in another world. It wasn't going to find an edge. There were no edges. The Oculus Rift is the first visual medium that doesn't have a frame around it.

Another demo put me in the driver's seat of an old-fashioned race car. Just sitting there, without even starting the engine, was a revelation. I leaned over and stuck my head out the window and admired the car's exposed left front wheel assembly. If I leaned in to the dashboard I could read the fine print on the gauges. When you're in the Rift you *become* the camera. You control the point of view with your body, the way you would in reality.

The Oculus Rift has limitations. The resolution isn't high enough yet, so you have a slight sense that you're viewing the world from inside a screened-in porch. Look down and you'll notice that something's missing: your entire body. Oculus can bring your eyes and, with headphones, your ears into the virtual world, but nothing else. You haunt the virtual world as a floating, disembodied ghost.

The news that Facebook was acquiring Oculus was not received with universal happiness in the gaming community that had backed the company in the first place. The announcement on Oculus' blog quickly grew a comment trail 900-plus posts long essentially arguing, in various ways, that Oculus had abandoned its hardcore hacker roots to become a bland, corporate, three-dimensional ad-serving platform. Markus Persson, the creator of *Minecraft*, was an early backer, and he visited the Oculus offices earlier this year. He summed up the attitude when he tweeted to his 1.54 million followers, "We were in talks about maybe bringing a version of *Minecraft* to Oculus. I just cancelled that deal. Facebook creeps me out."

Palmer Luckey (Oculus' creator) is quick, very quick, to assert that this isn't a pivot away from gaming toward something else. "Nope," he says. "No pivot. We're doing what we've always done. We're continuing to operate independently, and if anything, we're putting more resources into games, not less. This lets us invest in content, make better tools for content, better developer relations, and builds a much better platform for games."

Brendan Iribe (Oculus' CEO) points out one concrete benefit for users: cheaper headsets. Now Oculus can afford to sell them at cost. "It changes our priorities from making money to making virtual reality happen." Iribe rejects the idea that he and his colleagues sold out. "If anything, I think Facebook got an incredibly good deal," he says. "If we stayed independent, we could probably have made a lot more." Brian Blau, a consumer technology analyst at research firm Gartner, says, "They want to seed the market. They want to get it in front of more developers and more early adopters. And that's the way to do it, to give it away as cheaply as they can."

Passage 2

In the second passage, Joshua Kopstein gives his view on Facebook's purchase of Oculus Rift.

In Los Angeles, a journalist has built a virtual reality simulation that re-creates a night in 2010 when a Mexican immigrant was beaten and killed by the U.S. border patrol.

At a hacker convention in Las Vegas, an interactive theatre troupe is running a game in which players wearing special headsets must navigate a maze while looking down at their own physical bodies from a bird's eye view.

In Madrid, artists are using virtual reality technology for a project that allows participants to "switch bodies" with members of the opposite gender.

If you get the opportunity to use a virtual reality headset such as the Oculus Rift – and chances are you will, very soon – these are just a few of the intense, disorienting and profound experiences that await you. The Rift is shipping out to early adopters this month after a Kickstarter campaign raised money for the original prototype, and virtual reality enthusiasts see the technology as poised to finally enter the mainstream.

But for all its promise, the virtual reality revolution is haunted by the spectre of its newest and most intimidating stakeholder: Facebook.

The social media giant's $2 billion buyout of Oculus VR in March came as a shock to the gaming world. The backlash was immediate. Most of Oculus' crowdfunders assumed they were supporting a new gaming platform – not pumping its value for acquisition by the same company that lets "friends" spam you with invites to play "Farmville". Markus "Notch" Persson, an early Oculus backer and creator of the hugely popular "Minecraft", announced on Twitter that he was cancelling the upcoming version of his hit game for the Oculus Rift. "Facebook is not a company of grass-roots tech enthusiasts … Facebook has a history of caring about building user numbers, and nothing but building user numbers," he wrote.

The acquisition took on a more ominous tinge recently, when it was revealed that Facebook had secretly conducted a social experiment on hundreds of thousands of unwitting users. As part of a study in "massive-scale emotional contagion", the company altered nearly 700,000 news feeds to see if doing so changed the mood of the content those users decided to post.

That Facebook performed the experiment without users' consent and in conflict with its own terms of service was at once incendiary and unsurprising. Academics and commentators argued that the study was unethical, if not illegal. Kate Crawford, a prominent researcher at Microsoft, described it aptly as "a symptom of a much wider failure to think about ethics, power and consent on [online] platforms".

To anyone familiar with its business model, the reason Facebook would want data on manipulating users' emotions should be obvious. It's the same reason it wants a hand in virtual reality platforms such as the Oculus Rift, and it's also the reason the company has been moving in on social location apps, health tracking and the "quantified self" trend of turning one's lifestyle into a report card of easily digestible numbers.

To Facebook, any and all domains of human experience should be accessible for capture and monetisation.

This is particularly the case as Internet-connected devices such as Nest (a smart thermostat recently acquired by Google), FitBit (a wristband that tracks your exercise regime) and Google Glass make their way into our homes and onto our bodies, recording everything from our pulses to the temperature of our living rooms. The Zuckerbergian view (and, more broadly, that of the Silicon Valley church of Big Data) is one of data totalitarianism: there is no dimension of human activity that shouldn't be exploited, because where there are sensors, there's data to be mined and money to be made.

By establishing itself in VR, Facebook is likely setting itself up to harvest and experiment with intimate data from that domain as well. Unlike a website, where user activity is measured in relatively primitive ways, such as clicks and scrolls, a simulated environment allows for much more sophisticated monitoring of a user's every action. The head- and iris-tracking features that make gaming technologies like the Oculus Rift so immersive are treasure troves of data for a company like Facebook, giving it the ability to see exactly what you're looking at, and for how long.

Adapted from an article published on the Al Jazeera America website, July 2014

Passage 1 questions

1. Re-read paragraph 2.
Summarise the reasons why two billion dollars seems like a 'head-snapping' amount for Facebook to pay for Oculus Rift. **4**

2. **By referring to at least two features of language in lines 12–19,** analyse how the writer conveys the feelings he experienced while 'meeting' the Oculus Rift. **4**

3. Re-read lines 20–33.

(a) Identify three reasons why, according to the writer, Oculus Rift is succeeding in creating 'virtual reality'. **3**

(b) Analyse how the writer's language conveys the wonder he experienced during the trial of 'the Rift'. **4**

4. **By referring to one feature of language in lines 34–37,** analyse how the writer highlights the 'limitations' of Oculus Rift. **2**

5. **By referring to at least two features of language in lines 38–42,** analyse how the writer conveys the strength of feeling towards the Facebook buyout. **4**

6. Re-read lines 38–57.

(a) Explain why, according to lines 38–45, some are concerned about the deal with Facebook. **2**

(b) Identify two arguments in support of the Facebook deal. **2**

Passage 2 question

7. Both writers discuss the development of Oculus Rift. Identify areas in which they disagree. In your answer, you should refer in detail to both passages.

You may answer this question in continuous prose or in a series of developed bullet points. **5**

CfE Higher English

Practice Papers for SQA Exams

Exam C
Critical Reading

Duration – 1 hour 30 minutes

Total marks – 40

SECTION 1 – Scottish text – 20 marks
Read an extract from a Scottish text you have previously studied and attempt the questions.
Choose ONE text from either
Part A – Drama
or
Part B – Prose
or
Part C – Poetry
Attempt ALL the questions for your chosen text.

SECTION 2 – critical essay – 20 marks

Attempt ONE question from the following genres – Drama, Prose, Poetry, Film and Television Drama or Language.

Your answer must be on a different genre from that chosen in Section 1.

You should spend approximately 45 minutes on each section.

Section 1 – Scottish text – 20 marks

Choose one text from Drama, Prose or Poetry.

Read the text extract carefully and then attempt ALL the questions for your chosen text.

You should spend about 45 minutes on this section.

Text 1: Drama

If you choose this text you may not attempt a question on drama in Section 2.

Read the extract below and then attempt the following questions.

***The Slab Boys* by John Byrne**

(*Enter Jack Hogg. He has a bundle of mags.*)

Jack: Alan around?

Phil: Tall fat guy with scarlet fever and his nose in a sling?

Jack: Just tell him I've got those mags he asked about …

Spanky: What mags are these, Jacky boy?

Phil: Yeh … how come we never get to see them?

Spanky: Yeh … how come?

Jack: They're about design … I shouldn't think you'd be remotely interested …

Phil: Oh, is that right? Tell him, Spanks … are we interested?

Spanky: Not really.

Phil: So you think twice before lurching in here and accusing the brother and me of not giving a monkey's. The designing of carpets for the hoi polloi may mean nothing to you, Hogg, but it means a damn sight less to us. Right, Spanky?

Spanky: Roger.

Phil: Sorry … Roger.

Jack: You're so smart, aren't you? So bloody smart, the pair of you. You're just pea green if anyone takes an interest in things …

Spanky: Pea green? That's a new one …

Jack: You nobbled Hector when he first started, didn't you? He used to come out to my desk, we'd go through some carpet mags together … but, oh no, you soon put a stop to that … called him for everything … made his life a misery. A pair of bully boys, that's what you are. Hector could've been a pretty good designer by now … yes, he could! Better than either of you, anyway. When was the last time you were down the Showroom … eh? Neither of you takes the least interest in any trials that come up. In fact, I bet you don't even know what any of us is working on out there …

Phil: (*Producing tatty piece of carpet*) Fourteen and eleven the square furlong.

Jack: That's right … go on, make a fool of things. Some of us take a pride in what we do!

Phil: Ach, pish, Jack! 'Some of us take a pride in what we do' … You? You lot! You're a bunch of no-talent, no-hopers, arse-licking your way up the turkey runner to Barton's office, a fistful of brushes in this hand and the other one tugging at the forelock … 'Good morning, Sir Wallace, by Christ but that's a snazzy Canaletto print up there on the wall next to that big clock that says a quarter to eight … Suffering Jesus, is that the time already? My, but how time flies when you're enjoying yourself. Pardon me, while I flick this shite off my boot … Just after stepping on one of Jimmy Robertson's sketches … it'll wash off, I'm sure. What? No, no, not at all, Sir Wallace … of course I don't mind putting in a bit of unpaid overtime … it's results that count, isn't it?' Jack, you wouldn't know a good design from a plate of canteen mince. Interest? As soon as Barton starts revving up his Jag you're the first one out the door and the leg over the bike before Miss Walkinshaw's even got her teeth out of her water jug!

Jack: Yeh … yeh … very noble … very smart. Listen, you ned, I went to night school for three and a half years … I've got a Diploma in Wool Technology!

Phil: So, what does that mean?

Spanky: He's haun-knitted.

Jack: One day you're going to go too far, Farrell. When you do … watch out. That's all I'm saying … watch out. As for you, McCann … grow up. There's a real world out there. Some of us have to live in it. (*Exit.*)

Spanky: It's hard to believe he was ever a Slab Boy, isn't it? You don't suppose there's any truth in the rumour that he's really the love-child of Miss Walkinshaw and Plastic Man? No? Well, I think I'll stroll down the Showroom and have a look at the new rugs …

Phil: Eh?

Spanky: I'm going for a smoke … hold the fort. D'you want me to have a skite for Hector?

Phil: Christ, I forgot all about him …

Questions

1. Explain fully, with close reference to the extract, why Spanky and Phil find it hard to believe that Jack was ever a 'Slab Boy'. **2**

2. By referring closely to lines 19–25, explain the impact Jack feels Phil and Spanky have had on Hector. **4**

3. By referring to at least two examples from lines 28–40, analyse how the writer's use of language conveys Phil's attitude towards Jack. **4**

4. By referring to this extract and elsewhere in the play, analyse how Phil and Spanky use humour to distance themselves from their misfortune and uninspiring circumstances. **10**

Text 2: Drama

If you choose this text you may not attempt a question on drama in Section 2.

Read the extract below and then attempt the following questions.

The Cheviot, the Stag and the Black, Black Oil **by John McGrath**

Enter WHITEHALL, a worried senior Civil Servant.

WHITEHALL: You see we just didn't have the money to squander on this sort of thing.

TEXAS JIM: That's my boy.

WHITEHALL: And we don't believe in fettering private enterprise: after all this is a free country.

TEXAS JIM: Never known a freer one.

WHITEHALL: These chaps have the know how, and we don't.

TEXAS JIM: Yes sir, and we certainly move fast.

M.C.l.: By 1963 the North Sea was divided into blocks.

M.C.2.: By 1964 100,000 square miles of sea-bed had been handed out for exploration.

WHITEHALL: We didn't charge these chaps a lot of money, we didn't want to put them off.

TEXAS JIM: Good thinking, good thinking. Your wonderful labourite government was real nice: thank God they weren't socialists.

M.C. l.: The Norwegian Government took over 50% of the shares in exploration of their sector.

M.C.2.: The Algerian Government control 800k of the oil industry in Algeria.

M.C.l.: The Libyan Government are fighting to control 100% of the oil industry in Libya.

Guitar.

WHITEHALL: Our allies in N.A.T.O. were pressing us to get the oil flowing. There were Reds under the Med. Revolutions in the middle-east.

TEXAS JIM: Yeah, Britain is a stable country and we can make sure you stay that way. (*Fingers pistol.*)

WHITEHALL: There is a certain amount of disagreement about exactly how much oil there actually is out there. Some say 100 million tons a year, others as much as 600 million. I find myself awfully confused.

TEXAS JIM: Good thinking. Good thinking.

WHITEHALL: Besides if we produce our own oil, it'll be cheaper, and we won't have to import it – will we?

M.C.l.: As in all 3rd World countries exploited by American business, the raw material will be processed under the control of American capital – and sold back to us at three or four times the price -

M.C.2: To the detriment of our balance of payments, our cost of living and our way of life.

TEXAS JIM: And to the greater glory of the economy of, the U.S. of A.

Intro to song. Tune: souped-up version of 'Bonnie Dundee'. TEXAS JIM *and* WHITEHALL *sing as an echo of* LOCH *and* SELLAR.

TEXAS JIM & WHITEHALL:

As the rain on the hillside comes in from the sea
All the blessings of life fall in showers from me
So if you'd abandon your old misery
Then you'll open your doors to the oil industry

GIRLS (as backing group): Conoco, Amoco, Shell-Esso, Texaco, British Petroleum, yum, yum, yum. (*Twice.*)

TEXAS JIM:

There's many a barrel of oil in the sea
All waiting for drilling and piping to me
I'll refine it in Texas, you'll get it, you'll see
At four times the price that you sold it to me.

TEXAS JIM & WHITEHALL: As the rain on the hillside, etc.

(*Chorus.*)

GIRLS: Conoco, Amoco, etc. (*Four times.*)

WHITEHALL:

There's jobs and there's prospects so please have no fears,
There's building of oil rigs and houses and piers,
There's a boom-time a-coming, let's celebrate -cheers

TEXAS JIM *pours drinks of oil.*

TEXAS JIM: For the Highlands will be my lands in three or four years.

No oil in can.

Enter ABERDONIAN RIGGER.

A.R.: When it comes to the jobs all the big boys are American. All the technicians are American. Only about half the riggers are local. The American companies'll no take Union men, and some of the fellows recruiting for the Union have been beaten up. The fellows who get taken on as roustabouts are on a contract; 84 hours a week in 12 hour shifts, two weeks on and one week off. They have to do overtime when they're tellt. No accommodation, no leave, no sick-pay, and the company can sack them whenever they want to. And all that for £27.00 a week basic before tax. It's not what I'd cry a steady job for a family man. Of course, there's building jobs going but in a few years that'll be over, and by then we'll not be able to afford to live here. Some English property company has just sold 80 acres of Aberdeenshire for one million pounds. Even a stairhead tenement with a shared lavatory will cost you four thousand pounds in Aberdeen. At the first sniff of oil, there was a crowd of sharp operators jumping all over the place buying the land cheap. Now they're selling it at a hell of a profit.

Questions

5. At this stage in the play, we are introduced to Texas Jim who represents the American investors entering the Highlands. Explain in your own words the justification given by Whitehall for allowing American investment. **2**

6. By referring to two examples from the text, analyse how a contrast is created between Texas Jim and Whitehall. **2**

7. At this point, Texas Jim and Whitehall burst into song. By referring to at least two examples, analyse how this song is relevant to the themes of the play. **3**

8. From his opening speech, what is revealed about the Aberdonian Rigger's attitude towards working life on the rigs? You should support your answer with evidence from the text. **3**

9. Many of McGrath's characters are presented as clear stereotypes. With reference to this extract and elsewhere in the play, discuss how such characters are used to develop theme. **10**

Text 3: Drama

If you choose this text you may not attempt a question on drama in Section 2.

Read the extract below and then attempt the following questions.

***Men Should Weep* by Ena Lamont Stewart**

This extract is from Act III and is the end of the play. Jenny has returned home on Christmas Eve to offer her parents money for a council house.

JOHN: I tellt you tae keep oot o this!

LILY: Why should I? Maggie's ma sister! An I've had tae fight hauf your battles for ye, John Morrison, or the hale lot o ye would hae been oot on the street mair than once!

John cannot answer: his hatred of Lily and her truth turns his mouth to a grim line: his hands open and close, open and close. The others wait for him to speak.

MAGGIE: (*with a placating smile and a note of pleading*) John, it's juist a wee help till we get a Cooncil hoose wi a wee bit garden at the front and a real green tae hang oot the washin.

JENNY: (*holding out her fat roll of notes*) I've got the cash. Ca it a loan if ye like.

MAGGIE: There's plenty for the flittin and the key money.

JENNY: Fifty pounds. (*She comes forward and offers it to John*)

JOHN: Ye can tak that back tae yer fancy man. We're wantin nane o yer whore's winnins here.

MAGGIE: John!

LILY: (*shouting*) It's no for you! It's for Bertie an the ither weans, ye pigheided fool!

JOHN: (*to Jenny*) If ye'd earned it, I'd be doon on ma knees tae ye. But ye're no better than a tart. We tried wur best tae bring you up respectable so's ye could marry a decent fella –

JENNY: Marry a decent fella! I never had a chance! Every time I got whit you would ca a decent fella an he saw me hame frae the dancin, he'd tak one look at the close an that's the last I'd see o him. Did you ever provide me wi a hoose I could bring a decent fella hame to? Did ye?

JOHN: I done ma best! There's naebody can ca me a lay-about! I worked when there wis work tae get!

LILY: Oh, ye must mind, Jenny, he's no tae blame. Nae man's evertae blame.

It's they dirty rotten buggers in Parliament, or they stinkin rich bosses –

JOHN: Haud yer rotten tongue, ye frozen bitch!

JENNY: (*with a sudden sour laugh*) I've often thought the way it would be when I came hame. I was gonna make up for the way I left ye. An here we are, Christmas Eve, fightin ower ma – whit is it? – ma whore's winnins. I've been savin an savin so's I could help ye, an mak friends again, an be happy.

She cries, head bent, standing forlornly before John who looks down on her grimly. Maggie watches, waits: then suddenly she stops combing her hair and rises. She takes the money out of Jenny's hand and interposes herself between them.

MAGGIE: (*with uncharacteristic force*) An so we wull be happy! Whore's winnins, did ye ca this? An did I hear ye use the word "tart"? Whit wis I, when we was coortin, but your tart?

John is startled and shocked.

(*In an urgent whisper imitating the John of her "coortin" days*) Let me, Maggie, g'on, let me! I'll mairry ye if onythin happens –

JOHN: (*a hurried, shamed glance towards Lily*) Stop it, Maggie! Stop it!

He moves away from Maggie, but she follows, still whispering. Lily, arms akimbo, eyes a-gleam, laughs coarsely, and hugs herself.

MAGGIE: Aye, I wis your whore. An I'd nae winnins that I can mind o. But mebbe it's a right bein a whore if ye've nae winnins. Is that the way it goes, John? (*Pause. She draws breath and her voice is now bitter*) And don't you kid yersel that I didna see the way ye looked at yer ain son's wife trailin aboot the hoose wi her breasts fa'in oat o her fancy claes. (*Coming right up to him and completing his humiliation before Lily and Jenny*) I'm no sae saft I didna ken why it wis. (*Urgent whisper*) Maggie! Come on, quick, ben the back room … lock the door … it'll no tak minutes –

JENNY: Mammy, Mammy! Stop!

John has sunk into a chair. He covers his face with his hands. There is a silence: Maggie's breathing loses its harshness: she looks down upon him: she sags.

MAGGIE: Aw … aw … (*She wipes her face with her hands and sighs*) Aw, I shouldna have said they things.

LILY: Why no? Ye wouldna hae said them if they wisna true.

MAGGIE: (*shaking her head*) Naw. There's things atween husbands an wives shouldna be spoke aboot. I'm sorry. I lost ma heid.

JENNY: (*kneeling at her father's feet*) Daddy … Daddy … forget it. It disnae matter. Daddy? (*She tries to draw his hands from his face*) When I wis wee, you loved me, an I loved you. Why can we no get back?

He does not answer, but he lets her take one of his hands from his face and hold it in both of hers.

MAGGIE: Dinna fret yersel, Jenny. I can manage him … I can aye manage him.

She is still holding the roll of notes. She looks away into her long-ago dream and a smile breaks over her face.

(*Very softly*) Four rooms, did ye say, Jenny? (*Pause*) Four rooms. Four rooms … an a park forbye! There'll be flowers come the spring!

CURTAIN

Questions

10. Explain why John hates Lily and 'her truth', referring closely to the extract. **2**

11. Referring closely to the extract, explain why John will not take Jenny's money. **2**

12. Referring closely to the extract, analyse how the stage directions show a change in Maggie's character in lines 32–35. **2**

13. Referring closely to the text, show how Jenny's character is developed in this extract. **4**

14. Discuss the effectiveness of this ending to the play with detailed reference to this extract and the play as a whole. **10**

Text 1: Prose

If you choose this text you may not attempt a question on prose in Section 2.

Read the extract below and then attempt the following questions.

***The Painter* by Iain Crichton Smith**

We only once had a painter in our village in all the time that I can remember. His name was William Murray and he had always been a sickly, delicate, rather beautiful boy who was the only son of a widow. Ever since he was a child he had been painting or drawing because of some secret compulsion and the villagers had always encouraged him. He used to paint scenes of the village at harvest time when we were all scything the corn, or cutting it with sickles, and there is no doubt that the canvas had a fine golden sheen with a light such as we had never seen before. At other times he would make pictures of the village in the winter when there was a lot of snow on the moor and the hills and it was climbing up the sides of the houses so that there was in the painting a calm fairytale atmosphere. He would paint our dogs – who were nearly all collies – with great fidelity to nature, and once he did a particularly faithful picture of a sheep which had been found out on the moor with its eyes eaten by a crow. He also did paintings of the children dressed in their gay flowery clothes, and once he did a strange picture of an empty sack of flour which hung in the air like a spook.

We all liked him in those days and bought some of his pictures for small sums of money since his mother was poor. We felt a certain responsibility towards him also since he was sickly, and many maintained that he wouldn't live very long, as he was so clever. So our houses were decorated with his colourful paintings and if any stranger came to the village we always pointed to the paintings with great pride and mentioned the painter as one of our greatest assets. No other village that we knew of had a painter at all, not even an adult painter, and we had a wonderful artist who was also very young. It is true that once or twice he made us uncomfortable for he insisted on painting things as they were, and he made our village less glamorous on the whole than we would have liked it to appear. Our houses weren't as narrow and crooked as he made them seem in his paintings, nor did our villagers look so spindly and thin. Nor was our cemetery, for instance, so confused and weird. And certainly it wasn't in the centre of the village as he had placed it.

Questions

15. Explain the impact of Iain Crichton Smith's use of first person narration in the extract. **2**

16. With close reference to the text, analyse how the writer's use of language conveys the villagers' conflicting attitudes towards William's paintings. **4**

17. By referring to at least two examples, explain how the narrator makes it clear that William is different to the rest of the villagers. **4**

18. By referring to this and at least one other short story by Iain Crichton Smith, discuss his portrayal of rural island life. **10**

Text 2: Prose

If you choose this text you may not attempt a question on prose in Section 2.

Read the extract below and then attempt the following questions.

***The Wireless Set* by George Mackay Brown**

The first wireless ever to come to the valley of Tronvik in Orkney was brought by Howie Eunson, son of Hugh the fisherman and Betsy.

Howie had been at the whaling in the Antarctic all winter, and he arrived back in Britain in April with a stuffed wallet and jingling pockets. Passing through Glasgow on his way home he bought presents for everyone in Tronvik – fiddlestrings for Sam down at the shore, a bottle of malt whisky for Mansie of the hill, a secondhand volume of Spurgeon's sermons for Mr Sinclair the missionary, sweeties for all the bairns, a meerschaum pipe for his father Hugh and a portable wireless set for his mother Betsy.

There was great excitement the night Howie arrived home in Tronvik. Everyone in the valley – men, women, children, dogs, cats – crowded into the but-end of the croft, as Howie unwrapped and distributed his gifts.

'And have you been a good boy all the time you've been away?' said Betsy anxiously. 'Have you prayed every night, and not sworn?'

'This is thine, mother,' said Howie, and out of a big cardboard box he lifted the portable wireless and set it on the table.

For a full two minutes nobody said a word. They all stood staring at it, making small round noises of wonderment, like pigeons.

'And mercy,' said Betsy at last, 'what is it at all?'

'It's a wireless set,' said Howie proudly. 'Listen.'

He turned a little black knob and a posh voice came out of the box saying that it would be a fine day tomorrow over England, and over Scotland south of the Forth-Clyde valley, but that in the Highlands and in Orkney and Shetland there would be rain and moderate westerly winds.

'If it's a man that's speaking,' said old Hugh doubtfully, 'where is he standing just now?'

'In London,' said Howie.

'Well now,' said Betsy, 'if that isn't a marvel! But I'm not sure, all the same, but what it isn't against the scriptures. Maybe, Howie, we'd better not keep it.'

'Everybody in the big cities has a wireless,' said Howie. 'Even in Kirkwall and Hamnavoe every house has one. But now Tronvik has a wireless as well, and maybe we're not such clodhoppers as they think.'

They all stayed late, listening to the wireless. Howie kept twirling a second little knob, and sometimes they would hear music and sometimes they would hear a kind of loud half-witted voice urging them to use a particular brand of tooth-paste.

At half past eleven the wireless was switched off and everybody went home. Hugh and Betsy and Howie were left alone. 'Men speak,' said Betsy, 'but it's hard to know sometimes whether what they say is truth or lies.'

'This wireless speaks the truth,' said Howie.

Old Hugh shook his head. 'Indeed,' he said, 'it doesn't do that. For the man said there would be rain here and a westerly wind. But I assure you it'll be a fine day, and a southerly wind, and if the Lord spares me I'll get to the lobsters.'

Old Hugh was right. Next day was fine, and he and Howie took twenty lobsters from the creels he had under the Gray Head.

Questions

19. Referring closely to lines 1–2, analyse how George Mackay Brown presents the community of Tronvik. **2**

20. Show how the language of lines 16–17 conveys the amazement of the islanders. **4**

21. Referring to one example from the extract, explain why Howie believes that the 'wireless speaks the truth'. **2**

22. Explain the significance of the wireless weather forecast in this extract. **2**

23. George Mackay Brown wrote about Orkney, its past and its people, yet he used this 'small green world' to explore issues of universal significance. By referring to this story and at least one other story by George Mackay Brown, discuss how he achieves this. **10**

Text 3: Prose

If you choose this text you may not attempt a question on prose in Section 2.

Read the extract below and then attempt the following questions.

***The Trick Is To Keep Breathing* by Janice Galloway**

In this extract, Joy is in hospital and has just been discovered making herself sick.

One of the nurses hears me coughing up sandwiches in the bathroom and I shout through the inbreaths. Everything's fine. Jesus christ jesus leave me in peace. The petite blond with big eyes is there when I go out, hands behind my back. I smile- too wide and get brittle, walking away sooner than is polite. I have to go to the end room.

I want to be held

to be found

not to think

there is

no going back only further

going back only further

jesus

say there's nothing

say there's

jesus

jesus

on a grey table, eyes wide to the white light.

His chest slack with yellow bruises where they tried to make the heart

neck chain filled with water like fish eyes

fingers tinged with blue

refusing to come back to

what was it?

the past tense made me

A uniform doubles back, opens the door and looks. It goes.

I crawl out from under the window seat but cramp makes me limp and a junior arrives too soon. He is a stranger. Dark skin, white coat. He talks in a practised monotone until I stop shaking. He is calm and nice to me. I can't look him in the eye but he lets me sit, sharing the silence with me.

He says maybe I want to speak about

an ante-room after a lot of opening and closing doors. It felt tight and enclosed after the corridor, too full of people. The doctor made signs with his hand and an olive-skinned boy, about sixteen or so, came out from the middle of the huddle of white coats. I was saying Tell me he's all right, Tell me he's all right, not able to stop. The Spanish boy reached out his hand.

What was his name?

jesus

His voice came through everything else, finding my language. You must be still. You must try to be still.

The only thing you can do is be still.

I didn't even thank him.

I look up at the junior and he looks back; waiting. I say, I didn't even thank him.

He nods.

The uniform puts me to bed. Before long the teeth are rattling again. Chittering of the teeth that shakes the bed and makes you get up and out of this bloody thing it starts again

it

starts

again

especially for his *wife*
especially his wife

when you're in

love with a beautiful woman
it's hard

sometimes I get that
feeling of

your cheatin heart
will tell on

you

There is something more to
something more

when you think I've loved you all I can
There is always something

more

to COME

throwing off the
sheets and searching, raking through a spill of make-up bag, magazines, paper and pens. Pills are missing. A special collection over weeks and someone has taken the pills. The nurse comes, the Irish one with the face like fizz and wheels my locker away, returns with a full needle the bitch the bitch. Watching the blue ward light makes white rails across the aisle, the sound of wheels outside. Janey moaning in her sleep creak of springs while the drug

snakes cold
up the length of
an arm
My arm.
It's dawning on me where I am.

Questions

24. By referring closely to lines 1–22, analyse how Galloway uses sentence structure to develop a sense of Joy's fragile mental state. **2**

25. With reference to lines 24–26, analyse how Galloway evokes sympathy for Joy. **2**

26. Joy's flashback clearly reveals her great anguish. With close reference to lines 28–44, analyse how this is conveyed. **4**

27. At several points in this novel, Joy's use of drink and drugs heavily influences her emotions. With close reference to lines 60–69, examine how this incident develops the theme of substance use. **2**

28. Throughout this novel, the narrative becomes fragmented due to flashbacks and other breaks or interruptions. With reference to this extract and elsewhere in the novel, discuss how this is used to develop theme. **10**

Text 4: Prose

If you choose this text you may not attempt a question on prose in Section 2.

Read the extract below and then attempt the following questions.

Sunset Song **by Lewis Grassic Gibbon**

In this extract, which is from the Epilude, Chris, young Ewan and the folk of Kinraddie have gathered around the Standing Stones to witness the unveiling of the war memorial by the minister, Mr Colquohoun, to remember the four men from Kinraddie who died in the First World War.

And then, with the night waiting out by on Blawearie brae, and the sun just verging the coarse hills, the minister began to speak again, his short hair blowing in the wind that had come, his voice not decent and a kirk-like bumble, but ringing out over the loch:

FOR I WILL GIVE YOU THE MORNING STAR

In the sunset of an age and an epoch we may write that for epitaph of the men who were of it. They went quiet and brave from the lands they loved, though seldom of that love might they speak, it was not in them to tell in words of the earth that moved and lived and abided, their life and enduring love. And who knows at the last what memories of it were with them, the springs and the winters of this land and all the sounds and scents of it that had once been theirs, deep, and a passion of their blood and spirit, those four who died in France? With them we may say there died a thing older than themselves, these were the Last of the Peasants, the last of the Old Scots folk. A new generation comes up that will know them not, except as a memory in a song, they passed with the things that seemed good to them with loves and desires that grow dim and alien in the days to be. It was the old Scotland that perished then, and we may believe that never again will the old speech and the old songs, the old curses and the old benedictions, rise but with alien effort to our lips. The last of the peasants, those four that you knew, took that with them to the darkness and the quietness of the places where they sleep. And the land changes, their parks and their steadings are a desolation where the sheep are pastured, we are told that great machines come soon to till the land, and the great herds come to feed on it, the crofter has gone, the man with the house and the steading of his own and the land closer to his heart than the flesh of his body. Nothing, it has been said, is true but change, nothing abides, and here in Kinraddie where we watch the building of those little prides and those little fortunes on the ruins of the little farms we must give heed that these also do not abide, that a new spirit shall come to the land with the greater herd and the great machines. For greed of place and possession and great estate those four had little heed, the kindness of friends and the warmth of toil and the peace of rest – they asked no more from God or man, and no less would they endure. So, lest we shame them, let us believe that the new oppressions and foolish greeds are no more than mists that pass. They died for a world that is past, these men, but they did not die for this that we seem to inherit. Beyond it and us there shines a greater hope and a newer world, undreamt when these four died. But need we doubt which side the battle they would range themselves did they live to-day, need we doubt the answer they cry to us even now, the four of them, from the places of the sunset?

And then, as folk stood dumbfounded, this was just sheer politics, plain what he meant, the Highland man McIvor tuned up his pipes and began to step slow round the stone circle by Blawearie Loch, slow and quiet, and folk watched him, the dark was near, it lifted your hair and was eerie and uncanny, the *Flowers of the Forest* as he played it:

It rose and rose and wept and cried, that crying for the men that fell in battle, and there was Kirsty Strachan weeping quietly and others with her, and the young ploughmen they stood with glum, white faces, they'd no understanding or caring, it was something that vexed and tore at them, it belonged to times they had no knowing of.

Questions

29. With reference to the extract, explain why the time and place of this memorial service are particularly apt. **2**

30. With close reference to the extract, analyse how Grassic Gibbon's language reflects the greater significance of the deaths of these four men. **4**

31. Referring closely to the extract, show how atmosphere is created in lines 32–39. **4**

32. Lewis Grassic Gibbon uses symbolism a great deal in *Sunset Song*. Referring to this extract, and to the wider text, discuss how he does so and explain the effect. **10**

Text 5: Prose

If you choose this text you may not attempt a question on prose in Section 2.

Read the extract below and then attempt the following questions.

***The Cone-Gatherers* by Robin Jenkins**

In this extract, Neil and Calum are surprised at the beach hut by Lady Runcie Campbell and her two children.

The door was flung open to the accompaniment of the loudest peal of thunder since the start of the storm.

From a safe distance the little dog barked at the trespassers. The lady had only a silken handkerchief over her head; her green tweed costume was black in places with damp. In the midst of the thunder she shouted: 'What is the meaning of this?' Through astonishment, and perhaps dampness, made her voice hoarse, it nevertheless was far more appalling to the two men than any thunder. They could not meet the anger in her face. They gazed at her feet; her stockings were splashed with mud and her shoes had sand on them.

Neil did not know what to do or say. Every second of silent abjectness was a betrayal of himself, and especially of his brother who was innocent. All his vows of never again being ashamed of Calum were being broken. His rheumatism tortured him, as if coals from the stolen fire had been pressed into his shoulders and knees; but he wished that the pain was twenty times greater to punish him as he deserved. He could not lift his head; he tried, so that he could meet the lady's gaze at least once, no matter how scornful and contemptuous it was; but he could not. A lifetime of frightened submissiveness held it down.

Suddenly he realised that Calum was speaking.

'It's not Neil's fault, lady,' he was saying. 'He did it because I was cold and wet.'

'For God's sake,' muttered the lady, and Neil felt rather than saw how she recoiled from Calum, as if from something obnoxious, and took her children with her. For both the boy and girl were present.

The dog had not stopped barking. Even that insult to Calum could not break the grip shame had of Neil. Still with lowered head, he dragged on his jacket. 'Get out,' cried the lady. 'For God's sake, get out.'

Neil had to help Calum on with his jacket. Like an infant Calum presented the wrong hand, so that they had to try again. The girl giggled, but the boy said nothing.

At last they were ready.

'I'll have to get my cones,' whispered Calum.

'Get them.'

Calum went over and picked up the bag lying beside the hamper of toys.

Neil led the way past the lady, who drew back. He mumbled he was sorry.

Calum repeated the apology.

She stood in the doorway and gazed out at them running away into the rain. The dog barked after them from the edge of the verandah.

'You'll hear more about this,' she said.

In the hut Sheila had run to the fire, with little groans of joy. From the corner to which he had retreated Roderick watched her, with his own face grave and tense.

Their mother came in and shut the door.

'I shall certainly see to it,' she said, 'that they don't stay long in the wood after this. This week will be their last, whatever Mr Tulloch may say. I never heard of such impertinence.' She had to laugh to express her amazement. 'Your father's right. After this war, the lower orders are going to be frightfully presumptuous.'

'Did you see the holes in the little one's pullover?' asked Sheila.

'I'm afraid I didn't see beyond their astonishing impudence,' replied her mother. She then was aware that Roderick still remained in the corner. 'Roderick, come over to the fire at once. Your jacket's wet through.' She became anxious as she saw how pale, miserable, and pervious to disease he looked.

'You'll be taking another of those wretched colds.'

He did not move.

'What's the matter?' she asked.

His response shocked her. He turned and pressed his brow against the window.

Questions

33. By referring closely to at least two examples, analyse how the writer's use of language conveys Neil's emotions in lines 9–15. **4**

34. Explain fully what crimes Lady Runcie Campbell feels Neil and Calum have committed. **2**

35. By referring closely to lines 23–48, analyse Roderick and Sheila's contrasting reactions to the expulsion of the brothers from the beach hut. **4**

36. Class difference is a significant issue in the novel. By referring to this extract and elsewhere in the novel, discuss how this theme is developed. **10**

Text 1: Poetry

If you choose this text you may not attempt a question on poetry in Section 2.

Read the extract below and then attempt the following questions.

To A Mouse **by Robert Burns**

Wee, sleekit, cow'rin, tim'rous beastie,
O, what a panic's in thy breastie!
Thou need na start awa sae hasty,
Wi' bickering brattle!
I wad be laith to rin an' chase thee,
Wi' murd'ring pattle!

I'm truly sorry man's dominion,
Has broken nature's social union,
An' justifies that ill opinion,
Which makes thee startle
At me, thy poor, earth-born companion,
An' fellow-mortal!

I doubt na, whiles, but thou may thieve;
What then? poor beastie, thou maun live!
A daimen icker in a thrave
'S a sma' request;
I'll get a blessin wi' the lave,
An' never miss't!

Thy wee bit housie, too, in ruin!
It's silly wa's the win's are strewin!
An' naething, now, to big a new ane,
O' foggage green!

An' bleak December's winds ensuin,
Baith snell an' keen!

Thou saw the fields laid bare an' waste,
An' weary winter comin fast,
An' cozie here, beneath the blast,
Thou thought to dwell –
Till crash! the cruel coulter past
Out thro' thy cell.

That wee bit heap o' leaves an' stibble,
Has cost thee mony a weary nibble!
Now thou's turn'd out, for a' thy trouble,
But house or hald,
To thole the winter's sleety dribble,
An' cranreuch cauld!

But, Mousie, thou art no thy lane,
In proving foresight may be vain;
The best-laid schemes o' mice an' men
Gang aft agley,
An' lea'e us nought but grief an' pain,
For promis'd joy!

Still thou art blest, compar'd wi' me
The present only toucheth thee:
But, Och! I backward cast my e'e.
On prospects drear!
An' forward, tho' I canna see,
I guess an' fear!

Questions

37. Burns presents a vivid image of the mouse in lines 1–6. With reference to one example, explain how the mouse is presented and analyse how Burns does this. **2**

38. Burns is apologetic to the mouse in lines 1–36. Identify two reasons why he feels this way. **2**

39. Referring to one example, show how Burns' language suggests that he and the mouse are equals. **2**

40. The tone changes in lines 37–48. With reference to two examples, identify how the tone changes and explain why it does so. **4**

41. Burns was writing at a time when traditional hierarchies and class systems were being questioned. From your reading of this poem and at least one other poem by Burns, discuss how Burns deals with the issues of social justice and equality. **10**

Text 2: Poetry

If you choose this text you may not attempt a question on poetry in Section 2.

Read the extract below and then attempt the following questions.

***Valentine* by Carol Ann Duffy**

Not a red rose or a satin heart.

I give you an onion.
It is a moon wrapped in brown paper.
It promises light
like the careful undressing of love.

Here.
It will blind you with tears
like a lover.
It will make your reflection
a wobbling photo of grief.

I am trying to be truthful.

Not a cute card or a kissogram.

I give you an onion.
Its fierce kiss will stay on your lips,
possessive and faithful
as we are,
for as long as we are.

Take it.
Its platinum loops shrink to a wedding-ring,
if you like.
Lethal.
Its scent will cling to your fingers,
cling to your knife.

Questions

42. By referring closely to lines 1–6, analyse the use of poetic technique to establish an assertive tone. **3**

43. With reference to **two** pieces of evidence from the poem, analyse how Duffy highlights the conflicting nature of love. **2**

44. By referring closely to **one** example from the poem, analyse the poet's use of enjambment in these lines. **2**

45. Evaluate the effectiveness of the final stanza as a conclusion to the poem. Your answer should deal with ideas and/or language. **3**

46. In many of her poems, Duffy explores the depth and complexity of love. With reference to this poem and one other by Duffy, discuss the importance of this theme in her work. **10**

Questions

47. By referring to lines 1–11, analyse the use of poetic technique to establish a tense atmosphere. **4**

48. In lines 12–22 we are given a sense of the attitude the speaker has towards the mother. Identify the attitude displayed and analyse how this is conveyed. **2**

49. Analyse how the use of poetic technique in lines 23–35 conveys the power held by her 'rival'. **2**

50. Evaluate how effective lines 36–39 are as a conclusion to the poem. Your answer may deal with ideas and/or language. **2**

51. In many of Lochhead's poems, she establishes a strong sense of location. Referring closely to this poem and another poem or poems by Lochhead, discuss how the poet develops a theme or themes through her description of place. **10**

Text 4: Poetry

If you choose this text you may not attempt a question on poetry in Section 2.

Read the extract below and then attempt the following questions.

***Visiting Hour* by Norman MacCaig**

The hospital smell
combs my nostrils
as they go bobbing along
green and yellow corridors.

What seems a corpse
is trundled into a lift and vanishes
heavenward.

I will not feel, I will not
feel, until
I have to.

Nurses walk lightly, swiftly,
here and up and down and there,
their slender waists miraculously
carrying their burden
of so much pain, so
many deaths, their eyes
still clear after
so many farewells.

Ward 7. She lies
in a white cave of forgetfulness.
A withered hand
trembles on its stalk. Eyes move

behind eyelids too heavy
to raise. Into an arm wasted
of colour a glass fang is fixed,
not guzzling but giving.
And between her and me
distance shrinks till there is none left
but the distance of pain that neither she nor I
can cross.

She smiles a little at this
black figure in her white cave
who clumsily rises
in the round swimming waves of a bell
and dizzily goes off, growing fainter,
not smaller, leaving behind only
books that will not be read
and fruitless fruits.

Questions

52. By referring closely to lines 1–7, analyse MacCaig's use of poetic techniques to create a vivid sense of place. **3**

53. Look at **stanza 3**. By referring closely to lines 8–10, analyse MacCaig's use of poetic techniques to convey his feelings at this point in the visit. **2**

54. By referring to at least one example, analyse how MacCaig's admiration for the nurses is made clear in lines 11–18. **2**

55. Evaluate how effective lines 19–30 are in conveying the frailty of the woman in the hospital. **3**

56. By referring to this poem and at least one other by Norman MacCaig, discuss how he uses personal experience to explore theme in his work. **10**

Text 5: Poetry

If you choose this text you may not attempt a question on poetry in Section 2.

Read the extract below and then attempt the following questions.

***XIX I Gave You Immortality* by Sorley MacLean**

I gave you immortality
and what did you give me?
Only the sharp arrows of your beauty,
a harsh onset
and piercing sorrow,
bitterness of spirit
and a sore gleam of glory.
If I gave you immortality
you gave it to me;
you put an edge on my spirit
and radiance in my song.
And though you spoiled
my understanding of the conflict,
yet, were I to see you again,
I should accept more and the whole of it.

Were I, after oblivion of my trouble,
to see before me
on the plain of the Land of Youth
the gracious form of your beauty,
I should prefer it there,
although my weakness would return,
and to peace of spirit
again to be wounded.

O yellow-haired, lovely girl,
you tore my strength
and inclined my course
from its aim:
but, if I reach my place,
the high wood of the men of song,
you are the fire of my lyric –
you made a poet of me through sorrow.

I raised this pillar
on the shifting mountain of time,
but it is a memorial-stone
that will be heeded till the Deluge,
and, though you will be married to another
and ignorant of my struggle,
your glory is my poetry
after the slow rotting of your beauty.

Questions

57. Look at stanza 1 (lines 1–15). Explain how MacLean gives his subject 'immortality'. **2**

58. Maclean writes about a disappointed love. By referring closely to lines 16–31, discuss the speaker's attitude towards the 'yellow-haired girl'. **4**

59. Referring to at least two examples, analyse MacLean's language in lines 32–39 to reveal how MacLean feels about his poetry. **4**

60. MacLean writes this poem in the first person. Referring closely to this poem and to another poem or poems by MacLean, discuss the effect of the use of the first person in MacLean's poetry. **10**

Text 6: Poetry

If you choose this text you may not attempt a question on poetry in Section 2.

Read the extract below and then attempt the following questions.

***Two Trees* by Don Paterson**

One morning, Don Miguel got out of bed
with one idea rooted in his head:
to graft his orange to his lemon tree.
It took him the whole day to work them free,
lay open their sides, and lash them tight.
For twelve months, from the shame or from the fright
they put forth nothing; but one day there appeared
two lights in the dark leaves. Over the years
the limbs would get themselves so tangled up
each bough looked like it gave a double crop,
and not one kid in the village didn't know
the magic tree in Miguel's patio.

The man who bought the house had had no dream
so who can say what dark malicious whim
led him to take his axe and split the bole
along its fused seam, then dig two holes.
And no, they did not die from solitude;
nor did their branches bear a sterile fruit;
nor did their unhealed flanks weep every spring
for those four yards that lost them everything,
as each strained on its shackled root to face
the other's empty, intricate embrace.
They were trees, and trees don't weep or ache or shout.
And trees are all this poem is about.

Questions

61. By referring closely to lines 1–12, explain how Don Miguel created a 'magic tree' in his patio. **3**

62. There is a change of tone in the second stanza of the poem. With reference to lines 13–22, identify the tone and discuss how the poet conveys it through skilful use of poetic techniques. **4**

63. Evaluate how effective you find lines 23–24 as a conclusion to the poem. Your answer should deal with ideas and/or language. **3**

64. By referring to this poem and at least one other by Don Paterson, discuss the poet's use of extended metaphor to convey main ideas and theme in his work. **10**

[END OF SECTION 1]

Section 2 – Critical essay – 20 marks

Attempt ONE question from the following genres – Drama, Prose, Poetry, Film and Television Drama, or Language.

You may use a Scottish text but NOT the one used in Section 1.

Your answer must be on a different genre from that chosen in Section 1.

You should spend approximately 45 minutes on this section.

DRAMA

Answers to questions on **drama** should refer to the text and to such relevant features as characterisation, key scene(s), structure, climax, theme, plot, conflict, setting …

1. Choose a play in which a central character displays clear signs of instability or weakness on one or more than one occasion.
Briefly explain the reasons for their instability/weakness and discuss how the dramatist's presentation of this feature enhances your understanding of the play as a whole.

2. Choose a play in which emotions of one or more characters reach a clear climax.

By referring in detail to the climax, discuss in what ways it is important for your understanding of the play as a whole.

3. Choose a play in which a power struggle between two characters is an important feature.

Briefly explain how the dramatist establishes this power struggle and discuss how this feature enhances your understanding of the play as a whole.

PROSE – FICTION

Answers to questions on **prose fiction** should refer to the text and to such relevant features as characterisation, setting, language, key incident(s), climax, turning point, plot, structure, narrative technique, theme, ideas, description …

4. Choose a novel or short story whose setting in place and/or time is an important feature.

Explain how the writer establishes the setting and go on to discuss its importance to your appreciation of the text as a whole.

5. Choose a novel or short story in which an incident reveals a flaw in a central character.

Explain how the incident reveals this flaw and go on to discuss the importance of the flaw in your understanding of the character and your appreciation of the text as a whole.

6. Choose a novel in which there is a key incident involving a quarrel, an unexpected revelation or an emotional reunion.

Briefly explain the circumstances of the incident and go on to discuss to what extent the incident is important to your understanding of the text as a whole.

PROSE – NON-FICTION

Answers to questions on **prose non-fiction** should refer to the text and to such relevant features as ideas, use of evidence, stance, style, selection of material, narrative voice …

7. Choose a work of biography or autobiography which you feel is written with great insight and/or sensitivity.

Discuss, in detail, how the writer's presentation of the life leads you to this conclusion.

8. Choose a non-fiction text in which the writer puts forward a view on a social issue.

Briefly explain what the issue is and then discuss how effective the writer is in influencing you to share his or her point of view.

9. Choose a non-fiction text in which the style of writing is an important factor in your appreciation of the writer's ideas.

Discuss in detail how features of the style enhanced your appreciation of the text as a whole.

POETRY

Answers to questions on **poetry** should refer to the text and to such relevant features as word choice, tone, imagery, structure, content, rhythm, rhyme, theme, sound, ideas …

10. Choose a poem which deals with birth or adolescence or adulthood or any other relevant stage of life.

Discuss how the poet's exploration of the stage of life has deepened your understanding of it.

11. Choose a poem in which tone is important in developing theme.

Show how the poem creates this tone and discuss its importance in your appreciation of theme in the poem.

12. Choose a poem which features a character you admire or respect.

Show how, through the content and poetic techniques used, the poet creates a character who you admire or respect.

FILM AND TELEVISION DRAMA

Answers to questions on **film and television drama*** should refer to the text and to such relevant features as use of camera, key sequence, characterisation, mise en scène, editing, setting, music/sound, special effects, plot, dialogue …

13. Choose a film or television drama* in which there is a breakdown in the relationship between two characters.

Discuss how the film or programme makers' exploration of the breakdown of the relationship contributes to your understanding of character and/or the central concern(s) of the text.

14. Choose a film or television drama* which explores the tragic consequences of war.

Show how the film or television programme makers explore the tragic consequences and discuss to what extent they are successful in deepening your understanding of war.

15. Choose from a film or television drama* an important sequence in which tension is created by filmic technique or by action and dialogue.

Show how the film or programme maker creates this tension and explain why the sequence is so important to the film as a whole.

***"television drama" includes a single play, a series or a serial.**

LANGUAGE

Answers to questions on **language** should refer to the text and to such relevant features as register, accent, dialect, slang, jargon, vocabulary, tone, abbreviation …

16. Choose at least one example of live broadcasting.

Identify the key features of the language used in this particular example and discuss that area's contribution to effective reporting.

17. Choose at least one example of tabloid writing.

Identify some of the distinctive features of the language used and discuss to what extent these features contribute to effective communication.

18. Choose at least one example of a campaign speech which features emotive language.

By referring to specific features of language in this speech, discuss to what extent you feel the speech is successful in achieving its purpose.

[END OF SECTION 2]

Answers to Practice Exam A

WORKED ANSWERS — Practice Exam A

Reading for Understanding, Analysis and Evaluation

Question 1 (a)

See Hint R1.

- She believed that beauty was definable, that society imposes a definition on us which belongs only to an elite group (1).
- She believed that good looks are seen to diminish over time (1).
- Those who are not deemed as beautiful have to find other coping mechanisms/modes of compensating (1).

Question 1 (b)

See Hint R2.

Possible answers include:

Word choice

- 'fragile' – associated with delicate, vulnerable items. Suggests the writer herself felt weak, close to breaking due to poor confidence.
- 'ugly' – used as an insult, associated with traditional view of good and evil. Suggests the writer recognises herself as extremely unattractive.
- 'only recently been upgraded to beautiful' – use of qualifiers suggests how weak this status is, and how easily it could be lost to her. Suggests she remains hurt by how others treated her.
- 'nerdy' – associated with stereotypical view of those who are very intelligent but lacking in social graces, leaving them outcasts. Reveals the writer's lack of confidence in her own humour and awareness that she may be seen as 'goofy' or strange.
- 'my own personal motto' – typically associated with gangs/groups/clubs. Use of possessive reveals a growing determination/confidence. Suggests the writer feels passionate/committed to changing her self-perception.
- 'vowed'– associated with acts of chivalry and also religious unions. Reveals the power of her conviction and growing self-confidence.

Imagery

- 'ugly bin' – comparison suggests she felt her looks caused her to be discarded. Connotations of rejection.
- 'upgraded' – implies notion that she wasn't 'good enough' previously.
- 'My ego was still fragile' – implies weakness, vulnerability.
- 'pumped full' – reveals over-compensation, an excessive attempt to boost own confidence.

Tone

- Self-mocking ('ugly bin at school'; 'nerdy jokes') – see above.
- Zealous ('I will continue …'; 'I vowed …') – sense of deliberate, false over-confidence.
- Self-effacing ('What an idiot I was.') – reveals honesty, reflection revealing knowledge of own weakness.

Question 2

See Hint R2.

Possible answers include:

- 'wise age of 17 and 18' – use of 'wise' is ironic as wisdom is seldom achieved at such a young age.
- 'pontificated' – pompous tone, suggesting deeply spiritual thought.
- 'blabbered' – informal, suggests rambling/incoherent thought. This contrasts strongly with 'pontificated' to demonstrate the gap between her perceived wisdom and reality.

Question 3

See Hint R1.

- The writer is struggling (1) to come to terms with the changes in her own appearance (1).
- Comments which refer to the writer's use of beauty products may score 1 mark.

Question 4

See Hint R1.

- Beauty is a blessing which is given by nature and not achieved through effort (1) however,
- it is finite – it is not a life-long gift (1).
- It reaches its peak during youth, when its value cannot be appreciated (1).

Question 5

See Hint R2.

Possible answers include:

- 'To me,' – parenthesis emphasises the personal nature of her remarks.
- 'Yes, sorry,' – additional parenthesis demonstrates her conviction and defence of her argument.
- 'little shots … fat here and there' – rule of three; listing. Emphasises the number/range of procedures that can be carried out.
- Repetition of 'here and there' – sounds vague and helps to convey the notion that the procedures are minor and inconsequential. This helps to create a mocking tone, which shows the writer's disagreement with this line of thinking.
- 'Aging … accept' – contrast/balance.
- 'Aging … matter' – inversion. Draws reader's attention to the fact that ageing is a psychological as well as a physical battle.

Question 6

See Hint R2.

Reference + basic comment = 1 mark. Reference + detailed comment = 2 marks.

Possible tones: questioning/doubting/reflective; cynical/sarcastic/resentful.

Questioning/doubting/reflective

Possible answers include:

- 'That gave me pause.' – simple statement. Slows pace, reflecting contemplation and consideration.
- Use of rhetorical questions – reveals doubt.
- 'not a friggin' clue on how to achieve it' – informal use of language, contrasts with deeply reflective quest for self-acceptance.
- Repetition of 'true' – reinforces writer's search for real meaning.
- 'True confidence: the kind … looks.' – use of colon provides a definition, which she admits she has yet to achieve.

Cynical/sarcastic/resentful

Possible answers include:

- 'something I'm clearly not' – addition of comment reveals her vehement denial.
- '(dying young is a terrific way to achieve this, by the way)' – use of brackets to insert acidic, cynical comment.
- '– surprise, surprise–' – use of dashes to insert sarcastic, informal aside.

Question 7 (a)

See Hint R1.

- Madonna's youthful looks make her appear tough, strong-willed and ambitious (1),
- whereas Jamie Lee Curtis appears a generation older and yet seems to be glowing, self-assured and at peace with herself (1).

Question 7 (b)

See Hint R1.

- The writer is aware of her own vanity and lack of security (1) which will mean that she will not be able to find it within herself to choose to age naturally (1).

Question 8

See Hint R1.

- Madonna has fought the ageing process (1).
- 'graceful' implies acceptance, not resistance (1).

Question 9

See Hint R3.

	Area of disagreement	***Paulina Porizkova***	***Barbara Ellen***
1	Beauty has a finite life which is directly attributed to ageing.	Beauty 'trickles away' and is the gift that 'does NOT keep on giving'.	Discusses the 'shelf life for female beauty' imposed by industry.

2	Preoccupation with delaying ageing	Accepts that she will use various methods to 'battle' ageing.	Derisory towards women who are 'suckered' into believing women must fight ageing.
3	Source of paranoia around ageing	Women, individually and collectively, are responsible for their fears.	The modelling industry and men 'seek to keep them [women] paranoid'.
	Area of agreement	***Paulina Porizkova***	***Barbara Ellen***
1	*Society* believes women's beauty is dependent on youth	Introduces article with proverb: '*Old age is the revenge of the ugly ones*'.	There is a 'feeling' or 'pressure' that there is an 'ever-shortening shelf life' for females.
2	Beauty is directly linked to confidence	She names Jamie Lee Curtis as a 'heroine' for ageing naturally. She strives for the confidence to accept herself.	Women should be confident enough to notice when they're being duped by society.

WORKED ANSWERS – Practice Exam A

Critical Reading – Section 1: Scottish text

Drama, Text 1: *The Slab Boys* by John Byrne

Question 1

Reference + basic comment = 1 mark. Reference + detailed comment = 2 marks.

See Hint S2.

You may have chosen some of the examples below, although others are possible:

- 'All she done was' – litotes: expression suggests Phil's mother's actions will be reasonable/unobjectionable. This is followed by a shocking statement of irrational actions.
- 'run up the street … Co-operative windows' – Phil delivers this line matter-of-factly. The contrast between the straight delivery and shocking content creates black humour.
- 'Thought that was normal down your way?' – use of question. Hyperbole. Suggests actions of Phil's mum are representative of the people where he lives. Mocking Phil's background.
- 'Usual six weeks, I expect' – use of word 'usual' implies this sort of behaviour is a regular occurrence for Phil. He responds in the way another person might discuss the length of a holiday.
- 'Shocking' – use of pun. Inappropriate humour given topic.

Question 2

Reference + basic comment = 1 mark. Reference + detailed comment = 2 marks.

See Hint S2.

You may have chosen some of the examples below, although others are possible:

- 'Course he's hopeless' – suggests that Phil's father is unable to deal with her mental illness. The word 'course' implies that this inability to cope is a usual occurrence. 'Hopeless' has a double meaning: he is ineffective but also devoid of hope.
- 'thinks it's diphtheria or something' – Phil's father does not understand her illness. The phrase 'or something' conveys the vagueness of her condition to him.
- 'The doctors is doing their best, Annie … you'll be home soon' – these are meaningless platitudes. Suggests Phil's father is simply saying anything to appease her at that moment.
- '"You taking that medicine they give you?" Medicine?' – Phil's father has blind faith in the doctors. Phil's rhetorical question shows that he does not believe they are doing anything to help his mother. His cynicism makes his father appear naïve and gullible.

Question 3

See Hint S1.

- The use of inverted commas around 'Voluntary Patient' implies that the phrase is being used ironically (1).
- 'they gave her a jag to knock her out' – Phil's mother has been given an injection to make her unconscious. She is therefore unable to make decisions for herself and so it cannot be said that she submitted to being admitted to the hospital 'voluntarily' (1).

Question 4

Marks are allocated: 2 marks for commonality; 2 for comment(s) on this extract and 6 marks for comments on rest of text.

Reference + basic comment = 1 mark. Reference + detailed comment = 2 marks. Reference + insightful comment may score 3 marks.

See Hint S7.

You may have chosen some of the examples below, although others are possible:

Commonality

- Phil is often portrayed as an unsympathetic character.
- He is insecure about himself but uses humour and anger to mask this.

Extract

- This scene is effective in creating sympathy for Phil.
- His mother is a mentally unstable woman who engages in irrational acts such as running 'up the street with her hair on fire' and diving 'through the Co-operative windows'. Public scenes like this would be embarrassing for Phil.
- Phil's childhood memories are of staying with his mother in 'convalescent' homes, which are portrayed as unpleasant and demoralising places to be.
- We are also introduced to his father, who seems unable to cope with or fully understand his mother's illness.
- Phil's vulnerability is revealed when he asks Spanky whether 'going off your head's catching?' He is concerned that he may end up similarly afflicted.

Rest of text

- The scene acts as a contrast to much of the rest of the drama, where Phil is often portrayed in an unsympathetic light.
- Along with Spanky, he is cruel in teasing Jack. He calls him 'Plooky chops' and asks Hector to 'fling him the Dettol'. He also mocks Alan, refusing to call him by his real name.
- Phil is shown to be a lazy worker. Despite the fact that he claims he and Spanky 'take pride in what we do', during the play the audience do not see him perform any productive labour during the work day. Instead he spends his time joking and involved in antics with Hector's clothing.
- When he realises that Hector has been promoted while he has been fired, he lashes out at Curry, exposing his former manager's war lies and claiming he 'couldn't punch [his] way out of a paper bag.'
- The vulnerability identified in the extract is developed through the art school plot line. Phil tries to avoid confessing why he is late for work as he is afraid to reveal his dreams about furthering his education.

Drama, Text 2: *The Cheviot, the Stag and the Black, Black Oil* by John McGrath

Question 5

Reference + basic comment = 1 mark. Reference + detailed comment = 2 marks.

See Hint S2.

You may have chosen some of the examples below, although others are possible:

- 'sniffs the bucket, ignores the women, who are huddled under their shawls' – 'sniff' suggests that he is repulsed by the scent of the bucket and thus of the women themselves. This is compounded by the fact that he pays no attention to them. 'huddled' implies that they are cold and therefore suffering, which makes Sellar's dismissal even more cruel and contemptuous.
- 'They claim they have no money' – 'claim' indicates his suspicion and mistrust of the Highlanders, which in turn suggests his scorn.
- 'clearly they have enough to purchase the barley' – the use of an aside to reinforce what would be obvious to Loch reveals further contempt as it shows that Sellar is determined to justify his frustrations with the Highlanders.
- Referring to the 'terrible degeneracy in the character' of the Highlanders shows clear scorn as he is directly insulting them. Suggesting there is 'degeneracy' in their personality/lifestyle places them beneath him as people who are corrupt and immoral.
- 'aboriginals' – implication of a lack of civility and culture which therefore implies that Sellar sees them as savage/primeval.

Question 6

Basic comment = 1 mark. Detailed comment = 2 marks.

See Hint S2.

You may have chosen some of the examples below, although others are possible:

- Reference made to income (£120,000) – Highlights financial advantage of these men and the discrepancy that existed between classes. Helps us to understand the greed which motivated their actions.

- List of estates inherited in England and their corresponding industries – example of George Granville's inheritance reinforces inequality existing between the classes and the unjust nature of inheritance. Reinforces how easily wealth was passed between generations as well as power they had.
- 'he bought a large slice of the Liverpool-Manchester Railway' – 'slice' has harsh, aggressive connotations revealing careless, profit driven approach of those in the landed gentry. Reminds of the ease with which they could 'cut up' land and industry among themselves.
- 'From his wife … he acquired three-quarters of a million acres of Sutherland' – final remark creates impression that this particular inheritance was an afterthought. Giving such a specific number, and one of such considerable size reminds us just how vast the land was.

Question 7

See Hint S1.

Any two of:

- Loch believes that the Highlanders must engage in work which makes their lives more profitable, abandoning their traditional means of living as purely self-sufficient people ('To be happy, the people must be productive'). (1)
- Sellar believes that they must leave their homes and be forced into jobs in large organisations ('… be convinced that they must worship industry or starve').
  Both men believe that the Highlanders should be moved into new towns along the sea front, where it would be possible for them to earn money from fishing and mining ('perfect natural harbour … coal at Brora'). (1)
- Sellar is adamant that they must rid the land of its occupants, and proposes the option of moving them abroad in the belief that they are better tempered for lands which are yet untamed ('They are just in that state of society for a savage country'). (1)

Question 8

Basic comment = 1 mark. Detailed comment = 2 marks.

See Hint S2.

You may have chosen some of the examples below, although others are possible.

- 'They require to be thoroughly brought to the coast … they must worship industry or starve' – by suggesting that there should be no choice for the Highlanders but to accept the jobs presented to them, we are made aware of the aggressive pursuit of profit being made. There is no indication here of any care or concern for the well-being of the Highlanders.
- 'His Lordship should consider seriously the possibility of subsidising their departures' – assertive tone indicates that the land owners should go to any lengths in order to make the Highlanders leave.
- Bartering between Sellar and Loch and use of figures – revealing exactly how much profit can be made from sheep farming in the Highlands (£900,000) makes the small sums offered for rental of the land seem even more pitiful.
- 'His Lordship will have to remove these people at considerable expense' – dismissive tone. 'these people' suggests that Loch has no real interest or concern for them.

Question 9

Marks are allocated: 2 marks for commonality; 2 for comment(s) on this extract and 6 marks for comments on rest of text.

Reference + basic comment = 1 mark. Reference + detailed comment = 2 marks. Reference + insightful comment may score 3 marks.

See Hint S7.

You may have chosen some of the examples below, although others are possible:

Commonality

- McGrath uses the interjections of other voices/readers to present the audience with the 'truth', allowing them to see the contrast between what the upper classes believed and what the Highlanders experienced/felt.
- McGrath uses interjections to provide 'light relief' and humour.
- Songs used to highlight/develop the emotional intensity and tension in scenes.

Extract

- In this extract, Loch breaks character, allowing for an aside to be included which alerts the audience to the fact that the words spoken by the actors reflect on genuine accounts of comments from James Loch and Patrick Sellar. In doing so, McGrath is able to inject humour into the situation and poke fun at the lofty language used by these men. This is a central aspect of the play as a whole: McGrath makes the members of the upper class figures of fun in order to criticise their actions.
- The introduction of the song 'Bonnie Dundee' also provides a bitter irony to the scene. This particular song was written to celebrate John Graham, the 7th laird of Claverhouse, who led a Jacobite rising and won the Battle of Killiecrankie. This connection with a historical Scottish figure makes the use of the song as a backdrop to the negotiations over land heighten our awareness of the cruelty of this situation, given that lives had been lost in an attempt to secure the lands for Scottish nobles only to be bartered over and 'sold' by the landed gentry in years to come.

Rest of text

- Readers used to relay information regarding the efforts of women to fight the clearances. At this point, the women are complaining that there are no 'good men' to help fight their cause, and events are interrupted to recount details of actual events. The details we are given become increasingly graphic and disturbing ('they beat and kicked them while lying weltering in their blood'), allowing us both to understand the suffering which was inflicted upon the Highlanders at this time and to feel the injustice of these actions.
- Use of poem and song to interrupt trial of Patrick Sellar. Two contrasting songs are used: one celebrates the first Duke of Sutherland ('He tamed the torrent, fertilized the sand') while the other condemns him ('Nothing shall be placed over you / But the dung of cattle'). As the first was written by Lord Francis Egerton while the other is a Gaelic song, we are alerted to the conflicting views presented in history of those men at the centre of the Highland clearances. This reinforces how readily people accepted the clearances in the name of progress, forgetting the anger and suffering it inflicted upon those involved.
- Use of MC to interject during conversation between Texas Jim and Whitehall. As they justify the move to allow American investment in Scottish Oil, the announcers provide statistics which inform us of the extent of the takeover ('100,000 square miles') and the impact of this on those living in Scotland ('sold back to us at three times the price'). By contrasting the slick and sleazy approach of Texas Jim and the incompetence of Whitehall with the blunt statistics and facts, it reinforces the focus on profit and industry.

Drama, Text 3: *Men Should Weep* by Ena Lamont Stewart

Question 10

Reference + basic comment = 1 mark. Reference + detailed comment = 2 marks.

See Hint S1.

You may have chosen some of the examples below, although others are possible:

The house is untidy and disorganised

- 'Noo whaur did I lay it doon?'
- 'How you ever find onythin in this midden beats me.'
- 'It beats me tae sometimes.'

Maggie is slapdash in her manner

- 'D'ye no tak aff her dress tae wash her neck?'
- 'How you ever find onythin in this midden beats me.'

Maggie is overindulgent of her children

- 'She's old enough tae dae it herself.'
- 'The way you rin efter they weans is the bloomin limit.'

Maggie does not take good care of herself

- 'Nae wunner y're hauf-deid.'
- 'The difference is, I try.'
- 'Heve ye looked in the mirror since ye rose the morn?'

Question 11

Reference + basic comment = 1 mark. Reference + detailed comment = 2 marks.

See Hint S1.

You may have chosen some of the examples below, although others are possible:

- 'It beats me tae sometimes' – Maggie is easy going and accepts her situation with humour. Without humour she would find the conditions utterly intolerable and deeply depressing.
- 'Awa for Goad's sake! It's no Setturday nicht' – Maggie will not go to more effort than she needs to. It may be that Maggie does not have the energy left to be too scrupulous in the way that Lily would be.
- 'I'm no hauf-deid!' – this hot denial shows how much Maggie resents this accusation. She refuses to give in to self-pity or indeed consider her own situation.
- 'I havena time tae look in nae mirrors' – Maggie defends her appearance stoutly by inferring that she is so busy with her family that she does not need to be self-indulgent or overly anxious about her appearance.
- 'My lovin Johnnie's still ma lovin Johnnie, whitever I look like' – this is spoken with a firm authority which shows that Maggie feels quite secure, or wants to suggest that she is.

- 'ye jist canna resist a dig at him' – Maggie defends her husband and feels that Lily judges him too harshly. She is proud of John for going teetotal.
- 'My the tongue you have on you, Lily. It's a pity … couple a weans' – Maggie may feel that Lily is simply being spiteful and sees her attitude as bitterness because she, Lily, has never married and had children.
- 'Aye! I'm happy' – the emphatic nature of this answer suggests that this is the truth. Maggie is happy with her family and her struggles. She knows nothing else.
- 'Ye canna help havin a midden … I dae the best I can' – there is a fatalistic acceptance of her situation here which may make the audience empathise with her.
- 'You leave John alane! He does his best for us' – stout defence of John shows how united they are as a front, as well as how much Maggie refuses to criticise John's capabilities as a breadwinner, or his lack of help in the house.
- 'Aye. I still love John. And whit's more, he loves me' – the simplicity of these statements shows Maggie's certainty of these facts. Her relationship is strong and reciprocal.
- 'I'm sorry for you Lily. I'm right sorry for you' – Maggie feels pity for Lily as she has not experienced the depth and strength of love that she has.
- 'They're my weans! I'm workin for ma ain' – Maggie reclaims her children from Lily's bitter accusation and shows how important family is to her.
- 'Yer mind's twisted … You're daft!' – Maggie finds Lily's sweeping generalisation ridiculous.

Question 12

Reference + basic comment = 1 mark. Reference + detailed comment = 2 marks.

See Hint S2.

You may have chosen some of the examples below, although others are possible:

- 'Yin o they days your lovin Johnnie's gonna tak a look at whit he married and it'll be ta-ta Maggie.' – Lily suggests that men love with their eyes and that John will leave Maggie for someone better-looking. This contrasts sharply with the deep abiding love that Maggie says John has for her.
- 'That's whit he tells you, onywey' – Lily does not trust men, perhaps through her experiences of working in a pub.
- 'Lily holds out her sleeve and laughs up it' – Lily makes a joke out of Maggie's suggestion that she would have been happier married with children. Lily may be pragmatic about this – she is independent – or she may just be covering up her own real disappointment.
- 'If John wad gie hissel a shake' – a man's role is to provide for his family, according to Lily, and Maggie's desperate plight is down to him. She suggests that John could make more of an effort.
- 'I believe ye still love him!' – the disbelief in Lily's tone here suggests that she does not really believe in a strong, loving and enduring marriage. This suggests a cynicism and a deep mistrust of men.
- 'slavin efter a useless man' – the man is seen to have the upper hand here. Lily's use of the word 'slavin' shows that she thinks Maggie is subservient and looked down upon. She also judges John as 'useless' as he is not earning what he should, or helping enough with the children.
- 'Men! I'm wantin nae man's airms roon me. They're a dirty beasts' – Lily asserts her independence, but also shows her isolation. Her job as a barmaid has perhaps given her more of an insight into the world of working-class men at this time than Maggie has. She does not trust men.

- 'You're saft! You think yer man's wonderful and yer weans is a angels' – Lily is scornful of Maggie's staunch defence of her husband and family. She may feel that Maggie is either deluded or not wholly honest about John and her own situation.

Question 13

Marks are allocated: 2 marks for commonality; 2 for comment(s) on this extract and 6 marks for comments on rest of text.

Reference + basic comment = 1 mark. Reference + detailed comment = 2 marks. Reference + insightful comment may score 3 marks.

See Hint S7.

You may have chosen some of the examples below, although others are possible:

Commonality

- Lily and Maggie lead different lives and each feels pity for the other.
- Lily tries to draw her sister's attention to her faults though Maggie rarely listens.

Extract

- Maggie feels pity for her sister that she does not have a husband and a family of her own.
- Maggie will defend her husband and children even to Lily who is closest to her.

Rest of text

- Lily's support of the family both emotionally and materially in terms of food and medicine is key to their survival.
- Lily's great involvement in the Morrisons' family life is a mutually supportive one; Lily is part of a family and is protected from the loneliness and isolation she may feel by living alone.
- Lily uses typically hard words and plain speaking to defend Maggie and fight her corner during confrontations, such as those with Isa, Lizzie, John or Jenny. This can be contrasted with Maggie's rather helpless habit of 'raking' her hair.
- Lily's support of Maggie and her family shows her nurturing side.
- Maggie depends on her sister and does not take her for granted. Yet, despite this dependence, she firmly asserts her own opinions on her family life. Lily will always be an outsider to this aspect of Maggie's thinking and personality.
- Lily and Maggie are very different people; Maggie is easy going, slapdash and does not plan ahead whereas Lily is the opposite; Lily judges harshly yet shows tenderness and kindness in the support she provides for the family.
- Lily also sees that some of Maggie's problems are brought on Maggie by herself – Lily shows her frustration with this in the play, yet still shows her unfailing support for her sister.
- Lily does not expect Maggie to be assertive in a meaningful way, apart from in her verbal battles with Lily and with her neighbours. This is what makes Maggie's confrontation of John's double standards at the end of the play so interesting.
- Often in the play, Lily tries to open Maggie's eyes to the motives and actions of those around her. Yet she conceals the knife that Alec threatened Isa with from Maggie in order to protect her feelings.

- Lily supports Maggie's confrontation of John at the end of the play, though Maggie's response shows again her solidarity with her husband: 'things atween husbands and wives shouldna be spoke about'.

Prose, Text 1: *Mother and Son* by Iain Crichton Smith

Question 14

You should explain that John finally sees his mother not as someone superior and to be feared, but as a pathetic figure, shrunken by illness (1).

Reference + basic comment = 1 mark. Reference + detailed comment = 2 marks.

See Hints S2 and S3.

You may have chosen some of the examples below, although others are possible:

- 'mouth was open' – unattractive expression, implies dim-witted or simple-minded.
- 'little crumbs on her lower lip' – slovenly/unkempt, like a child.
- 'pecking at the bread' – comparison to a hen, an unintelligent creature.
- 'as if she were some kind of animal' – she has regressed to an animal state, incapable of the higher-order thinking of a person.
- 'this thing' – dehumanising her.
- 'What is she anyway?' – rhetorical question, John is questioning his assumption of her superiority.

Question 15

- He is angry with her for stealing his life and he begins to suspect that her illness may be a deception to keep him imprisoned with her.
- He is disgusted by her weakened figure and the revolting way she eats.

Reference + basic comment = 1 mark. Reference + detailed comment = 2 marks.

See Hints S2 and S3.

You may have chosen some of the examples below, although others are possible:

Anger

- 'flung' – this suggests the object was thrown forcibly, a sign of aggression.
- 'abrupt, savage gesture' – quick, ferocious movements.
- 'roaring' – onomatopoeic, suggests speed and noise.
- 'How he hated her!' – exclamation, alliteration: emphasises the intense strength of his feeling towards her.
- 'turmoil of hate' – suggests a state of turbulence/upheaval, as if his loathing is roiling inside of him.
- 'smash the cup … the house' – parallel structure, repetition: John wants to physically destroy the house and everything in it as it forms his prison.
- 'his hands clenched' – suggests having to physically restrain himself.

Disgust

- 'her scraggy neck' – hanging skin, unattractive image.
- 'chin wagging up and down' – implies she is prattling/blathering, no importance to her words; comparison to a dog's tail.
- 'stained with jam'/'flecked with ... crumbs' – soiled/unclean.

Question 16

See Hint S2.

You may have chosen some of the examples below, although others are possible:

- In the build-up to the final lines it seems John will stand up to his mother.
- 'He would show her' – we expect some sort of confrontation.
- 'He stood there ... his lips' – there is an implication that John will retaliate violently towards his mother as she lies there vulnerable, asleep.
- The final sentence is unexpected. John instead turns away from his mother to open the door. This gives a sense of anti-climax.
- 'stood listening to the rain' – the bleak weather reflects the bleakness of John's situation. It confines him to the house in the same way his duty to his mother does.

Question 17

Marks are allocated: 2 marks for commonality; 2 for comment(s) on this story and 6 marks for comments on other text(s).

Reference + basic comment = 1 mark. Reference + detailed comment = 2 marks. Reference + insightful comment may score 3 marks.

See Hint S7.

You may have chosen some of the examples below, although others are possible:

Commonality

- Crichton Smith portrays small highland and island communities as restrictive, repressing the individual.
- Individuals are only accepted if they conform to the unspoken rules of the community.
- Crichton Smith believes that sacrificing your individuality for acceptance is too great a price to pay.

Mother and Son

- In the story, John is repressed by his mother, a bitter, bed-ridden woman.
- In fulfilling his duty to his mother, John has been denied the opportunity to go out into the world and live his own life, like the other boys in the village. This has made him an isolated figure.
- John's mother controls him by undermining his confidence, constantly criticising him. This ensures that he will never have the courage to leave her, but has left John emotionally stunted and immature.
- John's unhappiness is clear in the story – he is frustrated by the confines of his existence and his mother's ungrateful attitude. Here Crichton Smith suggests that the sacrifice required – the suppression of one's own hopes and dreams – to fulfil bonds of duty is too high.

The Painter

- Crichton Smith takes on the perspective of a villager and tells the story of a painter who lived among them.
- The painter is shown to be different from the other villagers as he is weak and quiet, and cannot join in with the manual labour associated with rural life. This makes the painter an isolated figure.
- Although the village claims to be proud of having a painter among them, they are uneasy with his differences. This reaches a climax when the narrator, consumed by anger, destroys a picture the painter is working on.
- In the story, in order to reach his full potential and free himself from the restrictions imposed by the insular community, the painter is forced to leave.
- He must sacrifice the contentment and safety that comes with being embraced by a rural community to become fully himself.

The Red Door

- In the story, Murdo is a well-liked figure in, again, a small rural community. However, he has achieved this status through carefully adhering to the restrictions and expectations placed on him by the other villagers.
- When he awakes to discover that his door has been painted red overnight, he becomes afraid as he worries that this display of individuality may isolate him from his community in some way.
- However, he experiences a revelation when he realises obeying the unspoken rules of the village means he has never really been himself. He begins to be excited by the idea of becoming more of his own man.
- At the end of the story he makes the decision to follow his desires – rather than the desires of the villagers – and pursue Mary, a local spinster who is isolated by her creativity and individuality, traits which are not rewarded in his insular community.

Prose, Text 2: *The Eye of the Hurricane* by George Mackay Brown

Question 18

Reference + basic comment = 1 mark. Reference + detailed comment = 2 marks.

See Hint S2.

You may have chosen some of the examples below, although others are possible:

- 'deep rut' – suggests that the writing cannot progress, it is stuck in one place.
- 'sat most of the morning' – the period of writer's block lasts almost all of his writing time; he is genuinely stuck for inspiration.
- 'poised' – he is waiting for the writing to flow, yet he cannot write anything of worth. His pen cannot commit to paper as the ideas are not worth writing.
- 'dull, flaccid, affected' – his writing is lacking style, panache and real feeling.
- 'blankly' – Barclay's mind is vacant; he cannot connect with his feelings or imagination.
- 'tortured image' – the image of Christ lacks a deeper significance for Barclay here; he cannot connect with ideas of wider significance or great universal meaning.
- 'insults' – Barclay finds his inadequacy to convey his ideas as unworthy.

- 'a few more random thorns' – his paltry attempts to do justice to great ideas are seen as traitorous, mean and base.
- 'scored out everything' – Barclay does not feel his writing is worth keeping. He destroys all he has attempted to write that morning.

Question 19

Reference + basic comment = 1 mark. Reference + detailed comment = 2 marks.

See Hint S5.

Both aspects of metaphor must be commented on for full marks.

(i) Writers want to think of themselves as coming up with something original, much like explorers go into uncharted territory. They want to be the first to capture and describe something. They want their writing to be unique.

You may have chosen some of the examples below, although others are possible:

- 'explorers' – those who venture into uncharted territory. They are pioneers; doing things and going places where no one has gone before.
- 'probing into seas that have never been mapped' – this suggests that the incisiveness of writing can cut through, exploring aspects of life and human nature which have never before been made explicit.
- 'charted with only a few broken lines' – others' attempts to get at the essence or truth of an idea or feeling have been inadequate and merely sketch in the basics. The suggestion is that writers long to be able to capture unique, true meaning.

(ii) Yet so much has been written that there is no uncharted territory – there is nothing that has not been written about and written well. So instead, writers write about well-used themes and ideas, offering little that is new to excite or illuminate.

You may have chosen some of the examples below, although others are possible:

- 'the spacious days … are gone forever' – over time, literature has captured these experiences.
- 'There is nothing new to find' – all the universal truths and intricacies of human nature have been catalogued.
- 'every headland has been rounded' – every aspect of life and thought has been explored.
- 'every smallest ocean current observed' – even the minutiae of life and experience have been dwelt on.
- 'the deepest seas plumbed' – the darkest and most profound truths and ideas have been explored.
- 'charted human nature so well that really little is left' – other writers have captured what it is to be human completely.
- 'voyage along old trade routes' – writers now go along ideas which someone or many people have already dealt with. Their ideas are commonplace.
- 'in rusty bottoms' – suggests that there is no beauty in their writing; that it is a shabby vehicle to convey ideas.
- 'cargoes of small interest' – the import of the writing is very little; it has little real meaning or worth.

Question 20

Reference + basic comment = 1 mark. Reference + detailed comment = 2 marks.

See Hint S2.

You may have chosen some of the examples below, although others are possible:

- 'that was the devil talking' – Miriam sees Stevens' alcoholism as the devil's work, suggesting a strong belief in good and evil, heaven and hell.
- 'You should come to our Joy Hour' – she invites Barclay to a Salvation Army gathering, showing the merit and worth she sees in it. The name 'Joy Hour' suggests that this spiritual celebration is uplifting and allows one to connect with pure happiness.
- 'O, everybody's so happy!' – the exclamation shows her true feeling. 'Everybody' suggests that the feeling is universal. The very notion of shared happiness is a rare one in day-to-day life. This shows the strength of their shared conviction and the peace of mind which it gives to them.
- 'Her eyes drifted uneasily over the crucifix and the Virgin' – Miriam is true to her own religious observance which devotes itself to practical, pragmatic Christian work. She feels uncomfortable about religion being glamourised in the Catholic way. Her uneasiness shows her feeling that this is wrong.
- 'her plain little face shone for a moment like one of Botticelli's angels' – Miriam is transformed by her purity of spirit and Christian belief into a transcendent beauty, radiating goodness.
- 'she would be a devout Catholic girl' – the word 'devout' suggests her extreme religious conviction. She is a true believer.
- 'dearest treasures and delights' – the comparison here clearly indicates that Miriam's religious beliefs are the most important things to her and provide her with the most peace and tranquillity.
- 'touched the hem of Christ's garment' – Miriam's goodness and dedication bring her close to Jesus and show her to be a true believer.

Question 21

Marks are allocated: 2 marks for commonality; 2 for comment(s) on this story and 6 marks for comments on other text(s).

Reference + basic comment = 1 mark. Reference + detailed comment = 2 marks. Reference + insightful comment may score 3 marks.

See Hint S7.

Commonality

- Alcohol is destructive, weakening resolutions and putting characters in danger.
- Alcohol is a means of escaping from the drudgery of existence.
- Alcohol is intrinsic to society.
- Alcohol is part of the masculine culture of seafarers.

The Eye of the Hurricane

- Stevens' alcoholism is seen as 'the devil' by Miriam; as inevitable by Stevens himself. Barclay sees a more emotional cause in the death of Stevens' wife and son.
- Barclay battles whether to buy Stevens' rum for him or not – he ponders on what the right course of Christian charity would be in this instance.

Reference + basic comment = 1 mark. Reference + detailed comment = 2 marks. Reference + insightful comment may score 3 marks.

See Hint S7.

You may have chosen some of the examples below, although others are possible:

Commonality

- Joy's relationships highlight her vulnerability and how easily she can be exploited by others.
- Her relationships reveal her struggle with depression and how it has influenced her behaviour/attitude towards others.
- Through Joy's relationships we understand the extent of the impact losing her husband has had upon her.

Extract

- The 'domestic bliss' that Joy recalls at the start of the relationship highlights the impact of adhering to societal norms. There is a clear emotional detachment in their relationship, but while she is able to focus on being the ideal 'wife' ('The fridge was always well stocked and the cupboards interesting'), the flaws remain hidden. Joy's naïvety is evident.
- As the relationship between Paul and Joy progressed, we can see that there was a shift in power. This relationship has destroyed her confidence and there is evidence that it has caused her emotional turmoil. It is suggested that the relationship may have caused her paranoia ('... he could tell things by feeling the walls ...').
- There is the suggestion that the emotional neglect she felt during this relationship led her to become more vulnerable and susceptible to persuasion. ('The shoulder thought I might be more comfortable crying in bed.')

Rest of text

- Joy's relationship with Michael: develops central theme of loss. We learn that Joy was once content in an equal, committed relationship where there was compromise and understanding. Most importantly, it is Michael's death which leads to Joy's insecurity and emotional distress, and as she recalls his death and funeral we grow to understand her vulnerability and poor health.
- Joy's relationship with Tony: his desire for her reveals the vanity and arrogance which often prompts affairs. We see how vulnerable Joy is, as she feels unable to dismiss his advances, and as a result we are faced with the uncomfortable fact that he takes advantage of her.
- Joy's relationship with David: initially, their relationship seems to reveal Joy's struggle to connect emotionally and psychologically with her actions, and it seems this relationship serves a more physical purpose. With David's encouragement Joy grows stronger and learns to be more independent.

Prose, Text 4: *Sunset Song* by Lewis Grassic Gibbon

Question 26

Reference + basic comment = 1 mark. Reference + detailed comment = 2 marks.

See Hint S4.

You may have chosen some of the examples below, although others are possible:

- Long sentence conveys the number of actions Chris has to make before rescuing the horses and her panic to do everything quickly.
- The beginning of the sentence in line 17 builds tension as the clauses not only add detail but also force the reader to pause, to build a vivid and terrifying picture in their heads of the lightning.
- Use of main clauses in long sentences has a cumulative effect to show the speed of Chris and her panic.
- Use of simple connectives such as 'and' and 'then' create a long, breathless narrative to convey panic.

Question 27

Reference + basic comment = 1 mark. Reference + detailed comment = 2 marks.

See Hint S5.

You may have chosen some of the examples below, although others are possible:

- 'Blawearie's stones seemed falling about her ears' – the storm is so powerful, it could destroy the farmhouse around Chris.
- 'Kinraddie lighted up and fearful' – the personification of Kinraddie shows that it is in the grip of the storm; the storm has the power to destroy Kinraddie.
- 'a great beast moved and purred and scrabbled' – the metaphor suggests almost a mythological creature who roams the land as a mighty predator. There is a cat-like ferocity which suggests power and ruthlessness.
- 'suddenly it opened its mouth again' – speed and force are suggested here. Opening its mouth suggests that it will devour the countryside around it.
- 'roar' – clearly suggests volume, power and primitive rage.
- 'flash of its claws' – speed, power and violence suggested in this image. 'Claws' again links to the metaphor of the storm as a beast.
- 'tearing at the earth' – 'tearing' suggests brutality and rage. The 'earth' or land is the prey here, the storm the predator.

Question 28

Identification of attitude + reference + detailed comment = 2 marks.

Identification of attitude + reference + more basic comments = 1 mark.

See Hint S2.

You may have identified some of these possible opinions.

Chris:

- thinks Uncle Tam is childish and petulant
- does not find Uncle Tam's presence helpful
- does not want to argue with Uncle Tam
- will not do as Uncle Tam says
- considers him to be unmanly
- is surprised at Uncle Tam's fear.

You may have chosen some of the examples below, although others are possible:

- 'Funny Uncle Tam had never cried a word' – shows she expects him to be up and helping her, as her father would have done.
- 'maybe he was still in the sulks' – she considers him petulant and huffy, like a child.
- 'plumped head-first in' – Tam did not stop to think through Chris' decision; instead he impetuously chooses to show his displeasure in a childish sulk.
- 'she'd be glad to see them go' – Tam's presence has not been helpful; he is trying to control her which Chris does not like.
- 'she'd enough to do without fighting relations' – Chris does not want to fall out with Tam, nor will she do as he says. She seems to see any disagreement as pointless and childish.
- 'Chris stood as if she couldn't believe her own ears' – she is astonished by Tam's fear. This is not her experience of men around her. She had never considered fear as a reason for his behaviour.
- 'he wouldn't go out' – this is so adamant, it shows the depth of his fear. That he will not even contemplate trying to overcome his fear may be incredible to Chris and may make her pity him or look on him with contempt.

Question 29

Reference + basic comment = 1 mark. Reference + detailed comment = 2 marks.

See Hint S3.

You may have chosen some of the examples below, although others are possible:

- 'kye were lowing … stirks … stamping about in their stalls' – the animals' fear shows the danger of the situation.
- 'darkness complete and heavy flowed back on her again' – she is alone in the dark and cannot see what she is doing. This creates a sense of unease and danger.
- 'the barbed wire was alive' – the metaphor shows both the life of the electricity and also creates a sense of unnatural pernicious intentions.
- 'tremulous, vibrant serpent that spat and glowed and hid its head and quivered again to sight' – the power of nature is demonstrated in this metaphor. There is also a sense of fear, as though the electricity is fearful of its own power; it is an unnatural monster.
- 'they were finished' – the electricity will kill. This is a desperate situation.
- 'deathly still' – the silence is ominous and reflects the danger for Chris.
- 'crawl and quiver … and roar' – the natural world around Chris has turned on her, infused with the terrifying energy and power of the lightning. Nature is normally a refuge for Chris; here it threatens her.

Question 30

Marks are allocated: 2 marks for commonality; 2 for comment(s) on this extract and 6 marks for comments on rest of text.

Reference + basic comment = 1 mark. Reference + detailed comment = 2 marks. Reference + insightful comment may score 3 marks.

See Hint S7.

You may have chosen some of the examples below, although others are possible:

Commonality

- Chris takes practical, decisive action here and is not bound by what is conventionally accepted of a female.
- Chris is deft and purposeful in her movements and actions.
- Chris trusts her own instincts rather than what others expect of her or tell her to do.

Extract

- Chris gets up and thinks of the horses immediately, seeking to rouse her uncle, and is prepared to venture into the storm herself.
- She is practical in that she dresses for speed and takes only a lamp in order to see where the horses are.
- She does not listen to her Auntie and prepares to go out alone.
- She wastes no time and moves with urgency.
- She manages to keep the lantern intact, even when she trips and falls.

Rest of text

- Chris is often referred to as 'cool and calm' which demonstrates her quiet self-reliance and practicality.
- Chris makes her own decisions about her future after her father's death.
- Chris' decision to marry Ewan comes as a result of a moment of realisation in which she discovers that the love of the land is primitive and has more meaning to her than a life as a school-teacher. She is sure and certain that her decision is the right one.
- Chris copes with her father's incestuous intentions after her mother's death without becoming self-indulgent.
- Jean Guthrie says Chris should have been born a lad rather than a lass as she is practical and without artifice.
- Chris prefers the work of the fields and with the cows rather than the drudgery of housework.

Prose, Text 5: *The Cone-Gatherers* by Robin Jenkins

Question 31

See Hint S2.

You should explain that Neil is the leader of the two brothers. He makes decisions for Calum and takes responsibility for his care (1).

You may have chosen some of the examples below, although others are possible:

- 'To look after his brother, he had never got married' – the fact that Neil has to 'look after' Calum implies that he takes responsibility for Calum's care (1).
- 'We'd better get down' – Neil decides when the brothers will finish gathering cones for today (1).
- Neil is 'dependent on his brother' in the tree, but Calum does not see himself as superior because of this (1).
- Once on the ground, Neil 'immediately strode out', leading the way back to the hut (1).
- When they reach the snares, Neil has to give Calum a reminder 'to leave the snares alone' (1).
- When Duror confronted the brothers about rabbits freed from snares, Neil protected his brother and 'faced up to the gun' whereas Calum 'cowered against the hut' (1).

Question 32

See Hint S1.

- Calum finds talk a form of 'bondage' – a word which implies to be chained or bound by restrictive ties (1) – as his child-like brain often cannot follow complex ideas within conversations and he becomes confused and anxious (1).

Question 33

You should explain that Calum in the tree is agile and confident whereas Calum on the ground is clumsy and unsure.

Reference + basic comment = 1 mark. Reference + detailed comment = 2 marks.

See Hint S2.

You may have chosen some of the examples below, although others are possible:

Calum in the tree

- 'with consummate confidence and grace' – implies Calum is able to move with effortless skill through the trees; he is sure of his ability in this environment.
- 'Not once, all the long way down, was he at a loss' – the use of 'not once' and 'all the long way' emphasises the extent of Calum's assuredness and skill.
- 'find holds by instinct' – the word 'instinct' implies aptitude and natural intuition, as if Calum was born to be in the trees.
- 'Every time … act of love' – in the trees Calum is able to care for his brother in some small way.

Calum on the ground

- 'stumbled' – implies clumsiness and lack of coordination.
- 'Gone were the balance and sureness' – 'Gone' implies a complete lack of confidence and grace.
- 'If there was a hollow or a stone or a stick' – repetition of 'or' elongates the list, increasing the number of obstacles ready to trip Calum.
- 'scrambled' – suggests an anxiousness to Calum's movements.

Question 34

Reference + basic comment = 1 mark. Reference + detailed comment = 2 marks.

See Hint S2.

You may have chosen some of the examples below, although others are possible:

- 'pounded' – hard movement, implies desperation.
- 'choking' – connotations of suffocating and gasping. The rabbit was suffering greatly.
- 'moaned' – incoherent noise suggesting Calum cannot help but vocalise his pain over the rabbit's plight.
- 'solemn promise' – the word 'solemn' implies Calum understands the promise was serious and important.
- Repetition of 'remembered' – emphasises Calum is reminding himself of the reasons he must not act.

- 'expulsion' – suggests banishment or rejection.
- 'shared the suffering' – alliteration: Calum feels a kinship with the rabbit, he feels its pain.

Question 35

Marks are allocated: 2 marks for commonality; 2 for comment(s) on this extract and 6 marks for comments on rest of text.

Reference + basic comment = 1 mark. Reference + detailed comment = 2 marks. Reference + insightful comment may score 3 marks.

See Hint S7.

You may have chosen some of the examples below, although others are possible:

Commonality

- War is felt both at home and away.
- War instigates great change.
- War contributes to the downfall of Duror.
- War is terrible and evil.

Extract

- The wood that Calum and Neil are working in is being cut down to produce timber needed for the war effort. The war is not being fought in the estate in Scotland where they are, but it is impacting the landscape nonetheless.
- In order to replant the forest at a later date, Calum and Neil are being employed to gather seeds. The war has placed them in this environment, putting them under the baleful watch of Duror.
- 'You can make use of a tree, but what use is a dead man?' – Neil highlights the men risking their lives and dying at war. This emphasises the tragedy of war and the senseless loss of life that results from it.

Rest of text

- Because of the war, Lady Runcie Campbell is left alone to run the estate. Had her husband been home, lacking his wife's Christian compassion, the cone gatherers would likely have been expelled from the estate, sparing Calum his tragic death at the hands of Duror.
- Neil sees the war as an opportunity. Having all his life lived under the rule of his superiors, he hopes that a new order – a more equal order – might be created in the aftermath of the Second World War.
- Duror uses the war to justify his abhorrence of Calum. Although outwardly he condemns Hitler and his actions, he secretly believes that the Nazi attitude towards cripples is the correct one: he would like to murder Calum in the same way the Nazis were sending the physically disabled to the gas chambers.
- Using the Second World War as a backdrop serves to remind the reader that there is evil throughout the world, and that its presence in Duror in the wood is not isolated.
- The Second World War has added to Duror's mental instability. He wished to serve, but was thought too old. This rejection, added to the pressures of his wife's illness and his uncomfortable home life, may have contributed to his unreasonable hatred and fixation on the cone gatherers and, more specifically, Calum.

Poetry, Text 1: *A Poet's Welcome To His Love-Begotten Daughter* by Robert Burns

Question 36

You may have said: Warm/welcoming/protective (other answers are possible).

Attitude must be identified to score full marks.

Reference + basic comment = 1 mark. Reference + detailed comment = 2 marks.

See Hints S2 and S4.

You may have chosen some of the examples below, although others are possible:

- 'thou' – use of familiar term shows intimacy and conveys Burns' connection with the baby.
- 'welcome' – literally greeting the child, showing that she is gladly received.
- 'wean' – meaning child. This has connotations of innocence as well as the relationship between the two.
- 'mishanter fa' me' – Burns is almost swearing an oath here that terrible things should happen to him if he is ever ashamed of the baby.
- 'daunton' – Burns would be ashamed if he were ever to be frightened when thinking about his baby.
- 'My bonie lady' – incredibly tender. Possessive pronoun 'My' shows his connection with the baby clearly. 'bonie' suggests he finds her beautiful and is complimenting her. 'lady' shows that Burns gives his daughter rank; he does not see the child's illegitimate birth as shameful or dishonourable.
- 'blush' – Burns vows never to feel shame when talking of his daughter.
- 'Tyta or daddie' – affectionate diminutives of 'father' which show both his familial connection with the baby, but also show the sweet innocence of the child and her future perception of him.

Question 37

Identify the community's disapproval of Burns' behaviour and/or the suggestion that Burns should find the baby's existence shameful.

Reference + basic comment = 1 mark. Reference + detailed comment = 2 marks.

See Hint S1.

You may have chosen some of the examples below, although others are possible:

- 'daunton' – Burns' suggestion that he may be frightened by the mention of his daughter's name reflects the prejudices of his community.
- 'blush' – similarly, Burns' suggestion that he may be embarrassed by his daughter reflects the prejudices of his community.
- 'they ca' me fornicator' – the attitude of the community is negative towards love-making, instead focusing on it being a sin.
- 'tease my name in kintry clatter' – Burns' illegitimate child is the subject of gossip, showing how scandalous the community finds her birth.
- 'tho' your comin' I hae fought for, / Baith kirk and queir' – demonstrates that the church and its congregation have been against the birth of the baby.

Question 38

Reference + basic comment = 1 mark. Reference + detailed comment = 2 marks.

See Hints S2 and S4.

You may have identified one or more of the following points:

- Burns celebrates his enjoyment of love-making and despises the kirk's negative attitude to it.
- Burns acknowledges his own weakness but does not feel ashamed of it.
- Burns has great affection and feeling for his lover(s).

You may have chosen some of the examples below, although others are possible:

- 'ye're no unwrought for, / That I shall swear!' – he humorously says that he put a lot of effort into making the baby.
- 'Sweet fruit' – the child is a delightful result of many enjoyable occasions.
- 'mony a merry dint' – shows that he took many opportunities to have a good time with Betty, the baby's mother.
- 'My funny toil' – emphasises the joy and effort of lovemaking which produced the child. 'Toil' is a little tongue-in-cheek and adds humour which contrasts with the attitude of the kirk and community.
- 'My bonie Betty' – the possessive pronoun shows attachment and creates a connection between the two. He praises her beauty with 'bonie'. He openly acknowledges the connection between the two.

Question 39

Marks are allocated: 2 marks for commonality; 2 for comment(s) on this poem and 6 marks for comments on other text(s).

Reference + basic comment = 1 mark. Reference + detailed comment = 2 marks. Reference + insightful comment may score 3 marks.

See Hint S7.

You may have chosen some of the examples below, although others are possible:

Commonality

- Burns satirises Calvinism's hypocrisy in order to condemn and undermine it.
- Burns uses imagery effectively to expose the hypocrisy of the church.
- Burns suggests that the church represses love and does not value it highly enough.

A Poet's Welcome to his Love-Begotten Daughter

- The poem shows Burns' hatred of the kirk's negative attitude to love.
- He has been attacked by people representing the church who punish him for acknowledging his daughter.
- Religion is also presented as hypocritical here and perhaps obsessively focused on others' sins.
- Burns suggests that the ministers of the kirk enjoyed imagining the poet's 'sin'.
- Likewise, his connection of the 'priests' with 'hell' is a strong anti-church message – Burns may be implying that their destructive repression of others' earthly pleasures is, in fact, serving the devil, rather than God.

Holy Willie's Prayer

- Burns shows the hypocrisy of the church through the character of Holy Willie who condemns others for drinking and fornicating, and yet is not above indulging in these 'vices' himself.
- In this poem, Burns satirises the church by demonstrating how absurd Willie's beliefs and claims to Godliness are.
- Burns presents a strong visual image of Hell, as did the teaching of Calvinism.
- Burns seeks to expose this as a cheap device used by Calvinist ministers to keep the masses under control.
- The contrast between Willie's attitude to his potential illegitimate child with that of Burns' own in *A Poet's Welcome to his Love-Begotten Daughter* is marked; Willie, who claims to be an upstanding member of the kirk, refers to such a child as 'a livin' plague' whereas Burns, whom the kirk condemns as a 'fornicator', warmly welcomes his own daughter, promising to love and care for her as if he and her mother were married.

Address to the Deil

- Burns uses this humorous poem to indirectly attack Calvinism.
- He assumes a friendly, chummy tone with the devil which undermines the power of the devil.
- It is by graphic presentation of Hell and damnation that many Calvinist ministers sought to control their congregations: Burns subverts this.
- By also introducing the supernatural element and stories from folk-tales, he reduces the devil to a bogey-man figure – a creation designed to keep children from doing wrong.
- His depiction of the devil in the Garden of Eden echoes the lascivious attention that the ministers pay to Burns' indiscretions in *A Poet's Welcome to his Love-Begotten Daughter.*
- His address at the end of the poem shows how Burns imagines the devil, and his community, may be judging him.

Poetry, Text 2: *Anne Hathaway* by Carol Ann Duffy

Question 40

Reference + basic comment = 1 mark. Reference + detailed comment = 2 marks.

See Hint S2.

You may have chosen some of the examples below, although others are possible:

- Ambiguity of 'loved' – by leaving this open to interpretation it suggests both the emotional and physical love between them.
- Word choice: 'spinning' – suggests a vigorous, dizzying movement which therefore implies the relationship swept her off her feet.
- Metaphor of 'spinning world' – to imply that the bed is a 'world' suggests that they could have spent their whole lives there. The implication of size and space also conveys the magnitude of their relationship.
- Use of list – suggests the passion and creativity which existed between this couple. They created a magical, vibrant place together. The detail adds to the sense of intensity.
- Metaphor of 'we would dive for pearls' – the verb 'dive' suggests plunging, entering entirely and deeply into the relationship. 'Pearls' are precious, just as their moments together have clear value to her.

- Metaphor of 'My lover's words / were shooting stars' – the connection with fate and the Gods suggests the power of words.

Question 41

Reference + basic comment = 1 mark. Reference + detailed comment = 2 marks.

See Hint S2.

You may have chosen some of the examples below, although others are possible:

- Metaphor of 'my body now a softer rhyme / to his' – suggests a connection between husband and wife – like they complement each other. The fact that hers is 'softer' reflects that her words are more feminine, but also that his words would make her 'softer', more comforted, relaxed and loved.
- Connotations of 'echo' and 'assonance' – conveys the sense of mirroring, complementing that exists between the two.
- Metaphor of 'I dreamed he'd written me' – suggests he is incredibly creative and powerful to her. He is the 'author' of her life, creating emotions and influencing who she is.
- Metaphor of 'the bed / a page beneath his writer's hands' – shows a strong connection between his work and the passion he had with his wife. It implies that much of their romance then inspired his writing.

Question 42

See Hint S2.

- 'dozed' – suggests boredom. There is nothing passionate about their love (1).
- 'dribbling' – a disgusting image which contrasts with the beauty and poetry of the love between the speaker and her husband (1).
- 'prose' – reference to broad category could be said to be dull, compared to the specific references to 'Romance' and 'drama' which convey the heady love they shared (1).

Any of the above should be compared with:

- 'My living, laughing, love' – both 'living' and 'laughing' reveal the happiness and energy of their relationship. Alliteration of 'l' adds to the lightness, giving it a singing quality reinforcing the romance she felt (1).

Question 43

Marks are allocated: 2 marks for commonality; 2 for comment(s) on this poem and 6 marks for comments on other text(s).

Reference + basic comment = 1 mark. Reference + detailed comment = 2 marks. Reference + insightful comment may score 3 marks.

See Hint S7.

You may have chosen some of the examples below, although others are possible:

Commonality

- Duffy exploits symbolism as a means of exploring the many facets of her subject, revealing connected ideas and exploring its aspects in detail.
- Through a single symbolic object, Duffy is able to highlight the contrasts, conflicts and changes which occur as a result of her central idea.

Anne Hathaway

- In this poem, the bed itself is the central symbolic object. As the concept of a marital bed comes with the suggestion of love and commitment, Duffy is able to use this to present the view that Shakespeare and Anne Hathaway shared a loving relationship, contrary to popular belief. From the outset 'The bed we loved in' is the focus of the poem, and it becomes a place of wonder and magic.
- There are also symbolic references made to language, writing and specifically Shakespeare's work. Adopting the sonnet form – the form of love – suggests that this is an expression of romance. Mirroring Shakespeare's form supports the idea that there is a strong link between the couple.

War Photographer

- Religious symbols are used in this poem to alert us to the huge responsibility and challenge inflicted upon war photographers. By comparing the process of developing the photographs to a mass and the photographer himself to a priest, Duffy not only hints at the importance of his actions but also at his own desire to remember the dead and pay his respects.

Valentine

- The extended metaphor in this poem centres on an onion, which comes to embody the dual nature of love. Duffy uses this object to explore the hurt caused by love ('make your reflection / a wobbling photo of grief'), but also demonstrates the strength of love ('its fierce kiss').

Mrs Midas

- In this poem, the destructive power of ambition and greed is conveyed. A central symbolic object is Midas' hand. This connects the original myth with the breakdown in the relationship as throughout there are references to 'his touch' which provokes both her fear and longing as the couple ends up apart.

Poetry, Text 3: *Last Supper* by Liz Lochhead

Question 44

Possible conflicts include:

- determination versus uncertainty
- anger versus longing
- powerfulness versus anxiety.

Reference + basic comment = 1 mark. Reference + detailed comment = 2 marks.

See Hint S2.

You may have chosen some of the examples below, although others are possible:

- 'She is getting … ready to renounce' – ambiguity. 'renounce' suggests a strong desire to give up the relationship; the present tense plus the use of 'getting' implies that this is still in progress and therefore she is not quite 'ready' yet.
- 'Not just for lent. (For / Ever)' – bluntness of short sentence implies determination and focus on her goal; however the use of parenthesis weakens this as it seems to suggest a need to remind or reassert control. Use of capitals and enjambment reflect force/anger. Slightly excessive which again could hint at a deliberate attempt to seem strong.

- 'assembling the ingredients' – word choice implies a clear attempt to be organised and in control. Implies a cool, level-headed and focused approach to the situation.
- Use of parenthesis and rhetorical question – suggestion of uncertainty or hesitation in course of action. Use of a question also compounds the idea that this reflects the narrator's wavering determination.
- 'tearing foliage, scrambling / the salad' – hints at anger or aggression but also forcefulness. 'scrambling' hints at uncontrolled, hurried actions.

Question 45

See Hint S2.

1 mark for identification of central idea: anticipation of a gathering with friends where together they will gain satisfaction from dissecting the relationship.

1 mark for suitable reference plus comment.

- 'leftover hash' – suggests they will 'make a meal' out of the break-up, that it will feed them with some kind of emotional reward.
- 'when those three met again' – allusion to *Macbeth* suggests the power gained from the gathering and the potential menace they could cause.
- 'render from the bones' – also refers to cooking, making something out of the break-up to feed their needs. Reference to 'bones' is also somewhat sinister, suggesting perhaps the extremes they are willing to go to.

Question 46

See Hint S5.

1 mark for a suitable explanation of the purpose of extended metaphor.

- In this stanza, Lochhead compares the conversation between the women to a meal and uses this image to explore the delight and satisfaction which the women gain as they discuss the end of the relationship.
- It develops a powerful impression of the women and their connection.

A further 3 marks are available.

Reference + basic comment = 1 mark. Reference + detailed comment = 2 marks.

You may have chosen some of the examples below, although others are possible:

- 'spitting out the gristlier bits' – 'gristlier bits' suggests they are discussing the difficult, disgusting aspects of the relationship, while 'spitting' reveals the force and anger with which they are speaking. Conveys not only the power of these women, but also the fervour with which they will analyse a relationship.
- 'gnawing on … some intricate irony' – 'gnawing' reveals the almost animalistic, rough way these women are eating which reflects their relentless determination to discuss all aspects of the relationship. 'intricate irony' implies that they look into every minute detail in order to unearth a weakness in the partner or relationship.
- 'petit-gout mouthfuls of reported speech' – 'petit-gout mouthfuls' suggest that they have little to go on. 'reported' reinforces the idea that this information is second hand. This does not deter them, suggesting that they relish everything, even minor details.

- 'munching the lies, fat and sizzling as sausages' – 'munching' also implies a forceful, determined rumination on the information, but now we are introduced to the fact that they do not care for truth: more satisfaction can be gained from fallacy which is highlighted by the comparison with 'fat and sizzling' sausages which appear substantial and gratifying.
- 'gorged on truth' – 'gorged' implies an over-indulgence and thus we are reminded of the fact that these women relish the time together and discuss every aspect possible until there is nothing left.
- 'satisfied' – again this suggests the extent to which the discussion has been continued.
- 'somebody would get hungry' – implying these women are 'hungry' for a chance to ridicule a relationship. Reinforces the power of their collective bond and also their power as they are the ones seeking out the next 'prey'.

Question 47

Marks are allocated: 2 marks for commonality; 2 for comment(s) on this poem and 6 marks for comments on other text(s).

Reference + basic comment = 1 mark. Reference + detailed comment = 2 marks. Reference + insightful comment may score 3 marks.

See Hint S7.

You may have chosen some of the examples below, although others are possible:

Commonality

- The women in Lochhead's poems are often powerful, strong individuals with intense passions and loyalties.
- When faced with conflict or threat, the women demonstrate their determination.
- Lochhead demonstrates her admiration and respect for women.

Last Supper

- Lochhead defies traditional views of women and places them in a position of power. Rather than depicting them as emotionally weak and vulnerable following a break-up, she suggests that women relish the opportunity to end a failing relationship and can indeed achieve a sense of empowerment by taking control over the situation ('Already she was imagining it done with, this feast'). She also explores the collective power that women can feel when they come together, and shows the support they provide for one another in times of need.

My Rival's House

- Portrays a woman in a very powerful situation, but in this instance there is discord between members of the same sex. Lochhead looks closely at the matriarchal figure and the extent that she will go to in order to secure her position within the family (capped tooth, polished nail / will fight). Her portrayal of this woman effectively conveys the power of the maternal instinct, and the conflict which arises once the son falls in love.

For My Grandmother Knitting

- Offers a very moving description of the life of a woman, and the many aspects of being a wife and mother. Through this, Lochhead is able to subtly praise the strength and beauty of women, and acknowledge that these habits and instincts do not leave even with age. Lochhead paints the picture of the woman as a nurturer and provider, determined to do what she can for her family even when her body begins to refuse.

View of Scotland/Love Poem

- Involves yet another description of a mother, and Lochhead manages to take a humorous look at the effort and fervour they display when fulfilling the expectations of tradition. While her tone is slightly mocking, there is a sense of her admiration and respect for the woman 'jiffywaxing the vinolay', clearly keen to make sure her family face the new year in the best possible way in the hope of good things to come.

Poetry, Text 4: *Aunt Julia* by Norman MacCaig

Question 48

Reference + basic comment = 1 mark. Reference + detailed comment = 2 marks.

See Hint S2.

You may have chosen some of the examples below, although others are possible:

- 'spoke Gaelic / very loud and very fast' – repetition of 'very' emphasises her vitality and life. The use of straightforward language echoes Aunt Julia's straightforward, practical nature. The words 'loud' and 'fast' give the impression of energy.
- 'wore men's boots' – this highlights her practical nature and lack of femininity.
- 'strong foot' – suggests she was capable of physical work; the poet's admiration for her is clear.
- 'stained with peat' – highlights her connection with nature. The word 'stained' suggests long-term/ingrained; she is constantly working with the land.
- 'paddling with the treadle of the spinningwheel' – 'paddling' creates idea of movement and speed, indicating skill. The reference to the 'spinningwheel' reveals the simple nature of her lifestyle/working with her hands/ creativity.
- 'drew yarn / marvellously out of the air.' – indicates skill. The phrase 'out of the air' implies that she is magical/ gives the sense of being someone special.

Question 49

See Hint S2.

- It was the sole place where he felt safe at night, despite the confined space of a 'box bed'.
- Uniqueness of the old-fashioned lifestyle ('box bed').
- Describing the crickets as friendly indicates that there was a sense of peace and warmth at his aunt's house.

Question 50

Reference + basic comment = 1 mark. Reference + detailed comment = 2 marks.

See Hints S2 and S3.

You may have chosen some of the examples below, although others are possible:

- 'By the time I had learned / a little' – alliteration. The poet had learned some Gaelic, but also grown up and begun to more fully understand his aunt's way of life.
- 'silenced' – this is a contrast to Aunt Julia's natural, loud voice. She has been quietened by death and cannot speak to him now.

- 'absolute black' – refers to the 'absolute darkness' of the box bed. However, that was a comforting dark. Black is connected with mourning.
- 'a seagull's voice' – connecting Aunt Julia to nature, but also significant as he was unable to understand her.
- 'getting angry, getting angry' – repetition, conveys depth of emotion.
- 'so many questions / unanswered' – he could not connect with her through language, but he was also removed from the lifestyle and culture that she was a part of. Important message: MacCaig is fearful that we risk losing this rich cultural heritage.
- 'unanswered' – this final word of the poem is given a line of its own to emphasise its significance. He was unable to answer her in his youth, and now that she is gone he will never have any answers to the questions he had for her.

Question 51

Marks are allocated: 2 marks for commonality; 2 for comment(s) on this poem and 6 marks for comments on other text(s).

Reference + basic comment = 1 mark. Reference + detailed comment = 2 marks. Reference + insightful comment may score 3 marks.

See Hint S7.

You may have chosen some of the examples below, although others are possible:

Commonality

- MacCaig uses personal experience to convey loss.
- His use of language emphasises the pain of loss.
- MacCaig uses loss as a vehicle to explore the finality of death.

Aunt Julia

- Aunt Julia is remembered fondly by MacCaig, but the main theme in the poem is his frustration regarding his inability to communicate with her.
- He now regrets that, as she spoke Gaelic, he was never able to fully connect with his aunt. Even though he has rectified this gap in his knowledge, it is too late and she is gone.
- The description of his aunt being 'silenced in the absolute black' is effective as it contrasts with the vivid description of her life, which was full of energy. Death is seen as empty and bleak.
- In the final stanza of the poem, MacCaig mourns not only the loss of his aunt, who he was never fully able to connect with, but also the loss of the heritage and culture embodied in her Highland way of life, which he fears we risk abandoning.

Sounds of the Day

- In *Sounds of the Day*, MacCaig mourns the death of a relationship.
- Again, MacCaig uses the sounds of nature to signify life and energy. The pain of his loss leaves him shrouded in silence beside the 'quietest fire in the world'.
- He closes the poem by describing the impact of his loss: the sharp pain of the initial separation followed by the emotional numbness that leaves him detached from life.

Visiting Hour

- In this poem MacCaig describes a visit to a dying relative.
- He describes his discomfort with the hospital – which he associates with sickness and death rather than healing.
- His admiration for the nurses – whose 'slender waists miraculously' bear up under the constant burden of death – is clear. They are able to face every day something which he cannot bear to think about 'until / I have to'.
- He describes the person he is visiting as living in a 'white cave of forgetfulness', as if the colour is already leeching out of her world as she heads towards death.
- MacCaig struggles to deal with her pain and suffering, which he sees as a distance which 'neither she nor I / can cross', the forced extending of her life a 'fruitless torture'.

Memorial

- *Memorial* is an elegy, possibly to MacCaig's sister who died shortly before the poem was published.
- In the poem, MacCaig describes the all-consuming nature of loss: it is something he cannot escape.
- MacCaig reveals his fears about the 'nowhere' the dead woman in the poem is going into: he sees death as final and empty. This makes the poem more tragic as the loss is permanent and hopeless.
- In the final stanza MacCaig discusses his inability to move on: 'She makes me / her elegy'. He is so overwhelmed by grief that he has become nothing but his despair. He has lost both her and himself.

Poetry, Text 5: *An Autumn Day* by Sorley MacLean

Question 52

See Hint S1.

- A shell blast (1).

The other mark must come from one of these references with sensible comment.

- 'the screech' – describes the noise of the shell descending.
- 'out of the sun' – indicates the fact that the shell is falling on them from the sky.
- 'out of an invisible throbbing' – shows that initially they cannot see the shell itself but can hear its descent.
- 'flame leaped' – the shell has exploded, creating fire.
- 'smoke climbed' – smoke is created by the explosion.
- 'surged in every way' – shows the amount of smoke, caused by the explosion, enveloping in all directions.
- 'blinding of eyes' – the smoke of the explosion renders the poet sightless.
- 'splitting of hearing' – the noise of the impact temporarily deafens the poet.

Question 53

You must answer on both language and structure to secure full marks.

Reference + basic comment = 1 mark. Reference + detailed comment = 2 marks.

See Hint S3.

You may have chosen some of the examples below, although others are possible:

Language

- 'One Election' – refers to Calvinist beliefs in predestination in which it is already decided who will get to heaven. The sense is here that it is out of one's control – it was another's decision that these soldiers should die.
- 'and did not take me' – the poet questions why he is still alive; the 'decision' for him to survive seems arbitrary to him.
- 'without asking us' – there is no consultation, no control over one's destiny.
- 'which was better or worse' – the 'decision' over who lives or dies is not based on the hopes and fears of the soldiers.
- 'devilishly indifferent' – the deity who chooses who lives or dies seems to be completely unmoved by the personal feelings of the soldiers.
- 'as the shells' – the deity or fate representing the 'Election' is equated with the bombs which MacLean personifies. Neither has any personal connection or feeling about ending the lives of others.

Structure

- 'them', 'me', 'us' – position of these pronouns at the end of line places emphasis on them and highlights, paradoxically, the sense of 'sameness' and difference between MacLean and the dead soldiers. One is alive, the others are dead. There seems to be no reason why.
- Short lines – emphasise the simplicity of the ideas in the poem and highlights the enormous psychological strain of surviving war.
- Contrast between 'them' / 'us' and 'better' / 'worse' – shows the polarity of the fates which makes the arbitrariness of the choice of who lives or dies seem all the more absurd.
- 'One Election' / 'shells' – the opening and closing words of the stanza equate these two, echoing a notion of a destructive, cruel God.

Question 54

Reference + basic comment = 1 mark. Reference + detailed comment = 2 marks.

See Hint S2.

You may have chosen some of the examples below, although others are possible:

- Single syllable words – have directness and heavy emphasis which shows both the strength and the horror of the memory of this incident.
- Repetition – of the word 'dead' conveys the horror of the incident.
- Number – the number of men who died is repeated three times. This emphasises not only what MacLean remembers in detail and the number of dead men behind MacLean but also makes the poet's survival seem all the more miraculous and important.
- 'at my shoulder' – this specific notion of place shows the proximity of death to MacLean, makes his survival seem incredibly lucky and also connotes a sense of camaraderie which emphasises the horrid arbitrariness of survival in war.
- 'on an Autumn day' – the contrast of the gory subject matter with this bucolic ideal (autumn days have connotations of mildness, peace and abundance), further emphasises the horror of the experience.

Question 55

Marks are allocated: 2 marks for commonality; 2 for comment(s) on this poem and 6 marks for comments on other text(s).

Reference + basic comment = 1 mark. Reference + detailed comment = 2 marks. Reference + insightful comment may score 3 marks.

See Hint S7.

You may have chosen some of the examples below, although others are possible:

Commonality

- MacLean is preoccupied by the transitory nature of life as well as the legacy that lives on after death.
- MacLean sees time as both the barrier to and the means of connecting with his past and his ancestors.
- MacLean's poetry is a means of trapping time, of memorialising an incident, place or person.

An Autumn Day

- Specific time of the title is echoed in the final lines. This shows the contrast between the connotations of an autumn day and the poet's experience of this particular day and emphasises the wistful horror of the remembrance.
- Specifics of time such as 'morning', 'midday' and 'evening' emphasise the brutal continuity of war.
- MacLean's precision in identifying time reflects his preoccupation with this near-death experience and his possible disillusionment with war.

Hallaig

- MacLean's metaphor of time as a deer presents time as a living entity that lives in Hallaig.
- Time dissolves in Hallaig and all generations can be seen simultaneously.
- The poem is set at twilight, a time between day and night. The suggestion is that the world of the living becomes permeable to the world of the dead and the past at this time.
- The haunting beauty of deserted Hallaig makes it easier for the poet to connect to the past.

Heroes

- Time loosely referred to through the poem to indicate that time is running out for this particular hero. The finite span of life and the inglorious manner in which one can die is suggested.
- The man's efforts will not be remembered; they will not stand the test of time. MacLean hints at the notion that soldiers in war are seen as expendable.
- The man's death so far from home creates pathos and a sense of disillusionment with the 'glory' of war.

I Gave You Immortality

- MacLean sees his poetry as a legacy that lasts until the end of time, overcoming the mundane confines of mortality.
- MacLean immortalises the 'yellow-haired' muse, capturing her beauty. He turns something fragile and transient into something permanent and everlasting.
- MacLean's poetry is so universal that it will endure; he is capturing the very essence of frustrated love.

Poetry, Text 6: *Nil Nil* by Don Paterson

Question 56

See Hint S1.

- The title is missing the dash expected in the score line, making a double negative (1). 'Nil Nil' is both nothing and everything. It has metaphorical meaning, reflecting the idea in the poem that man's life and achievement, when time passes, becomes nothing but is also absorbed into the fabric of the world – everything (1).
- 'Nil Nil' is a score line, which is a reference to the main topic of the poem: the fall in fortunes of a football club (1).

Question 57

Reference + basic comment = 1 mark. Reference + detailed comment = 2 marks.

See Hints S2, S3 and S5.

You may have chosen some of the examples below, although others are possible:

- 'From the top, then, the zenith' – both 'top' and 'zenith' connote the peak of something. This was the football club at the height of its success.
- 'majestic' – word choice: connotations of greatness and dignity. Implies McGrandle was an outstanding, skilful player.
- 'balletic toe-poke' – oxymoron. 'balletic' connotes graceful and elegant, whereas 'toe-poke' implies a lack of skill. There is a nostalgic romanticism in his description of the play.
- 'nearly bursting the roof / of the net' – hyperbole. Implies strength and power.
- 'shaky pan' – refers to the early era of television, gives a sense of history to the club.
- 'a plague of grey bonnets' – metaphor: gives a sense of the sheer number of fans – the football club was very well supported at this point.
- 'falls out of the clouds' – metaphor: the stands full of supporters went to the skyline, there is no view of the rest of the city; gives a sense of the stadium being its own world. Also implies heavenly/angelic, as if the fans have come down from heaven to watch the game.

Question 58(a)

Reference + basic comment = 1 mark. Reference + detailed comment = 2 marks.

See Hint S4.

You may have chosen some of the examples below, although others are possible:

- Use of list ('McGrandle, Visocchi and Spankie') to highlight number and quick succession of players abandoning the club.
- Use of list ('pitch-sharing / pay-cuts, pawned silver') using alliteration and rhythm to highlight the consequences of the team's plummeting popularity.
- Use of list with parallel structure ('*the* Highland Division / *the* absolute sitters… / *the* dismal nutmegs, *the* scores so obscene') to emphasise the amount and range of calamities experienced by the club.
- Use of long sentence creates pace to emphasise the speed of the club's demise.

Question 58(b)

Reference + basic comment = 1 mark. Reference + detailed comment = 2 marks.

See Hint S2.

You may have chosen some of the examples below, although others are possible:

- 'down'.../ ...'descent' – connotations of falling, highlights the failing fortunes of the club.
- 'foot' – implies being at the bottom; the worst.
- 'ballooned' – implies missed by a clear margin, showing lack of skill/luck.
- 'dismal nutmegs' – suggests appalling/poor. A nutmeg is to put the ball between the other player's legs; implies the team were being mocked by their opponents.
- 'obscene' – connotations of being shocking or disgusting. Implies the team were often soundly beaten; gives a sense of embarrassment.

Question 59

Marks are allocated: 2 marks for commonality; 2 for comment(s) on this poem and 6 marks for comments on other text(s).

Reference + basic comment = 1 mark. Reference + detailed comment = 2 marks. Reference + insightful comment may score 3 marks.

See Hint S7.

You may have chosen some of the examples below, though others are possible:

Commonality

- Structure helps to indicate points of change in Paterson's poems.
- Paterson uses structure to mirror the speed or magnitude of events, emphasising theme/ideas.

Nil Nil

- The poem is made up of only two stanzas. The long opening stanza emphasises the monumental fall of the football team.
- The second, shorter stanza widens the scope of the poem and highlights a key theme: life is meaningless and everything eventually fades to nothing (the successful team becomes no more than two boys playing kick-about / the brave pilot becomes a stone they play with), but at the end of our life we also return to the earth to become a part of everything.
- The use of long sentences and enjambment creates pace and rhythm to highlight the speed of the club's descent.
- The use of lists emphasises the number and continuous occurrence of difficulties and problems experienced by the club.

11:00 Baldovan

- The poem is written in short stanzas of two lines. When viewed from the side this creates a repeated pattern of 11 on the page. This emphasises the momentous nature of the bus journey to the two boys: it is almost a rite of passage on the road to adulthood.

Question 3 (b)

See Hint R2.

Possible answers include:

- 'deceptively airy fairy' – mocks the assumption that there is little substance to the practise. 'deceptively' suggests its hidden complexities and therefore its merit.
- 'make no mistake' – assertive tone. Reflects writer's confidence in its complexity.
- 'isn't about chanting' – creates a caustic tone, dismissing possible assumptions about the validity of mindfulness.
- 'no cross-legged spirituality involved' – sarcastic, also undermining the false assumptions many would make about mindfulness.
- '(hardly a bastion of hippiedom)' – tongue-in-cheek. Use of contrasting formality/informality helps to convey mocking and therefore highlight the absurdity of questioning the US army's use of mindfulness.
- 'effective form of mental discipline' – 'discipline' implies extreme dedication in order to achieve success. This then hints at the rigorous and challenging nature of mindfulness.
- 'dedicated' – reveals that Oxford University has placed a significant amount of resources into the development of mindfulness.
- Reference to Harvard and Oxford – both are highly respected institutions. Indicates their support for mindfulness makes us recognise its significance.

Question 4 (a)

See Hint R1.

- 'advances in neuroscience and psychology … 15 years' – our understanding of the brain and behaviour has improved and now there is a greater knowledge of mental health issues (1).
- 'current economic situation' – global financial instability/financial crashes have deeply affected our lives and left many struggling to cope (1).

Question 4 (b)

See Hint R1.

For full marks, there must be a gloss of the problem and the solution.

- Gloss of 'prone to overthinking' – we spend too much time considering what has happened and what may happen (1).
  OR
- Gloss of 'ruminating' – we mull over things too much (1).
- Gloss of 'develop a way of stilling our minds' – we need to learn methods that will allow us to calm our thoughts and think in a more methodical manner (1).

Question 5 (a)

See Hint R2.

Word choice

- 'manage' – implies control and stability. Suggests that mindfulness will be of great benefit in allowing people greater strength.
- 'remarkable' – emphasises the impressive extent of change brought through mindfulness.
- 'transformed' – suggests the extent of the change offered through mindfulness will be significant. Mindfulness could allow people to change completely.
- 'flexibility' – highlights how challenging our lives can be and our need to adapt, which mindfulness allows.
- 'rather than thinking strategically' – by implication this suggests that mindfulness will allow us to work systematically and more efficiently.
- 'profound effect' – suggests that mindfulness can result in awe-inspiring change.
- 'crucial tools' – suggests that mindfulness is vital to the lives of young people.
- 'empowering' – suggests that mindfulness offers something magical to our children, making them stronger.

Sentence structure

- Balance in 'from an unhappy … in the moment' – creates the impression that all the difficulties mentioned are overcome/tackled.
- Complex sentence in 'Mindfulness-based … half of all cases.' – emphasis is placed on the recommendation by the National Institute for Clinical Excellence which promotes its status and highlights the calibre of the commendation as opposed to its success rate.
- Short statement 'Such findings have been backed up by neuroscience.' – stating that it has been scientifically proven to work highlights that it should be widely recognised and used.
- Use of colon and single sentence paragraph in 'It's not just … performance in class.' – links the two arguments together and builds the argument that mindfulness has the potential to help everyone.

Other features

- Reference to the National Institute for Clinical Excellence – elevates the standing of mindfulness as a practice and consolidates the idea that it has medical benefits.

Question 5 (b)

See Hint R1.

Any four of:

- Mindfulness helps to calm us which in turn means that the brain is no longer producing as much cortisol – a chemical which causes us to feel strained/concerned.
- It helps to reduce the build-up of tissue in areas of the brain linked with stress and anxiety.
- It has been shown to increase the build-up of tissue in other parts of the brain that are associated with processes that are beneficial to us. This includes areas that allow us to retain information and focus as well as understand and connect with others.
- It helps to improve children's sense of worth and self-belief.
- It helps them to improve their attainment in class and work better.
- It helps them to feel less stressed by their studies.
- It helps them to feel more confident and assertive.

Question 6

See Hint R3.

	Area of agreement	*Judith Woods*	*Kate Pickert*
1	Mindfulness is increasing in popularity.	Woods refers to the numerous organisations that are adopting the practice including the US army and she highlights that it 'may well be coming to a classroom near you.'	Pickert promotes the rise of mindfulness in schools also: 'Educators are turning to mindfulness with increasing frequency'.
2	Mindfulness offers an antidote to the stresses of modern life.	Woods refers to the 'relentless pressure and information overload' that affects us all.	Pickert interviews Silverman who speaks of the huge pressures he was under at work ('hundreds of phone calls and emails each day') and the 'life-changing experience' he encountered when going on a mindfulness retreat.
3	Both acknowledge the benefits of mindfulness with regard to how it influences our brain.	Woods refers to the physical impact on our brains, allowing it to strengthen areas that are beneficial to us and reducing pressure on those which cause us strain.	Pickert refers to the fact that mindfulness can change the 'structure of the brain itself' and therefore allows us to counteract the negative effects caused by our stressful lives.
4	The benefits of mindfulness are widely acknowledged and supported by respected bodies.	Woods refers to many organisations that are very well respected and refers to the scientific studies by organisations such as Nice, which support mindfulness.	Pickert interviews Professor Kabat-Zinn who is advocating the use of mindfulness.
5	Mindfulness has the potential to help everyone.	Woods refers both to professionals using mindfulness, including a list of companies such as Google, Pricewaterhouse-Coopers and the Home Office and she also interviews Claire Kelly who praises its 'tangible effect' on children.	Pickert refers to the significant uptake of mindfulness in schools ('300,000 pupils, and educators in 43 countries') while also interviewing professionals who speak of the need for mindfulness to help them cope.

WORKED ANSWERS – Practice Exam B

Critical Reading – Section 1: Scottish text

Drama, Text 1: *The Slab Boys* by John Byrne

Question 1

You need to establish that Spanky, while competent, has an almost contemptuous attitude towards his work. He is aware that it is not a highly skilled role and knows that his chances for promotion depend as much on luck and nepotism as they do on merit. Jack, on the other hand, is very serious about his work. He appears boastful about his knowledge and is keen to reveal his importance to the company.

Reference + basic comment = 1 mark. Reference + detailed comment = 2 marks.

See Hints S2 and S3.

You may have chosen some of the examples below, although others are possible:

Spanky's attitude

- 'I'm busy, Jack.' – Spanky is not interested in aiding the company by developing new employees, or impressing Jack with his willingness to help.
- 'OK, OK … you get the stuff, pap it on the slab, water, gum, bingo … you grind away till you feel like a smoke.' – the use of 'stuff' is vague and imprecise. We know that Spanky is capable and knowledgeable so this is an attempt to prove to Alan that he doesn't care. The phrase 'till you feel like a smoke' reveals Spanky's laid back attitude. He is motivated not by the workload or company deadlines, but by his personal desires.
- 'That is it.' – by avoiding the contraction, Spanky highlights the simplicity of his job.
- 'Texture … seldom varies. Rough … that goes for the lot.' – Spanky speaks in broken sentences, giving him an off-hand manner and highlighting his lack of care.

Jack's attitude

- 'Aha … all on your ownio, Georgie? What … nobody pulling the strings? Thought Alan here might come back and do another spot in the Slab …' – Jack's forced joviality with Spanky – who does not return the humour or friendliness – is intended to show Alan how many connections he has at the company, to make himself look like an integral figure in the factory.
- 'Source materials … pigmentation … texture … density … all that sort of guff … fugitive colours … wrist technique.' – Jack lists facets of the slab boys' job, proving to Alan that he is knowledgeable in all areas of the company.
- 'I'd love to show you myself but the Boss has just hit me with a half-drop for Holland.' – Jack makes an excuse designed to show Alan (and Spanky) how important he is, that the 'boss' would give him an important, international job to complete.

Question 2

Reference + basic comment = 1 mark. Reference + detailed comment = 2 marks.

See Hints S2 and S3.

You may have chosen some of the examples below, although others are possible:

- 'The floor's just been mopped.' – this suggests that Alan is incapable of helping. The only job he could do – mopping the floor – has already been done. It may also be a snide insult, insinuating that Alan (who is educated and more upper class than Spanky) is a wet mop.
- 'I'm busy, Jack.' – Spanky does not want to take time out from working to show and help Alan. Given how little work Spanky has done in the play up to this point, this does not seem a valid reason to the audience.
- 'Spanky works on. Alan watches. Silence.' – Spanky, who has worked there for almost three years, makes no attempt to speak to Alan or put him at ease, indicating he does not want him in the slab room.
- 'Sure, sure ... anything you say ... kiddo.' – by calling Alan 'kiddo' immediately after the other character has asked him to stop, Spanky shows a teasing side to his character. However, the term 'kiddo' is derogatory, implying Alan is young and unknowledgeable, and so there appears a snide side to Spanky's teasing.
- '(Waiting till he's finished) Enough gum in it?' – Spanky deliberately allows Alan to make a mistake before correcting him. Again, this could be seen as teasing, but as Alan is new and does not have an established relationship with Spanky, this appears slightly cruel – especially as Spanky does it twice in quick succession.

Question 3

Reference + basic comment = 1 mark. Reference + detailed comment = 2 marks.

See Hint S2.

You may have chosen some of the examples below, although others are possible:

- 'Starts going over the list of colours in his head' – Spanky knows his job so well that he has the full list – which we can see by the following dialogue is extensive – by memory.
- 'Starts working quickly and methodically' – Spanky works at speed and proceeds systematically, implying he knows the process intimately.
- 'Adjusts Alan's grip' – Spanky knows his job and the slab process to the extent that he can train others and see small flaws in their method such as Alan's hold on the equipment.

Question 4

Marks are allocated: 2 marks for commonality; 2 for comment(s) on this extract and 6 marks for comments on rest of text.

Reference + basic comment = 1 mark. Reference + detailed comment = 2 marks. Reference + insightful comment may score 3 marks.

See Hint S7.

You may have chosen some of the examples below, though others are possible:

Commonality

- Education and background can create divides in society.
- Education is an important factor in success.
- Achievement in education involves personal responsibility.

Extract

- In this scene we can see Spanky's struggle for promotion. As an uneducated slab boy he is reliant on unfair factors such as 'if they take to your features … how many desks are free … how the Boss is feeling … what the Berlin situation's like …' to get ahead.
- Workers like Alan, however, who are educated, gain automatic entry to a 'desk'.
- We are also told about Phil's educational history.
- At first it seems that Phil's attitude towards education was positive: he stayed on at school to try to get his Highers.
- However, he sabotaged his own progress by 'smacking the French teacher in the mouth with a German biscuit', showing a lack of real commitment to learning.

Rest of text

- The advantages of education are made clear in the play by contrasting the opportunities available to Alan with those that present themselves to Spanky and the slab boys.
- Alan is automatically given access to the higher echelons of the company whereas the slab boys have to toil for years in the slab room before being considered for promotion.
- However, it is difficult for the audience to sympathise as we are told that Phil threw away his opportunity at gaining his Highers and can see the lack of work ethic present in all of the slab boys. Alan, by contrast, seems very keen to learn.
- Despite Phil's cavalier attitude towards his school years and poor work ethic in the slab room, we can see that furthering his education is very important to him – so important he attempts to hide his application to art college from his friends for fear of failure.
- He arrives late to work, not having told anyone about his application, and goes along with Spanky's hastily constructed cover story when his boss, Curry, complains about his lateness.
- He is outraged and embarrassed when he discovers that Curry and Alan have been looking at his portfolio, then shocked almost speechless, muttering 'Christ …', when he realises he's been unsuccessful.
- Phil blames losing his job on his attempts to better himself, claiming Curry was antagonised by the fact that Phil 'might just have the savvy to realise there was more to life than giving myself housemaid's fucking knee on them slabs!' and attempting to get into art school.
- Curry, who also, by his mannerisms and speech, appears to be uneducated, justifies his place in the management by boosting his self-importance through fabricated war stories.

Drama, Text 2: *The Cheviot, the Stag and the Black, Black Oil* by John McGrath

Question 5

Your answer should demonstrate an understanding of 'humour' and why it is appropriate.

- The Sturdy Highlander is a character for whom we are made to feel great sympathy. By creating humour, we are able to engage with this character and find him more likeable (1).
- The use of humour also helps to exaggerate the character of the Northwest Trader, making him seem even more unpleasant (1).

You may have chosen some of the examples below, although others are possible:

Commonality

- Additional accounts/voices used to highlight the reality of the struggle facing the Highlanders and critique the actions of the upper classes.
- Range of voices emphasises the impact of the actions carried out by the landed gentry.
- Appearance of additional voices/characters allows McGrath to highlight the 'truth', dispelling the myths spread by the upper classes.

Extract

- In this section, the pause of action to include a speech from Lord Selkirk helps to emphasise how disconnected those in charge were from the events facing the Highlanders living in the colonies. Allowing the audience to hear the self-satisfied, arrogant view of Lord Selkirk as he assumes that the Highlanders are 'accustomed' to such conditions alerts the audience to the injustice facing those sent to the colonies against their will.
- Voices of Indians used to create further humour in this scene but also illustrate the stereotyping/lack of knowledge about the colonies. There is clear criticism throughout the play of the tendency for those in the landed classes to show little interest or involvement with the lands they 'own'.

Rest of text

- Descriptions of the Highland clearances involving voices of two girls, old man and readers – the words of the young girls are supported and developed by the factual accounts provided by the readers. We are made aware of their heroism in the face of eviction and the strength with which they fought and even died. This engages our sympathy, forcing us both to 'witness' and accept the harsh reality of the brutality inflicted upon the Highlanders.
- Meeting in Skye – 'Scene 5'. Many different ages and several different men and women appear at this moment to share their frustrations regarding their treatment at the hands of the factors. We see how young and old were all equally mistreated, but that they unified. In the same section we are made to appreciate that despite the numbers, they were powerless against the factors.
- Use of multiple MCs and singers to recount changes in the Highlands between late 1800s and 'present day'. The number of speakers helps to emphasise the numerous obstacles facing those living in the Highlands as their way of life was destroyed. It allows a seamless transition between the different locations and times to indicate the continued, widespread attempts at rebellion and suppression.

Drama, Text 3: *Men Should Weep* by Ena Lamont Stewart

Question 10

Reference + basic comment = 1 mark. Reference + detailed comment = 2 marks.

See Hint S2.

You may have chosen some of the examples below, although others are possible:

- 'soiled, tawdry negligee' – that Isa is still in nightclothes in the afternoon suggests that she is idle, choosing to stay in bed all day, with or without Alec

- 'hair about her shoulders' – again this emphasises the fact that she has just risen and has done nothing about her appearance. In the 1930s, hair was more formally 'done' and set with pins or curlers. This makes Isa's dishevelled appearance more shocking and emphasises her defiant, independent, but rather slatternly character.
- 'cigarette hanging from her lip' – it's not a classy look and emphasises the rakishness of Isa's character. She is far from a conventional wife and cares little for it.

Question 11

Reference + basic comment = 1 mark. Reference + detailed comment = 2 marks.

See Hints S2 and S4.

You may have chosen some of the examples below, although others are possible:

- Alec threatens Isa and tries to assert his dominance over her in a bid to get the upper hand in the relationship.

  'I'm tellin ye, Isa, I'll no staun much mair!'

  'You say Peter Robb tae me again an I'll kill ye! I wull! I'll kill ye!'

- Alec tries to appease Isa and take her mind off their troubled relationship hoping that she will forget all about it.

  '(Placating)'; 'I'll hae plenty again, you'll see'

  'I'll get ye onythin ye want … a fur coat and crockydile shoes'.

- Alec uses physical violence against Isa as a means of trying to assert some power and control over her.

  'He gets hold of her by the throat: she makes strangling noises.'

- Alec grovels apologetically, horrified at his behaviour. He does not have the 'courage' to see his murderous intentions through.

  '(He panics and drops her.)'

  'I didnae mean tae hurt ye – I lost ma heid.'

  'Isa, I'm sorry. I jist see red when ye talk aboot Peter Robb'.

- Alec makes promises that he can't keep to convince Isa to stay with him in a childish way.

  'I'll get ye onythin ye want … a fur coat an crockydile shoes … I proamise, Isa!'

  'If ye'll stay wi me … I love ye, Isa'.

- Alec shows his need for Isa and desperation that she stays with him, resorting to begging at the end of this extract as none of his other tactics have worked. This has the opposite effect and makes Isa despise him even more.

  'I'm no fit for onythin when ye're oot o ma sight'

  'I'm … lost waitin on ye comin back'.

Question 12

Reference + basic comment = 1 mark. Reference + detailed comment = 2 marks.

See Hints S2 and S4.

You may have chosen some of the examples below, although others are possible:

- The audience sees Alec and Isa in a state of undress, which suggests that they have been in bed together. And, it is the middle of the afternoon!

  'Afternoon'

  'soiled, tawdry negligee'

  'hair about her shoulders'

- Isa has clearly got Alec involved in mugging people in order to fund her lifestyle and the pair talk about the robbery without qualm or conscience.

  'I flung it ower a wa'

  'I'm needin a bag'

  'Three quid and a handful o coppers!'

  'Why the Hell did ye no pick on a toff!'

  'Next time, I'm no jookin up a lane, I'm stayin wi ye.'

- Isa's taunts of Peter Robb and her openness about her infidelity would provoke a strong response in the audience. This, combined with the insulting way in which she talks to Alec and the way in which she talks of sex so flippantly would shock the audience as it goes against conventional ideas of love and shows a tough, cynical hardness to Isa's character.

  'If I'd went wi Peter Robb I'd hae a fur coat'

  'cairryin oan wi him'

  'if ye wis hauf a man, ye'd have kicked his teeth in last night'

  'fancy me mairryin a rat like you'

  'Love! Hee-haw! There's nae sich thing. There's wantin tae get intae bed wi someone ye fancy … Don't kid yersel.'

  'If I'm behaving masel? Well, hauf the time, I'm no.'

  'I canna staun yer fumbling aboot – unless I'm canned.'

Question 13

Marks are allocated: 2 marks for commonality; 2 for comment(s) on this extract and 6 marks for comments on rest of text.

Reference + basic comment = 1 mark. Reference + detailed comment = 2 marks. Reference + insightful comment may score 3 marks.

See Hint S7.

You may have chosen some of the examples below, although others are possible:

Commonality

- Isa is in control of Alec for the most part, contrasting with Maggie and her relationship with John. This develops the theme of the role of men in the play.
- Isa's attitude to love and relationships sharply contrasts with Maggie's, or even Jenny's. This bitter mercenary attitude may be a product of survival at the time. Lily's attitude to love is equally cynical.

Extract

- Alec and Isa's relationship provides the most dramatic moment in the whole play – that of the strangling of Isa. This open demonstration of domestic violence and the poverty and crime that surround the couple would make for compelling and thought-provoking watching.
- Alec shows, through his desperate negotiations with Isa, that he is weak, silly and lacking in self-respect. The audience may feel more distaste for the character after this scene in which he alternately grovels and threatens violence. His character is not one worthy of respect. The fact that he does not kill Isa is one of his few redeeming features.
- The audience can see from the way that Isa talks to Alec that she really cannot stand him. This makes his desperate attempts to keep her even more pitiful.

Rest of text

- Alec and Isa's presence puts a huge strain on the Morrison family; the young children, including the ill Bertie, have to share their already cramped beds with the pair. Isa is open with Maggie about Maggie's dislike of her, creating a difficult and uncomfortable atmosphere and heightening the tension at crucial points in the play.
- Isa plays with John, enjoying making him uncomfortable by the way she walks around in revealing clothing and also revelling in the fact that he is undoubtedly noticing her 'attractions'. This, too, puts pressure on Maggie.
- Raises the theme of what it is to be a man as Alec is clearly at the mercy of Isa. Alec has been spoiled by his mother and has grown up to be idle, weak and lacking in the cheerful toughness which characterised the men with whom he has grown up.
- Isa's attitude to love contrasts with Maggie and John's lasting relationship. Hers is a cynical, tough understanding of relationships. For Isa, a sexual relationship is a commercial exercise which works on the principles of money or sexual attraction. Nothing else is relevant. Isa is a survivor. Her callousness perhaps indicates that life has taught her not to be sentimental – she is a product of her time and place.
- Alec and Isa show another aspect of working-class Glaswegian life which is perhaps not so heart-warming to the audience. They steal, drink, lie, connive and cause problems in the Morrison family.
- Isa is seen to encourage Jenny in her plans to leave home, causing pain to both Maggie and John. She and Jenny show that they are not willing to live the lives their mothers did, living in a slum and struggling with innumerable children. Both girls, Isa and Jenny, are seen to survive, despite their break from tradition and their own assertion of their independence, of a sort.

Prose, Text 1: *The Crater* by Iain Crichton Smith

Question 14

You might refer to two of the following in your answer. However, there are other possibilities that you could discuss:

- He has integrity (1).
- He is nervous and inexperienced in trench warfare (1).
- He is brave despite his fear (1).

Reference + basic comment = 1 mark. Reference + detailed comment = 2 marks.

See Hints S2 and S3.

You may have chosen some of the examples below, although others are possible:

Integrity

- '"All right," he said. "We're going for him. Come on."' – he refuses to leave a man behind (1).
- 'He couldn't leave a man to die in a pit of green slime.'/'It wasn't right that a man should die in green slime' – he cares about the soldiers under his command, does not want to leave Morrison to such an undignified death (1).

Nervous/inexperienced

- 'He was terrified … after all?' – simple sentence, repetition, use of question: reveals uncertainty, he is afraid of the hostile environment (1).
- 'For Christ's sake don't let me go' – use of curse: reveals fear (1).
- 'a sight so terrible he nearly fell' – he has not yet hardened himself to the hideous sights of war (1).

Bravery

- 'Robert hung over the edge of the crater' – despite his fear of the 'green depth', he risks his life in the rescue attempt (1).
- 'the others hung at his heels' – alliteration, word choice of 'heels' emphasises full body hanging into the crater (1).

Question 15

Reference + basic comment = 1 mark. Reference + detailed comment = 2 marks.

See Hints S2 and S3.

You may have chosen some of the examples below, although others are possible:

- 'The voice was like an animal's' – comparison to an animal makes the soldier appear inhuman, suggests regression to an instinctive state.
- 'an obscene mermaid' – metaphor suggests repugnant or indecent.
- Use of pronoun 'it' – makes soldier appear as a thing, inhuman.
- 'monster of the deep'/'the monster below' – metaphor, a large creature, suggestion of primeval beast.
- 'a sight so terrible' – implies abhorrent, disgusting.

- 'emerging from the deep' – gives impression of repulsive birth.
- 'all green, all mottled' – repetition of 'all' emphasises soldier is engulfed in mud.
- 'mottled' – smeared and streaked, distasteful connotations.
- 'stench' – unpleasant aroma.
- 'The face … the teeth' – use of definite article in place of pronoun 'his'.
- 'like a body which might have come from space' – he appears alien.
- 'green and illuminated and slimy' – repetition of 'and', unpleasant connotations of 'slimy'.

Question 16

Basic comment = 1 mark. A more insightful, detailed comment = 2 marks.

See Hint S1.

- Given the lengths Mackinnon and the others went to – and the risks they took – in order to rescue Morrison from the crater, the reader expects a happy ending. This is thwarted when the soldier is saved only to die as soon as he is out.
- This conveys the futility and arbitrary nature of war – men live or die according to no rules of nature, simply luck and chance.

Question 17

Marks are allocated: 2 marks for commonality; 2 for comment(s) on this story and 6 marks for comments on other text(s).

Reference + basic comment = 1 mark. Reference + detailed comment = 2 marks. Reference + insightful comment may score 3 marks.

See Hint S7.

You may have chosen some of the examples below, although others are possible:

Commonality

- Crichton Smith uses contrasting characters to emphasise character traits in his main protagonists.
- Contrasting characters are used to develop main ideas/themes in his short stories.
- Tension and conflict are created through the use of contrasting characters.

The Crater

- Lieutenant Mackinnon is nervous and inexperienced, plagued by doubts.
- This is shown in the questions he asks in his internal dialogue: 'What am I doing here?' and 'Will we need the ladders?'
- Sergeant Smith is a pragmatic character who simply gets on with what needs to be done.
- After the rescue, when Mackinnon is revelling in the triumph of getting the soldier out of the crater, Smith concentrates on practical matters: checking whether Morrison is alive or dead.
- He enjoys the fraternity of war. He returns to fight after being sent home 'invalided', something the other soldiers hope for in order to allow them to escape the fighting.

The Telegram

- The character Sarah is narrow-minded and insular.
- She is described as a 'fat domestic bird' suggesting she lacks ambition and possesses a limited intelligence/outlook. She pretends to be content in her situation, but her resentment of the thin woman reveals this to be false.
- The thin woman is driven and determined.
- She is described as a 'buzzard', able to scratch out a survival under difficult circumstances. She has sacrificed for her son and is a more sympathetic character, but is also contemptuous of Sarah and the other islanders.

The Painter

- William Murray is quietly intelligent. He is able to see the village for what it is, examining below the veneer of idealism the villagers would like to portray.
- He is a feeble, 'sickly' boy who is not able to take part in hard manual labour, further isolating him from the community.
- In contrast, Red Roderick is a loud and brash character. When sober, he is jovial and popular.
- Despite the fact he abuses his family and can be a violent drunk, he is accepted by the community whereas William is ostracised.
- Again contrasting William's frailty, Red Roderick is a physically strong character who feels overshadowed because his father-in-law is well-known for his strength.

Mother and Son

- John is a fully grown man; however, he is down-trodden and kept under his mother's thumb.
- He has been forced to put his life on hold in order to care for her and she has slowly eroded his self-confidence.
- The mother is a sickly character, physically much weaker than John.
- However, she has a sharp tongue and is able to control and manipulate her son. She enjoys the feeling of power of having him run after her.

The Red Door

- In *The Red Door* Murdo describes two women to whom he is romantically attached. The first spinster is seen as unattractive and under the thumb of her religious mother.
- She is negatively portrayed as 'stout' and deemed an unsuitable prospect by Murdo after she serves him unpalatable food.
- The second spinster, Mary, is shown to be independent, intelligent and artistic.
- It is hinted in the story that she is responsible for painting Murdo's door red, an invitation to him to explore his own individualism.
- Also in *The Red Door* Murdo himself contrasts with Mary, whom he admires. Murdo has always adhered to the village's expectations, allowing them to dictate his actions and even his clothing.
- Mary, though ridiculed by the villagers, is creative and individual. She writes poetry and takes evening strolls, and is seen to be more educated than those around her, given that she has 'read many books'.

Prose, Text 2: *The Whaler's Return* by George Mackay Brown

Question 18

Reference + basic comment = 1 mark. Reference + detailed comment = 2 marks.

See Hint S2.

You may have chosen some of the examples below, although others are possible:

- 'in a ditch' – suggests that Flaws has just lain down by the side of the road in a damp and dirty ditch to sleep. The inference is that he is surprised to find himself here.
- 'in broad daylight' – Flaws has slept long as a result of his drunkenness. He must be feeling hungover.
- 'Painfully' – Flaws feels the effects of the beating from the previous night as well as from his uncomfortable night's sleep.
- 'bones creaked' – Flaws is sore; his body is protesting.
- 'Water ran out of his sleeve' – clearly this is unpleasant. Flaws may be disgusted or surprised at this.
- 'his tongue lay in his mouth like a filthy rag' – Flaws feels not only thirsty, but disgusted at himself for drinking when he promised he would not.

Question 19

Reference + basic comment = 1 mark. Reference + detailed comment = 2 marks.

See Hint S2.

You may have chosen some of the examples below, although others are possible:

- 'You're in better shape than I expected'/'There are thirty-four ale-houses in the town of Hamnavoe …' – Peterina not only knows the tradition of sailors visiting every pub in town on their way home, she does not expect Flaws to do anything otherwise. She has no expectations of him that lie outwith her experience of men returning from the sea.
- 'We move in in November' – Peterina has already planned ahead for the beginning of their married life.
- 'Here's some bread and ale' – Peterina sees to Flaws' hunger and thirst without being asked.
- 'That will be the last week of September' – similarly, Peterina has thought through their future life together and planned it well.
- 'I will try and be a good wife to you, Andrew Flaws' – Peterina knows what is expected of her and is prepared to fulfil her side of the bargain.
- 'Before that time … we must be ready at all times' – Peterina prepares for practicalities of marriage, childbirth and the unknown eventuality of death. Her head is not filled with dreams, more pragmatic plans for what is likely to happen and in what order.
- 'I tarred the boat down at the beach' – Peterina has taken practical steps to prepare for Flaws' arrival and to ensure they have an income straight away.
- 'You'll fish until such time as we reap our first harvest at Breck' – again, Peterina has prepared for their future life, securing a livelihood until they can make a living from the land.

Question 20

Reference + basic comment = 1 mark. Reference + detailed comment = 2 marks.

See Hints S2 and S3.

You may have chosen some of the examples below, although others are possible:

- 'He drank the last of the ale' – the extract shows how alcohol undoes Flaws' good intentions and makes his journey back to Peterina last longer than expected. It is fitting that he should finish the story enjoying a final drink at home before his work as a crofter begins.
- 'It was the sweetest drink he had ever tasted' – finally Flaws' thirst is quenched, literally and metaphorically. He is content and happy with Peterina and his future life. The fire and oblivion offered by the other drinks on the road do not compare – they do not represent happiness in the way that Peterina's home-made ale does.
- 'I'll maybe catch a few haddocks' – Flaws intends to get out to sea again that very day to provide for himself and Peterina. He is happy and willing to accept his new life with alacrity.
- 'The laird will be wanting harvesters tomorrow or the day after' – Flaws' couple of boozy days' celebration are coming to an end; he is ready to take up work, working for another to provide for himself and Peterina. It is a practical and happy ending. Flaws has no wish to prolong his drinking binge.

Question 21

Marks are allocated: 2 marks for commonality; 2 for comment(s) on this story and 6 marks for comments on other text(s).

Reference + basic comment = 1 mark. Reference + detailed comment = 2 marks. Reference + insightful comment may score 3 marks.

See Hint S7.

You may have chosen some of the examples below, although others are possible:

Commonality

- Flaws and Peterina's lives are dictated by the seasons just as many of George Mackay Brown's characters who live on the land are in tune with nature.
- George Mackay Brown shows that death and new life are an accepted part of the natural cycle.

The Whaler's Return

- The lives of Flaws and Peterina will be dictated to by the seasons. The harvest is the main source of their livelihood. Flaws feels an easy comfort and security in this pattern.
- The items that Peterina feels she must weave – the bedcover, the blanket for the baby and the shrouds – show an intrinsic awareness of the cycle of birth and death as well as a recognition that this cycle may be a short one.
- Flaws' good intentions are easily put aside under pressure from companions and alcohol. This can be human nature; we aspire to perfection, and yet we may fail.

A Time to Keep

- References are made throughout this short story to time in relation to the seasons to show how essential they are to the crofter's way of life.

- Bill's lack of success as a crofter, in the course of the story, is partly due to his lack of luck with the land and the seasons. Mackay Brown shows how farming people are at the mercy of the seasons. Bill is dependent on his lambs living and his crops being successfully harvested. The happiness and livelihood of the couple depend on this.
- Mackay Brown shows the fruitfulness of Bill's success in comparison with Ingi's growing capability as a housewife, improving her skill in baking and brewing as well as other household chores. We see the cycle of learning in connection with both as they begin to master their craft. This is a universal theme.
- Ingi's death shortly after childbirth follows the idea of the natural cycle. The idea that only the strong survive in this hard crofting life is reflected.
- Bill's remarriage to a more pragmatic, practical woman is noted without emotion and the inference is that this will be successful. Anna is in tune with the seasons and understands the role of a crofter's wife. There is a sense of the ceaseless renewal of the natural cycle within human lives as well as within the farming calendar.

The Wireless Set

- The community in Tronvik are rural crofters, set in a seemingly ageless community, who follow the pattern of the seasons and have been, until the arrival of the wireless, relatively isolated from national events and politics.
- The crofters' resilience and self-sufficiency, created from a life in tune with the seasons and the natural world, removes them from the sense of deprivation felt by mainland Britain.
- Betsy and Old Hugh receive the news of Howie's death with stark simplicity which is reflected in their speech. His death, part of an unnatural cycle caused by the foreign politics of war, is not commented on. Instead his parents fall into the cyclical, repetitive but comforting work of the crofter, ruled by the weather and the seasons. There is a sense of inevitability about their fate which is reflected in much of Mackay Brown's work.

The Bright Spade

- Here Mackay Brown synthesises the natural cycle with that of the human world. The story covers a winter in which many people die on the island, showing how the harsh conditions have a direct impact on the survival of the island's inhabitants.
- Death is seen to come to old and young, strong and weak, as they battle with the elements.
- The poor harvest brings famine to the island, resulting in many deaths, in combination with the harsh winter.
- The end of the story links the coming of spring with the end of the cycle of death on the island as Jacob puts aside his spade until harvest.

Prose, Text 3: *The Trick Is To Keep Breathing* by Janice Galloway

Question 22

See Hint S1.

For full marks, both aspects must be explained in your own words.

- Like Christian in Bunyan's *Pilgrim's Progress*, she feels as though she has to face many challenges before she will achieve her goal (1).
- Like Christian, she believes she is learning a great deal/looking towards spiritual enlightenment (1).
- Like Dorothy, she is hoping that she will eventually wake up to discover her experience has been a dream (1).
- Like Dorothy, she feels she is on a journey/mission that will eventually lead her 'home' (1).

Question 23

Reference + basic comment = 1 mark. Reference + detailed comment = 2 marks.

See Hints S2, S4–S6.

You may have chosen some of the examples below, although others are possible:

- Use of many successive statements including 'I thought if I could smell his aftershave he must be around somewhere' – suggests conviction/strength of her belief.
- 'I saw him in cars, across the street, in buses, roaring past on strange motorbikes, drifting by the glass panel of my classroom door.' – use of list helps to emphasise how pervasive his image is in her mind.
- Use of questions – reveals that she is challenging logic/reality.
- Use of italics in 'Of course he wasn't *dead.*' – places emphasis on key idea, suggesting the strength of her rejection of reality.
- 'I knew he wasn't just a carcass liquefying in a wooden box but an invisible presence hovering in a cloud of Aramis above my bed.' – reveals strong rejection of reality and belief that he is now something ethereal/heavenly.

Question 24

See Hint S1.

One mark is awarded for evidence of understanding:

- Joy is surprised by her ability to deceive herself/deny reality/convince herself that things are different (1).

The other mark is awarded for your explanation. This could be supported by:

- 'I had put it there myself ages ago so I could reach for it and smell his neck …' – this proves that she was consciously aware of her own actions and had therefore chosen to delude herself (1).
- 'Then I must have knocked it over and been too wilful to admit to what it was later.' – this is a clear recognition of her 'guilt' and a confession that she decided to deceive herself (1).

Question 25

Understanding of the term 'conflict' must be evident.

Reference + basic comment = 1 mark. Reference + detailed comment = 2 marks.

See Hints S1 and S2.

You may have chosen some of the examples below, although others are possible:

- 'Please god make boulders crash through the roof'/'I shiver and wish the phone would ring.' – the first quotation would indicate that she is wishing for death/destruction and yet the second hints at a wish for rescue.
- Explanation of the 'paradox' that exists in her life – Joy recognises that her thoughts and wishes completely contradict one another. She is afraid of others and yet hopes/wishes they would help her.
- 'At work I never speak but I want to be spoken to.' – recognises that while she is painfully shy she craves company.

- 'I'm scared of the phone yet I want it to ring.' – fears speaking to others but still hopes they will reach out to her.

Question 26

Marks are allocated: 2 marks for commonality; 2 for comment(s) on this extract and 6 marks for comments on rest of text.

Reference + basic comment = 1 mark. Reference + detailed comment = 2 marks. Reference + insightful comment may score 3 marks.

See Hint S7.

You may have chosen some of the examples below, though others are possible:

Commonality

- We are made to sympathise with Joy as we see her struggle to cope with the emotional turmoil she experiences on a daily basis.
- Joy is clearly a very vulnerable person, and her struggle to maintain strong relationships makes her seem even more at risk.
- Her honesty and bluntness reveal her to be a very likeable character, which makes us saddened by her distress.

Extract

- 'I wanted to be no trouble. I wanted to be brave and discreet' – in this extract we see how determined Joy has been to take charge of her own recovery. It is clear that she is in no way malicious and only wishes to get better.
- She is clearly very vulnerable and desperate. The incident in which she describes her self-deception reveals the extent that she has gone to in order to survive. It is also saddening to realise that she is struggling with the acceptance of her partner's death.
- Humorous reference to the Health Visitor – rather than be spiteful or aggressive in her dislike, Joy pokes fun at herself and the situation (*'Well, she'll say, We're not doing so well today, are we?'*) making her humility evident and her character more endearing.

Rest of text

- Flashbacks to Michael's death reveal how shocking this event was for her and her struggle to fully engage with the situation. The fact that she seems detached makes her more vulnerable and therefore more sympathetic as a character as she can't comprehend the tragedy.
- Myra's visit shows us how intimidating her sister is and the abuse that she has suffered. It is revealed that Joy has faced both physical and emotional abuse.
- Time in hospital reveals Joy's battle to submit to care and also her fear of the implications of good health – that she may end up lonelier as a result.
- Relationship with Tony – he clearly takes advantage of her. While she submits to his wishes we see that she is vulnerable and detached from what is happening.

Prose, Text 4: *Sunset Song* by Lewis Grassic Gibbon

Question 27

See Hint S2.

To gain full marks, candidates must have identified both horns of Chris' dilemma in their own words.

- Chris is looking forward to getting her education and living an independent life away from farming and the control of men. *(+ suitable supporting evidence = 2 marks)*
- Yet Chris also feels an essential connection with the land that renders all her ambitions worthless. *(+ suitable supporting evidence = 2 marks)*

You may have chosen some of the examples below, although others are possible:

- 'glad she'd be … Aberdeen University getting her B.A.' – Chris is relishing the thought of her education and the qualification that she will attain; it is a validation of her worth that she does not get at home on the farm from her father.
- 'school of her own' – here Chris will be in charge, shaping young minds and providing an outlet and opportunity for others as this had been done for her. 'Her own' clearly suggests ownership and independence.
- 'the English Chris' – Chris sees her very self as being divided, split between her heart and her ambitions.
- 'father and his glowering and girning forgotten' – Chris is under her father's control and at the mercy of his bad-temper.
- 'brave house of her own' – 'her own' suggests that the independence is appealing to Chris, not only the physical space itself. Chris wants to be free.
- 'wear what she liked' – again, Chris longs for independence and the opportunity to make her own choices, not to have them imposed upon her.
- 'never a man vexed with sight of her' – John Guthrie's attitude has affected Chris; she is fed up of being under male control and made to feel inadequate by the dominant male in her life.
- 'or maybe she wouldn't' – Chris' reflections turn very quickly to the contrary. She is aware that her dreams and aspirations are perhaps fleeting things and may not reflect what will truly make her happy.
- 'queer that she never knew herself for long' – Chris is aware of the mercurial shifts in her mindset and is bemused by them.
- 'she was no more than ploughed land still' – Chris' future life has not been mapped out at this point.
- 'the furrows went criss and cross' – this metaphorically reflects the conflicting ambitions in Chris' head.
- 'you wanted this and you wanted that' – 'this' and 'that' reflect the contrary ambitions or aspirations of Chris. The tone here is also reflective of the lingering childishness of Chris.
- 'books and the fineness of them … empty gabble sometimes' – sometimes she adores learning and the elevated realm to which books take her, and at another time she sees them as void of real meaning compared to the life of the land.
- 'sharn and the snapping … drove you back to books' – the labour, stink and drudgery of farming, especially under John Guthrie, makes Chris long for the world of the mind and the imagination which books represent.

Question 28

Reference + basic comment = 1 mark. Reference + detailed comment = 2 marks.

See Hints S2 and S3.

You may have chosen some of the examples below, although others are possible:

- 'hot as ever it was' – the heat connotes danger or violence which foreshadows the news of Jean Guthrie's death.
- 'dark was a foul, black blanket' – there is no repose in sleep; instead, the darkness is seen as suffocating and oppressive.
- 'It had died off, the wind' – the lack of wind creates an eerie stillness which increases anticipation.
- 'the sky crackled behind her'; 'a long flash zig-zagged across the Grampian peaks' – the electricity of the lightning reflects Chris' terror and perhaps also the 'unnatural' act of Jean poisoning her own babies as well as herself. This lightning splits the atmosphere in the way that Jean's death destroys Chris' lazy dreams and ambitions.
- 'she heard a hiss of rain' – the onomatopoeia of 'hiss' is suggestive of malice or fear; it is as though the natural world conveys Chris' fearful anxiety and also the cruelty of a life that drove her mother to suicide.

Question 29

Reference + basic comment = 1 mark. Reference + detailed comment = 2 marks.

See Hint S2.

You may have chosen some of the examples below, although others are possible:

- 'far below' – the perspective makes Dod and Alec appear distant and almost insignificant in relation to Chris' thoughts about her own future. This is a sharp juxtaposition to the news that they are bearing and its future impact on Chris.
- 'waving up at her' – the boys are trying to catch her attention. There is a desperate childishness in this gesture which reminds the reader that they are still children. This heightens the pathos of the moment.
- 'They were crying her name excitedly' – the fear and panic in the boys' voices shows just how much they will need and depend on Chris to take their mother's place.
- 'it sounded like the lowing of calves that had lost their mother' – the simile is effective as it not only makes the agricultural connection, but captures the mournful tone in the boys' voices, emphasising their distress.
- 'she went slow to tease them till she saw their faces' – Chris' initial response emphasises Dod and Alec's status in the family, those of little brothers, who both annoy and are there to be annoyed. This is then sharply juxtaposed by the horror on their faces reflecting their animal terror.

Question 30

Marks are allocated: 2 marks for commonality; 2 for comment(s) on this extract and 6 marks for comments on rest of text.

Reference + basic comment = 1 mark. Reference + detailed comment = 2 marks. Reference + insightful comment may score 3 marks.

See Hint S7.

You may have chosen some of the examples below, although others are possible:

Commonality

- Chris is at the Standing Stones, as she always is at the end and the beginning of a section. This location marks the enduring nature of the land and its timelessness in the endlessly changing seasons and the relentless passage of time.

Extract

- Chris is reflecting on the end of her secondary schooling and her hopes for the future; this shows a change in Chris in itself as she can see her own independence lying ahead.
- The natural cycle referred to in 'the weary pleiter of the land and its life while you waited for rain or thaw!' shows itself in the constant shift of the seasons and the need for change in life.
- Chris' realisation that something terrible has happened, and the suggestion that something has happened to her mother, marks the end of her childhood and the beginning of a new, unthought-of stage in her life.
- The breaking of the weather in the lightning storm with the rain shows that all things come to an end; change is inevitable.

Rest of text

- The structure of the novel reflects the endless cycle of birth, growth, death and renewal to which Lewis Grassic Gibbon constantly refers. Only the land endures, all the rest falls away.
- The ancient civilisations that Chris studies, in her Greek and Latin lessons, have all fallen away. They have not endured – they are voices from the past.
- The Standing Stones mark timelessness, paradoxically, although the civilisation which raised them is gone and largely forgotten. Through the stones, Chris connects with the past, and time, and also connects with a more natural sense of order and understanding of the universe.
- Marriage to Ewan brings a change to Chris' life, a happy one, one of fulfilment and understanding of herself.
- The conception of young Ewan brings change to Chris; she is conscious of an end to a certain type of existence and the need of her child for her.
- The war brings great change to Kinraddie.
- Change can be seen in Ewan on his return on leave. This change is then reflected in Chris.
- The landscape of Kinraddie reflects change.
- The change of the political age can be seen in the rise of support for socialism as the old ideals of conservatism fall away with the loss of the independent farmers. The need for social justice marks an end of a more innocent patriarchal society which had faith in those in power and which dies with the atrocities of the First World War.
- Chris' reconciliations with her father and with Ewan after their deaths show the change that takes place in one's understanding when one truly considers and learns about other people and can examine their actions after the passing of time.

Prose, Text 5: *The Cone-Gatherers* by Robin Jenkins

Question 31

Reference + basic comment = 1 mark. Reference + detailed comment = 2 marks.

See Hint S2.

You may have chosen some of the examples below, although others are possible:

- 'sharply' – implies her tone of voice was angry, abrupt.
- 'It was an accusation.' – suggests she is suspicious, always thinking negatively of Duror.

- '"Thanks," he said, and stood still.' – Duror speaks only one word during their conversation. The fact that he 'stood still' implies that he is awkward and uncomfortable.
- 'There was no pity in her question, only condemnation' – Mrs Lochie feels no sympathy for Duror, trapped in his marriage to a bed-ridden wife. Instead she castigates him for struggling to cope with his situation.
- 'It's a pity … peace.' – Mrs Lochie's words, said with a 'smile', appear to be a trap for Duror, as if daring him to agree.
- 'He did not deny … nor did he try to explain' – Duror does not – or cannot – freely communicate his feelings to Mrs Lochie; perhaps he knows he will gain no understanding from her.
- 'With a shudder' – it is unclear whether Duror's 'shudder' is an involuntary reaction to dealing with Mrs Lochie's poisonous presence, or the thought of moving on to deal with his wife.

Question 32

Reference + basic comment = 1 mark. Reference + detailed comment = 2 marks.

See Hint S2.

You may have chosen some of the examples below, although others are possible:

- 'haunting' – metaphor: suggests echoes remain.
- 'great wobbling masses' – the use of 'great' and 'wobbling' emphasises the sheer size of Peggy. The word 'wobbling' has connotations of quivering jelly.
- 'pallid' – negative connotations of being sickly and pale.
- 'grotesqueness' – suggests she is monstrous and gross.

Question 33

Reference + basic comment = 1 mark. Reference + detailed comment = 2 marks.

See Hint S2.

You may have chosen some of the examples below, although others are possible:

- 'voice was squeaky with an inveterate petulance' – she sounds sulky and childish when she speaks to Duror, revealing her frustration at her bed-ridden state.
- 'I've still to wash … rabbits' – Duror tries to avoid touching Peggy, leaving her simpering and almost begging for his affections.
- '"Fine for some folk," she whimpered.' – alliteration: Peggy's reply reveals her bitterness that others can enjoy the outdoors while she cannot.
- 'You know … herself' – by beginning 'you know' Peggy makes her words an accusation.
- 'I was thinking of a day at Fyneside long ago' – given Peggy's current bed-ridden state, she is forced to live in the past where she has joyful memories.
- 'The rowans are just about past' – Duror, who is still able to live in the world, refuses to be drawn into the past with Peggy, further isolating her.
- 'He saw … respond to it' – Peggy and Duror's relationship has deteriorated to the extent that he can no longer even give her emotion and love for pity's sake. She is as trapped in a loveless marriage as him.

Question 34

See Hint S1.

- Duror is able to see that his house is far superior to Calum's hut – it is much larger and cleaner than the hovel in which the brothers live (1).
- However, there is a sense of contentedness and homeliness about the hut as he imagines it in his mind – Calum sits 'carving happily' – that his own home lacks. He is jealous of what Calum has (1).

Question 35

Marks are allocated: 2 marks for commonality; 2 for comment(s) on this extract and 6 marks for comments on rest of text.

Reference + basic comment = 1 mark. Reference + detailed comment = 2 marks. Reference + insightful comment may score 3 marks.

See Hint S7.

You may have chosen some of the examples below, although others are possible:

Commonality

- Female characters attempt to manipulate Duror.
- Duror's wife and mother-in-law make home an uncomfortable place for him.
- Female characters use Duror as an outlet for their own insecurities and frustrations.

Extract

- Mrs Lochie, Duror's mother-in-law, lives with Duror and his wife to help with Peggy's care. However, her own bitterness about her daughter's misfortune and her anger at Duror for his continued distance from Peggy mean she makes the house an uncomfortable place for the gamekeeper.
- Peggy is bed-ridden and, lacking company except for her mother, is desperate for Duror's affections.
- Peggy has let herself get grossly overweight and this, along with the sulking petulance her situation has instilled in her, means that Duror does not want to be with her.

Rest of text

- Both Peggy and Mrs Lochie make the house an uncomfortable place for Duror to be, meaning he spends more and more of his time in the woods to escape from them. The cone gatherers' existence in the wood ruins this place of peace for him, quickening his mental collapse.
- Mrs Lochie also conspires to make life difficult for Duror by maliciously confiding to Lady Runcie Campbell that Duror brought home a naked doll. This act was intended to discredit Duror in the eyes of his employer and create suspicion that he was involved in indecent behaviour.
- Mrs Morton is a jovial character who thinks well of Duror. When he intimates that he might be interested in having an affair, she encourages him. However, she also defends Calum when Duror attempts to badmouth him with lies, then – after Duror has further convinced her – beseeches him to keep it to himself. She does not encourage his callous plans for the brothers.

- Lady Runcie Campbell gives power to Duror's hatred of the brothers – and in particular Calum – by turning to him for advice on several occasions about how to deal with the cone gatherers. Her own doubts about them lend credence to Duror's own obsessive thoughts.
- Lady Runcie Campbell is also complicit in the cone gatherers' involvement in the deer drive. She decides she cannot allow them to dictate to her and so goes along with Duror's plans to re-establish class boundaries. This leads to Duror having an episode where he confuses a deer with his wife and viciously murders the animal by slitting its throat.

Poetry, Text 1: *Tam o'Shanter* by Robert Burns

Question 36

See Hint S6.

Tone must be identified and supported with reference and comment for 2 marks:

Humorous/indulgent/wondering/affectionate.

You may have chosen some of the examples below, although others are possible:

- 'Inspiring bold John Barleycorn' – the personification of ale in John Barleycorn shows familiarity and affection.
- Use of exclamation marks – shows the exaggerated wonder and affection for drink and lightens the tone.
- 'we' – the plural pronoun creates shared experience with the reader, engages and creates wonder/affection/indulgence.
- Hyperbole of 'face the devil' and 'fear no evil' – creates humour.
- Rhyme of 'noddle' and 'boddle' creates a jaunty humorous tone.

Question 37

Reference + basic comment = 1 mark. Reference + detailed comment = 2 marks.

See Hint S2.

You may have chosen some of the examples below, although others are possible:

- Long stanza – allows the narrative to flow on uninterrupted and press forward into a mood of sudden excitement and astonishment.
- List – all the eerie and hellish characters that Tam sees serve to create a catalogue of horrors.
- Rhyming couplets – uninterrupted by stanza breaks, gather in intensity which mirrors the frenzied dancers and increases its horrific and yet comedic effect.

Question 38

Reference + basic comment = 1 mark. Reference + detailed comment = 2 marks.

See Hints S2 and S3.

You need to provide an example and explanation for both vigorous and terrifying.

You may have chosen some of the examples below, although others are possible:

Vigorous

- 'dance' – suggests movement and energy.
- 'hornpipes, jigs, strathspeys and reels' – lively Scottish dancing.
- 'life and mettle' – clear connotations of spirit and energy.
- 'music' – the music that is being played is lively and energetic.
- 'skirl' – the shrieking of the pipes suggests both volume and excitement.

Terrifying

- 'warlocks and witches' – traditional supernatural beings.
- 'auld Nick' – the devil himself.
- 'beast' – unidentified animal which makes it more sinister.
- 'black, grim, and large' – connotations of darkness, power and strength.
- 'coffins' – designed to contain the dead, not to release them. Should be below ground, out of sight, not part of this display.
- 'the Dead' – the collective and the capital serve to make this group seem more sinister.
- 'cauld hand' – cold emphasises the fact that these are the dead. The hands are 'alive' and clutching lights; the impossibility of this contrast creates horror.
- 'murderer's banes' – this man took another's life, terrifying in itself. Bones of the skeleton are clearly frightening.
- 'gibbet-airns' – the murderer was hung for his crimes and hangs now perpetually on the gibbet, trapped in irons. He suffers eternal punishment for his crimes.
- 'twa span-lang, wee, unchristened bairns' – the horror of these tiny dead babies is made all the more ghastly by the fact that they are innocent. They are only in hell as they were not christened in time. There may be an implied criticism of traditional religious views of Hell here.
- 'new-cutted frae a rape' – the thief has been hung and has just been cut down. The horrific manner in which he died and the vivid imagery create horror.
- 'his gab did gape' – the graphic image of the thief struggling for breath, combined with the idea of his mouth hanging slack when dead make this frightening.
- 'blude red-rusted' – the blood is thick and richly-coloured, representing the savagery and the horror of the crime.
- 'murder crusted' – the metonymy of 'murder' for 'blood' emphasises the horror of these implements.
- 'a babe had strangled' – death of a child is in itself horrific. 'Strangled' suggests a grim, horrific death. Connotations of 'babe' are all designed to evoke feelings of tenderness and love. The juxtaposition renders this horrific.
- 'a father's throat had mangled' – patricide emphasised by the term 'father'. Terrifying as this goes against natural familiar bonds. 'Mangled' suggests violence and atrocity of the crime.
- 'the grey-hairs yet stack to the heft' – the strength of the blow drove the knife deep into the parent's head. The age of the father seen by the 'grey'.
- 'rotten, black as muck' – connotations of lacking in goodness, being foul and evil.
- 'stinkin, vile in every neuk' – suggesting rot, evil, the odour is almost pernicious. 'every neuk' suggests that the crimes of the priests are covert, hiding, and yet are common.

Question 39

Marks are allocated: 2 marks for commonality; 2 for comment(s) on this poem and 6 marks for comments on other text(s).

Reference + basic comment = 1 mark. Reference + detailed comment = 2 marks. Reference + insightful comment may score 3 marks.

See Hint S7.

You may have chosen some of the examples below, although others are possible:

Commonality

- Common man repressed by kirk/marriage or society.
- Failings of common man are treated with humanity, compassion and humour.
- Common man represented as one whose life should be treated with dignity and respect.

Tam o'Shanter

- Tam has a nagging wife from whom he escapes to the pub. The difficulties of marriage and, perhaps some of the unrealistic expectations we have of others, may be universal notions. The tone is affectionate and indulgent of Tam. Burns does not censure Tam for his drinking, rather sees the appeal of drink as universal and that Tam tends to get what he deserves from his nagging wife anyway.
- The love of drink is clearly seen; Tam finds he can access the best of his own self when he is drunk. The friendship that Tam experiences when he is in the pub may also be of universal significance. It is a reprieve from real life.
- Supernatural beliefs are celebrated in this poem, harking back to the folktales of Burns' youth and own community. This creates not only a sense of a more richly-coloured world, but also attempts to make some sense of life and death themselves.
- The temporary nature of earthly pleasures is noted with wry amusement. All good things come to an end; the intoxication wears off, the night draws to a close and it is time to face up to whatever you were avoiding thinking about.

Address to the Deil

- The common man is kept in thrall of the devil – kirk uses the image of hell to 'scaud poor wretches' and to oppress the common man.
- Burns satirises the power of the devil by using a humorous tone and matey approach – this helps to subvert the power of the kirk and the devil.
- Burns shows the difficulties of the working classes, blaming the devil for them.

Man's A Man For A' That

- Burns suggests that wealth, which equals rank or social class, is not a measure of a man's worth.
- Burns refers to the food and clothing of the poor, again emphasising that this should not suggest their worth.
- Burns says honesty is worth more than anything.
- Burns champions individual thinking, rather than following someone's ideas simply because they are more powerful than you or richer than you are.
- Burns contrasts the aristocracy with the common man.

- Burns says that revolution will come bringing with it freedom and equality. The poor but honest man will then prevail.

A Poet's Welcome to his Love-Begotten Daughter

- The poet delights in the birth of his first child, despite the trouble her birth has caused him with the church and the community.
- Burns himself was under the power and at the mercy of the kirk and had to undergo a shame-inducing punishment as a result of fathering the child.
- Burns is honest about earthly pleasures and does not censure or condemn.
- Burns sees no difference in a baby born out of wedlock and one born within it – in either appearance or personal qualities. Again he challenges the way contemporary society judged people.

To A Mouse

- Burns presents the mouse as an allegory for the labouring classes, who can be turned out of their homes by cruel landlords or factors, and highlights the insecurity of both the mouse and human beings.
- Burns shows how those who worked on the land were at the mercy of the elements – a poor season could wipe out a harvest.
- Neither the mouse nor mankind can plan ahead or make provision against such unforeseen disasters; they are at the mercy of both nature and those who have more power than them.

Holy Willie's Prayer

- Burns shows how hypocritical and absurd the kirk and Calvinism are. The kirk exerted huge power over the common man.
- By subverting the kirk, Burns presents human 'failings' such as lechery, drink, swearing and gambling as part of life's rich tapestry and that they should be accepted as such.

Poetry, Text 2: *Mrs Midas* by Carol Ann Duffy

Question 40

Reference + basic comment = 1 mark. Reference + detailed comment = 2 marks.

See Hints S2 and S4.

You may have chosen some of the examples below, although others are possible:

- Use of minor sentence ('Separate beds.') – reflects speed, also appears very dramatic and unexpected.
- 'petrified' – suggests the intensity of her emotions, seeming somewhat surprising given that she is referring to her emotion towards her husband.
- Use of 'petrified' could be contrasted with 'halcyon days', 'unwrapping each other' etc. – reflects dramatic shift in their relationship from one of passion to fear.
- 'But now …' – use of conjunction indicates sudden and true shift.

Question 41

Reference + basic comment = 1 mark. Reference + detailed comment = 2 marks.

See Hint S2.

You may have chosen some of the examples below, although others are possible:

- 'perfect' – use of adjective reveals the adoration and love she would feel.
- 'ore limbs' – suggesting the child would be made of rock makes it seem unnatural, heavy and cold. However, there are also implications of value due to connection with precious metals.
- 'little tongue' – 'little' suggests vulnerable and cute, thus implying her affection.
- 'precious' – direct reference to value revealing protective maternal instinct.
- 'amber eyes' – reference could be made to both emotions. The precious, beautiful nature of the stone could reveal her love; however connotations of stones also hint at a cold, inhumane and unfeeling nature.
- 'holding their pupils like flies' – reference to fossilisation hints at something powerful and somewhat threatening about the child.
- 'burned in my breasts' – ambiguous. This could hint at the pain and suffering, but there is also perhaps a sense of the aching of desire which lingers.

Question 42

See Hint S1.

For full marks, reference should be made to:

- the connection with Greek gods and mythology that is central to this poem (1).
- Pan, as the god of shepherds and flocks, is also an isolated figure like Midas (1).

Question 43

See Hint S2.

Reference should be made to:

- repetition of 'hands' – central aspect of myth directly referred to, but this also reflects the lack of connection between husband and wife (1).
- closing phrase 'his touch' – again this connects both the Midas myth with the mixture of emotions Mrs Midas experienced – the fear of his curse but the longing for a closer relationship (1).

Question 44

Marks are allocated: 2 marks for commonality; 2 for comment(s) on this poem and 6 marks for comments on other text(s).

Reference + basic comment = 1 mark. Reference + detailed comment = 2 marks. Reference + insightful comment may score 3 marks.

See Hint S7.

You may have chosen some of the examples below, although others are possible:

Commonality

- Several of her speakers reveal the conflicting nature of love.
- Duffy uses the change/development in the speaker's attitude to explore the complexity of human emotions.

- However, he qualifies this by saying his one experience was 'enough' – he doesn't want to repeat the performance (1).

Question 51

Reference + basic comment = 1 mark. Reference + detailed comment = 2 marks.

See Hint S2.

You may have chosen some of the examples below, although others are possible:

- 'a rock' – metaphor: implies that the shark is solid/immovable; an inanimate object with no intelligence.
- 'slounge' – onomatopoeia: the shark moved in a slow rise out of the waves; implies it is lazy or unhurried.
- Contrast – the shark is described as 'roomsized' and yet its brain is that of a 'matchbox'. This emphasises a lack of intelligence.
- 'monster' – implies the shark is low on the evolutionary scale; the word suggests the creature was frightening.

Question 52

Reference + basic comment = 1 mark. Reference + detailed comment = 2 marks.

- The creature was so large that it moved the water around MacCaig's boat, causing him to be 'shoggled' or shifted about on the sea (1).
- However, the phrase also has a metaphorical meaning. MacCaig feels that he was sent back in time by the experience, able to appreciate evolution and how both man and the shark have developed (1).

Question 53

Reference + basic comment = 1 mark. Reference + detailed comment = 2 marks.

See Hint S2.

You may have chosen some of the examples below, although others are possible:

- Use of rhetorical question: 'So who's the monster?' Initially in the poem he found the shark monstrous because of its size.
- However, on reflection, he questions whether it is not man who is the monster. He says 'The thought made me go pale', acknowledging that humanity is the more destructive force. MacCaig is uncomfortable – turning 'pale' – as he is no longer sure that he is the superior being in the encounter.
- 'sail after sail' – repetition/metaphor: conveys size/shape/vastness. Comparing the shark's fins to sails is appropriate as both are connected to water.
- 'slid' – implies a smooth, fluid movement. After initially describing the shark as a 'rock', MacCaig has changed his perspective. He now sees it as something graceful.
- 'and then the tail' – MacCaig is emphasising the time it took the shark to swim away, highlighting its great size and flowing movement.
- MacCaig uses lots of long vowels (sail/tail/tall/away) to further emphasise the time it took for the shark to pass by.

Question 54

Marks are allocated: 2 marks for commonality; 2 for comment(s) on this poem and 6 marks for comments on other text(s).

Reference + basic comment = 1 mark. Reference + detailed comment = 2 marks. Reference + insightful comment may score 3 marks.

See Hint S7.

You may have chosen some of the examples below, though others are possible:

Commonality

- MacCaig uses nature to help us understand more about ourselves.
- MacCaig associates nature with life and energy and beauty.
- MacCaig uses nature to consider the natural order of the world.
- Nature is associated with goodness.

Basking Shark

- MacCaig uses his encounter with the basking shark to pose questions about man's supposed superiority over all creatures.
- He initially depicts the shark as a clumsy, unintelligent creature, having failed to reach the same level of evolutionary development as humanity.
- However, as the experience continues he begins to realise that there is a grace and majesty about the basking shark, and he appreciates the beauty of its movement.
- He also comes to the conclusion that it is harmless, posing him no threat. MacCaig is shocked to realise that the same cannot be said for humanity. He thought the shark monstrous for its size, but in fact we are the monsters in the way we destroy nature and the natural world for our own gain.

Sounds of the Day

- The poem is about MacCaig's sense of loss, about his pain and hurt at the end of a relationship.
- He uses nature in the opening stanza to create a feeling of life and energy. Horses 'clatter' across a bridge and even the air 'creaked'. Water is described as both a gentle 'snuffling' and then a 'black drum' as it topples down a waterfall.
- This is used to contrast the absolute silence MacCaig feels when he is left alone next to 'the quietest fire in the world'.

Aunt Julia

- Aunt Julia is a relation who MacCaig remembers fondly, although he rues his inability to communicate with her as she spoke Gaelic and he could not.
- Aunt Julia was a sturdy, practical woman and many of MacCaig's memories of her are connected to nature as she worked with the land.
- Her foot is remembered as being 'stained with peat' and he associated her with 'water', 'winds' and 'brown eggs'. MacCaig further associates her with nature when he says she had a 'seagull's voice'.

Memorial

- *Memorial* is an elegy, likely written for MacCaig's sister who died in 1968.
- In the second stanza of the poem, MacCaig uses nature to explore the idea of death and how it disrupts the natural order of the world. In death, he says 'bird dives from the sun, that fish / leaps into it'.
- He also highlights the beauty and delicacy of nature, comparing its perfection and gentle touch to the way her death has marked him, saying 'No crocus is carved more gently / than the way her dying / shapes my mind'.

Poetry, Text 5: *Hallaig* by Sorley MacLean

Question 55

Reference + basic comment = 1 mark. Reference + detailed comment = 2 marks.

See Hints S2 and S3.

You may have chosen some of the examples below, although others are possible:

- 'I will wait for the birches to move' – this happens in Hallaig; the trees turn into those who once populated the area.
- 'If it doesn't, I'll go to Hallaig' – Hallaig is where the poet meets the dead.
- 'To the Sabbath of the dead' – Hallaig is a sacred place for those who have passed. It is also silent – like a Raasay Sabbath.
- 'Down to where each departed / Generation has gathered' – Hallaig is a place where the past comes to life; the dead from all ages return to repopulate and reclaim Hallaig.
- 'Hallaig is where they survive' – the ghosts and echoes of the past people can be keenly felt in Hallaig.
- 'All the MacLeans and MacLeods' – these are the poet's people; members of his own clan. It is his own people who have been evicted from their home and heartland.
- 'The dead have been seen alive' – the past comes to life here in Hallaig. They appear as ghosts yet are full of life and vibrancy.

Question 56

Reference + basic comment = 1 mark. Reference + detailed comment = 2 marks.

See Hint 2.

You may have chosen some of the examples below, although others are possible:

- 'Sabbath' – has connotations of silence in Free Presbyterian Raasay, which echoes the idea of desertion.
- 'the road is plush with moss' – the road is not used anymore; no one is there to use it.
- 'noiseless procession' – the girls are silent and ghostly.
- 'shrouded' – clear connotations of death, silence and the echoing emptiness of the place.

Question 57

Reference + basic comment = 1 mark. Reference + detailed comment = 2 marks.

See Hint S5.

You may have chosen some of the examples below, although others are possible:

'Love's loaded gun will take aim' – poet uses the paradoxical metaphor of love as a gun, which is effective as love and hope seems to conquer in this deserted place. Imagery of hunter and hunted is effective, as the people of Hallaig have been hunted by the landowner and run from the land they have lived and worked on for centuries. MacLean sees himself in this poem as the hunter, rather than the hunted; shooting time, trapping it, preserving the memory of these people and this place for eternity.

- 'It will bring down the lightheaded deer' – time is personified as a deer. By shooting or stilling time, MacLean is preserving a sense of place and creating a timelessness in which the ghosts and echoes of the past can be felt for eternity.
- 'his eye will freeze' – time is stilled; it does not continue its linear progression.
- 'while I live / His blood won't be traced in the woods' – this is a bloodless killing, a killing of love. Paradoxically, the 'death' of time preserves the sense of place and people and captures the emotion of the land itself. The poet's intense connection to the past and his people allows him to capture and still time in the poem, thus preserving the past and its people and showing a sense of timelessness in the cleared township of Hallaig. The history of the clearances is not forgotten.

Question 58

Marks are allocated: 2 marks for commonality; 2 for comment(s) on this poem and 6 marks for comments on other text(s).

Reference + basic comment = 1 mark. Reference + detailed comment = 2 marks. Reference + insightful comment may score 3 marks.

See Hint S7.

You may have chosen some of the examples below, although others are possible:

Commonality

- MacLean uses the landscape to represent its people, both past and present.
- MacLean shows the connection between the landscape and time or a sense of history.
- MacLean uses the landscape to symbolise his own poetic transcendence.

Hallaig

- MacLean uses trees, native to Raasay, to symbolise the people who once lived in Hallaig.
- Birch is a symbol of recovery and regeneration as it can be the first to be regrown in an abandoned area.
- Pine is not native and may represent the landowners or enemies of the islanders.
- MacLean refers to place names and specific geographical features such as 'beach', 'Burn', 'hills' and 'Dun Cana' to emphasise the location and, in this instance, create an eerie ghostly sense of loss and timelessness. Shows a connection with land and nature.
- The shore and/or island location of Hallaig shows a connection between land and the sea.

Shores

- MacLean uses specific locations in this poem and particularly sand and sea to capture the intensity of his feeling.

Question 7

See Hint R3.

Area of disagreement	*Lev Grossman*	*Joshua Kopstein*
Extent of backlash to Facebook buyout	Acknowledges there was some concern, including Minecraft's drop out.	Highlights the instant anger caused in response.
Oculus' and Facebook's priorities	Mentions the focus on game development as well as on producing affordable handset.	Argues that their only interest is in data gathering.
Benefit of Facebook buyout	Highlights that access to greater funds will allow the company much more flexibility.	Argues that Facebook is only interested in profit.
Extent of Facebook's control over Oculus	Highlights that this purchase will not mean a shift in focus or control over activity.	Suggests that Facebook will exploit the device unethically.

WORKED ANSWERS – Practice Exam C

Critical Reading – Section 1: Scottish text

Drama, Text 1: *The Slab Boys* by John Byrne

Question 1

See Hints S1 and S2.

- Spanky and Phil, as slab boys, pride themselves on their poor work ethic and nonchalance over the company and its workings outside their small environment in the slab room (1).
- Jack reveals himself to be dedicated to developing himself – 'I went to night school for three and a half years … I've got a Diploma in Wool Technology!' – and is keen to involve himself in the progress of the company. Phil feels that Jack's supposed work ethic is in fact a farce ('As soon as Barton starts revving up his Jag you're the first one out the door'), an attempt to impress the bosses. He has compromised himself in an attempt to get ahead (1).

Question 2

Reference + basic comment = 1 mark. Reference + detailed comment = 2 marks.

See Hints S2 and S3.

You may have chosen some of the examples below, although others are possible:

- 'You nobbled Hector when he first started' – 'nobbled' means to influence by underhand or unfair methods. Implies Spanky and Phil were acting against Hector's interests.
- 'we'd go through some carpet mags together … but, oh no, you soon put a stop to that' – looking over 'carpet mags' with Jack suggests that Hector was interested in design and saw the job as more than just a pay packet, but Jack implies that Spanky and Phil tried to quash his enthusiasm.

- 'called him for everything' – this implies that Phil and Spanky called Hector names in an attempt to embarrass him out of showing an interest.
- 'made his life a misery' – 'misery' suggests that Hector's working life was uncomfortable and unpleasant when he first started. It is implied that this continued until he fitted in with the poor attitude shown to work by the other two slab boys.
- 'Hector could've been a pretty good designer by now … yes, he could!' – suggests that Phil and Spanky have impeded Hector from making progress within the company.

Question 3

Reference + basic comment = 1 mark. Reference + detailed comment = 2 marks.

See Hints S2 and S3.

You may have chosen some of the examples below, although others are possible:

- 'Ach, pish, Jack!' – Phil is derisory of Jack's assertion that he takes 'pride' in working for the carpet factory. The use of an expletive emphasises his strength of feeling.
- 'You? You lot!' – the use of a rhetorical question reveals Phil's scorn. The repetition of 'you' highlights his disbelief that those on desks are truly hard-working and actually care about the company.
- 'a fistful of brushes in this hand and the other one tugging at the forelock …' – Phil suggests that the 'fistful of brushes' is merely a prop to pretend to the management that Jack and his cohort are working. The phrase 'tugging on the forelock' is scornful, implying that the designers care more about being seen to be respectful and subservient workers in order to impress the 'boss'.
- 'Good morning, Sir Wallace, by Christ but that's a snazzy Canaletto print' – Phil's impersonation of Jack is mocking and suggests that he attempts to curry favour with management.
- 'No, no, not at all, Sir Wallace … of course I don't mind putting in a bit of unpaid overtime' – the series of negatives ('No, no, not') and addition of' of course' suggests that Jack fawns as he agrees readily with the unreasonable demand in Phil's imagined conversation. The use of 'Sir' makes Jack appear a grovelling servant. Phil is disdainful of this attitude.
- 'you wouldn't know a good design from a plate of canteen mince' – although Jack makes an effort to develop himself, Phil believes that his supposed superior knowledge is false. The use of contrast ('good design'/'canteen mince') emphasises the strength of Phil's dismissal of Jack's skills.
- 'Interest?' – rhetorical question – the use of a single word adds power to Phil's derision, suggesting Jack's interest is false.
- 'As soon as Barton starts revving up his Jag you're the first one out the door' – Phil's observation implies that Jack's enthusiasm is merely for show and not genuine.

Question 4

Marks are allocated: 2 marks for commonality; 2 for comment(s) on this extract and 6 marks for comments on rest of text.

Reference + basic comment = 1 mark. Reference + detailed comment = 2 marks. Reference + insightful comment may score 3 marks.

See Hint S7.

You may have chosen some of the examples below, although others are possible:

Commonality

- Phil and Spanky use humour to downplay their frustration at their lack of advancement in the factory.
- They make fun of others to (falsely) show that they do not wish to join the ranks of the 'desks'.

Extract

- Phil and Spanky are insulted that Jack doesn't offer to show them the design mags, both of them asking 'how come?', but then play to the stereotype assigned to them (uncaring and idle): 'The designing of carpets for the hoi polloi may mean nothing to you, Hogg, but it means a damn sight less to us. Right, Spanky?'
- When Jack reveals the way he has tried to develop himself, gaining his diploma in Wool Technology, they mock his achievement, saying 'He's haun-knitted.' This serves to cover up their own lack of progress from the slab room.
- When Jack leaves, Spanky attempts to deflect the tension caused by the truth in Jack's words – they are stuck in the slab room while he's free to leave – by mocking him: 'You don't suppose there's any truth in the rumour that he's really the love-child of Miss Walkinshaw and Plastic Man? No?'
- The scene closes with a final joke: Spanky mocks Jack and his enthusiasm one final time by pretending he's going to go and look at the showroom when in fact he's going to skive.

Rest of text

- When Spanky, Phil and Hector are asked to show Alan how the slab room works in the opening scene, they turn it into a pantomime production. This is in part to cover up the lowly position they hold in the company and lack of skill required to work in the slab room.
- Curry berates both Phil and Spanky for their lack of work ethic, pointing out how much better the slab room was run when Jack was in charge of it. In response (after he has left) they avoid the truth of his words by laughing at him. Spanky asks 'D'you think that might've been a good moment to ask him for a desk, Phil?' By making fun of Curry and their situation they are able to avoid the truth of their unglamorous job and self-imposed poor prospects.
- In the final scene of the play, Phil waltzes out of the slab room with great pomp and energy, performing a short comic routine, in order to prove that he is not upset at losing his job, failing to get into art school, or being passed over for promotion (Hector, instead, is given the desk).

Drama, Text 2: *The Cheviot, the Stag and the Black, Black Oil* by John McGrath

Question 5

See Hint S1.

You may have chosen some of the examples below, although others are possible:

- It was believed that the British Government did not have the finances to spend on exploring the land and digging for oil (1).
- As the United Kingdom believes in capitalism and the importance of encouraging industry, they did not want to prevent investment from foreign companies (1).

- As the oil industry was already well established in America, its companies would have the skills and information essential to create success in Scotland (1).

Question 6

When asked to identify contrast, it is important that the evidence you provide clearly demonstrates a difference between the two characters. 1 mark for appropriate comment on each character.

See Hint S2.

You may have chosen some of the examples below, although others are possible:

- 'These chaps have the know how, and we don't.' / 'we didn't want to put them off' – suggests Whitehall is anxious/uncertain. There is the suggestion that politicians feared the loss of investment in the Highlands.
- 'Yes sir, and we certainly move fast' – suggests Texas Jim is confident/sleazy. His 'politeness' seems somewhat insincere given his clear motivation is accumulating wealth.
- 'Our allies in N.A.T.O. were pressing us …' – suggests Whitehall is keen to avoid conflict/scared of potential threats.
- '… we can make sure you stay that way. (*Fingers pistol*).' – suggests Texas Jim is aggressive and determined to secure profit even if it involves use of force.
- 'I find myself awfully confused' – suggests Whitehall is naïve/stupid. There is the suggestion that the United Kingdom has no understanding of the consequences of its actions.
- 'And to the greater glory of the economy of the U.S. of A.' – suggests Texas Jim is manipulative/intelligent. It is clear that he is very aware of the benefits it will bring and has no concern for those negatively impacted in Scotland.

Question 7

Reference + basic comment = 1 mark. Reference + detailed comment = 2 marks.

See Hint S2.

You may have chosen some of the examples below, although others are possible:

- Use of traditional song (*Bonnie Dundee*) which is changed to suit their meaning can be linked to the issue of exploitation as they are adapting/destroying something which is a part of Scottish culture.
- 'So if you'd abandon your old misery' / There's boom-time a-coming' reminds us of the historical arrogance displayed by the upper classes with regard to the lifestyle and culture of the Highlanders.
- 'All waiting for drilling and piping to me … At four times the price you sold it' demonstrates the financial exploitation of the Highlands to the benefit of 'outsiders'.
- 'For the Highlands will be my lands in three or four years.' Indicates the sense of possession felt by those investing in the land.

Question 8

Reference + basic comment = 1 mark. Reference + detailed comment = 2 marks.

See Hint S2.

Question 12

Maggie stops being the peacemaker or the passive victim and instead takes charge of the situation, acting decisively and with authority.

Reference + basic comment = 1 mark. Reference + detailed comment = 2 marks.

See Hint S2.

You may have chosen some of the examples below, although others are possible:

- 'suddenly she stops combing her hair and rises' – Lamont Stewart uses Maggie's habitual raking of her hair to show her anxiety and her feelings of helplessness. That this 'suddenly … stops' shows a resolution in Maggie; she does not waver and is decisive in her action.
- 'she takes the money out of Jenny's hand' and 'interposes herself between them' – her body language and positioning clearly shows that she is a physical and emotional buffer between Jenny and John.
- 'with uncharacteristic force' – Maggie's tone of voice conveys her resolution and shows that she is not to be taken lightly. Here the audience sees that Maggie can fight for her family when the need arises.

Question 13

Reference + basic comment = 1 mark. Reference + detailed comment = 2 marks.

See Hints S2 and S3.

You may have chosen some of the examples below, although others are possible:

- '(holding out her fat roll of notes)' – Jenny returns to the Morrison household, not only penitent and hopeful of a reconciliation with her family, but also as their potential saviour.
- 'Ca it a loan if ye like' – Jenny understands that John may not want to take charity and offers him a way of accepting the money.
- '(She comes forward and offers it to John)' – she comes with the means to get them out of their cramped, unsanitary conditions and into a council house.
- 'I never had a chance!'/ 'he'd tak one look at the close and that's the last I'd see o him' – Jenny reveals how the dirt and poverty of the slum she lived in put any potential 'respectable' suitors off, leaving her no choice, she says, but to go a more alternative route.
- 'I've often thought the way it would be when I came hame' / 'I was gonna make up for the way I left ye' – the audience sees that Jenny truly repents her previous callous treatment of her mother and the rest of her family and has dreamed of this moment of reconciliation.
- 'I've been savin an savin so's I could help ye and mak friends again, an be happy' – Jenny has been saving her money, earned from her job, in order to rescue her family from the dire conditions in which they live.
- 'She cries, head bent, standing forlornly before John' – Jenny sobbing before John clearly shows their strong connection.
- 'Mammy, Mammy! Stop!' – Jenny, by begging her mother to stop, is defending her father, despite all he has said to her.
- '(kneeling at her father's feet)' – this gesture clearly shows penitence and subservience. She needs his approval.

- 'Daddy ... Daddy ... forget it.' – Jenny shows that she has a forgiving spirit. John means everything to her.
- 'When I wis wee, you loved me, and I loved you. Why can we no get back?' – the simplicity of this renews the connection between Jenny and John.
- 'he lets her take one of his hands from his face and hold it in both of hers' – Jenny's action shows her willingness to forgive and to build bridges with John. There is tenderness in the action as she holds his hand in 'both of hers'.

Question 14

Marks are allocated: 2 marks for commonality; 2 for comment(s) on this extract and 6 marks for comments on rest of text.

Reference + basic comment = 1 mark. Reference + detailed comment = 2 marks. Reference + insightful comment may score 3 marks.

See Hint S7.

You may have chosen some of the examples below, although others are possible:

Commonality

- John's treatment of Jenny is harsh and judgemental, as is his attitude to Lily, and highlights his own perception of himself as the man in the household.
- John and Maggie's relationship provides the underlying tension in the play.
- The theme of the role of men within the working class is explored in John's prejudice, abuse of his own power and in the ways in which he does not conform to the stereotypical expectation.
- The theme of family and the divisions that can arise in close family units is explored in Jenny's defection and reconciliation as well as in many other incidents in the play.
- The living conditions of the Morrisons contribute to their emotional burden as a family and highlight the plight of the working classes.

This extract

- Jenny's return and reconciliation with her family restores the family and heals the rift within it that her absence and silence has caused.
- Her return also gives cause for optimism that there is hope for Maggie and John's children – they will not all turn out like Alec.
- Maggie's confrontation of John's hypocrisy and her assertive challenge to him shows hope for the future. Maggie may take charge of her family and fight for them more herself.
- John's covered face suggests shame certainly, and possibly also tears. This is a neat link with the title which conveys the multiplicity of Lamont Stewart's observations about Glaswegian tenement life.

Rest of text

- The prospect of a council house lifts Maggie as she can see a window of hope rather than just the drudgery of existence and survival in her cramped slum. The living conditions of the Morrisons have been a key element in the play, showing the tension and the challenging circumstances under which these people tried to live their lives.

- Lily's presence at the end of the play is fitting as she is a lynchpin of the family and without her support they would not survive.
- The argument between Jenny and John and the way Lily and John interact maintains the thread of tension and heightened emotion that is present throughout the play. The anger and love of the final scene reminds the audience once more of how volatile relationships are in the family and how easily situations get out of control.
- Maggie has deferred to John previously and turned a blind eye to his failings.

Prose, Text 1: *The Painter* by Iain Crichton Smith

Question 15

- The use of the possessive pronoun in expressions such as 'our village' creates a sense of unity and togetherness in the village community (1).
- The narrator also creates a sense of the community as a sentient entity with mutual feeling. He says 'we all liked him' and 'he made us uncomfortable' to imply a collective identity (1).

Question 16

You need to establish that the villagers were pleased to have a painter in the village/were proud of William's art, then go on to make it clear that elements of his work unnerved them.

Reference + basic comment = 1 mark. Reference + detailed comment = 2 marks.

See Hints S2 and S3.

You may have chosen some of the examples below, although others are possible:

The villagers were proud/admired William's work

- 'the villagers … encouraged him' – suggests they enjoyed/gained satisfaction from his paintings.
- 'fine golden sheen' – he portrayed their labours in a positive light.
- 'such as … seen before' – William was unique and special.
- 'a calm fairytale atmosphere' – he imbued the village with a magical/enchanting feel.
- 'great fidelity to nature' – implies skill/attention to detail.
- 'particularly faithful picture' – his pictures were truthful/honest.
- 'colourful paintings' – suggests bright and lively.
- 'pointed … great pride' – alliteration, use of 'great' to emphasise depth of pride.
- 'one of our greatest assets' – use of possessive pronoun implies ownership, 'assets' shows he had value in the village despite his infirmity.
- 'No other … painter at all' – he made them feel unique/special.
- 'wonderful artist' – inspires delight.

William's paintings at times disconcerted the villagers

- 'strange picture … a spook' – the villagers were practical people who did not understand some of William's unusual subjects.

- 'once or twice … uncomfortable' – the villagers were disturbed by some of William's paintings.
- 'insisted … as they were' – they did not always appreciate the stark realism of his work (when it was unflattering).
- Use of negatives (weren't/nor/wasn't) to deny the truth of William's paintings.
- 'less glamorous' – they resented the pictures which portrayed the village in a negative light.
- 'narrow and crooked'/'spindly and thin'/'confused and weird'– critical of William's portrayal.
- 'made them seem' – accusing tone.

Question 17

Reference + basic comment = 1 mark. Reference + detailed comment = 2 marks.

See Hints S2 and S3.

You may have chosen some of the examples below, although others are possible:

- 'sickly, delicate, rather beautiful boy' – his fragility and beauty are out of place in amongst the hardy, hard-working villagers.
- 'He used to paint scenes of the village … we were all scything the corn' – contrast: sedate, artistic activity versus hard manual work.
- 'many maintained that he wouldn't live very long, as he was so clever' – William's intelligence is seen as a weakness, the villagers value physical strength.
- 'once or twice … things as they were' – William's ability and determination to see and portray reality contrasts with the villagers' desire to present an idealised version of themselves.

Question 18

Marks are allocated: 2 marks for commonality; 2 for comment(s) on this story and 6 marks for comments on other text(s).

Reference + basic comment = 1 mark. Reference + detailed comment = 2 marks. Reference + insightful comment may score 3 marks.

See Hint S7.

You may have chosen some of the examples below, although others are possible:

Commonality

- Island life is restrictive, repressing the individual.
- Island communities are insular.
- Island living is a harsh way of life.

The Painter

- In this story, the restrictiveness of island life can be seen in the character William, who has to leave in order to embrace his individualism. His intelligence is not valued, the villagers instead preferring physical strength – an advantage in manual labour.
- The harshness of island life can be seen in the way the villagers ostracise William after the incident with Red Roderick. He has always been an isolated figure due to his fragility, but was tolerated. After the fight, he is further distanced from his community.

- Unusually, in *The Painter* Crichton Smith uses first person narration to counter-balance the outsider's perspective adopted in *Mother and Son* and *The Red Door*. The narrator is a part of the community and Crichton Smith highlights the sense of belonging that can develop in such a small, isolated place.

The Red Door

- Similarly to William, Murdo in *The Red Door* has had his individualism repressed by the expectations of the villagers.
- He feels the need to conform and allows his community to mould his every action – down to the clothing that he wears.

The Telegram

- The small-mindedness and tension of rural communities can be seen in the interactions between Sarah and the thin woman.
- The thin woman is seen as an 'incomer' even though she has lived in the village for thirty years.
- Sarah delights in spreading gossip about her neighbours, reflecting the pettiness that can occur in isolated, small communities.

Mother and Son

- In *Mother and Son* this harshness is shown in the bleak landscape. The constant wind and rain and working the land is described as 'monotonous and uncomfortable'.
- The suffocating nature of John's relationship with his mother also reflects the restrictiveness of rural life.
- She is shrewd and manipulative, and has prevented John from experiencing life, trapping him. This can be seen to mirror the way isolated communities can act as a trap, isolating individuals from the wider world.

Prose, Text 2: *The Wireless Set* by George Mackay Brown

Question 19

Reference + basic comment = 1 mark. Reference + detailed comment = 2 marks.

See Hint S2.

You may have chosen some of the examples below, although others are possible:

- 'valley of Tronvik' – rural community; small area (relatively) is identified. This presents the community as being isolated.
- 'Orkney' – island location in the north suggests remoteness, being 'cut off' or distant from London and its politics.
- 'son of Hugh the fisherman and Betsy' – identifying the family connection shows how small and close the community is. It suggests that everyone knows one another.

Question 20

Reference + basic comment = 1 mark. Reference + detailed comment = 2 marks.

See Hint S2.

You may have chosen some of the examples below, although others are possible:

- 'For a full two minutes' – alliteration emphasises the two minutes' silence. 'Full' highlights how long a time this is, in reality, to go without speaking which shows the islanders' amazement.
- 'nobody said a word' – the emphatic nature of 'nobody' and 'a word' indicates how universal this reaction is and how completely silent the islanders are due to their surprise and wonder.
- 'They all' – emphasises how universal the reaction is – all are amazed.
- 'stood staring' – 'staring' clearly connotes shock, surprise and wonder. The islanders cannot believe their eyes.
- 'it' – the indefinite article shows how foreign and unusual the wireless is to the islanders.
- 'small round noises of wonderment' – the islanders do not have the words to explain their astonishment; they can only ooh and aah to show their amazement.
- 'like pigeons' – this simile not only suggests the gentle noises of surprise the islanders are making, but also may suggest their naïvety and ignorance as they are dehumanised and compared instead to birds.
- Simple sentence – emphasises the content of the sentence. Allows the reader to appreciate the meaning of the two minutes' silence.
- Complementing phrases – develops the visual image of 'all stood staring', emphasises the simile 'like pigeons' and creates an almost comic picture of the islanders' astonished reactions to the wireless.

Question 21

See Hint S2.

Reference + basic comment = 1 mark. Reference + detailed comment = 2 marks.

You may have chosen some of the examples below, although others are possible:

- 'posh voice' – suggests education and authority. Howie might equate these things with being trustworthy.
- 'in London' – the capital city of Britain which connotes power, influence, authority.
- 'Everybody in the big cities has a wireless' – 'everybody' suggests a universality which in turn may suggest to Howie that wirelesses are valued by urbanites and therefore trustworthy. 'big cities' hints at sophistication, progress, technology and industrialisation. Howie may feel that technology such as the wireless is not only desirable, but that it is symbolic or representative of urbanity and civilisation and is therefore trustworthy.
- 'loud … voice' – this suggests authority and confidence which in turn may suggest trustworthiness.

Question 22

See Hint S1.

- The significance is that the wireless is not to be trusted (1); instead, trusting one's instincts and understanding of the world in which one lives is most important (1). There is as much, or more, value in a traditional, natural way of life as there is in a modern technological one (2).

Question 23

Marks are allocated: 2 marks for commonality; 2 for comment(s) on this story and 6 marks for comments on other text(s).

Reference + basic comment = 1 mark. Reference + detailed comment = 2 marks. Reference + insightful comment may score 3 marks.

See Hint S7.

You may have chosen some of the examples below, although others are possible:

Commonality

- The universal issues of life and death are explored at length in many of George Mackay Brown's stories. Largely this is seen as part of a natural process. However, modern warfare and modern technology are seen to be disassociating Orkney's people from their traditions and disrupting the natural pattern of life.
- The impact of war on families and communities is explored across time – from *The Wireless Set* to *Tartan*.
- Those in power are not to be trusted – the church, state or institutions like the BBC – as they oppress the working man.

The Wireless Set

- The issue of modernity and how it impacts on a culture and society thousands of years old is explored.
- The notion of truth and lies; we should not trust everything that we are told by those in authority.
- Impact of war on both families and communities. Old Hugh blames the wireless; he sees it as a bringer of falsehood as well as a symbol of modernity.
- The natural pattern of life and death is seen in the parents' muted reactions to the death of Howie. They focus on various jobs they have to do on the croft to survive.

A Time To Keep

- The unforgiving yet enduring cycle of life and death – Ingi dies giving birth, despite the fact she has had little time to grow into her role as wife and mother.
- Oppression of the working class by the aristocracy and the church – Bill feels punished for his hard work on the farm – the laird profits from it. The censure of the church and church-going members of the community is felt.
- Jealousy within small communities – Bill is shunned for marrying above his station. Ingi is not a crofting girl. Bill's house, boat and equipment are all new. This, and his success fishing, causes some resentment in the community.
- Marriage and its realities are explored – Ingi is not used to the hard crofting lifestyle. Bill notices her inadequacies as a housewife. The gap between their love for each other and their expectations of each other is revealed.

Tartan

- The realities of war – the islanders are not equipped to defend themselves against the Vikings; they have learned not to oppose them by bitter experience. The Vikings take their beasts and their precious goods as if it were their right. They would rape the females given a chance.
- The insignificance of life and death – Kol's death is not mourned; it is accepted as being a reality of war. The people of Durness are aware of how easily their lives can be taken by the Vikings. A dead child in one of the cottages shows death is not simply for the old.

The Bright Spade

- Connecting with the cycle of life and death within a small community. Death can strike anyone – young or old; rich or poor; strong or weak.
- Nature and the community's connection with the natural rhythms – events are noted in connection with the natural calendar. Harsh winter and poor harvest have an impact on the population of the island.

The Eye of the Hurricane

- The nature of belief is explored through Barclay's Catholicism and Miriam's membership of the Salvation Army. Both try to be forces for good with varying degrees of success. Miriam's belief is almost transcendent and emphasised in the final lines.
- The loss of love – the narrator has never got over his passionate affair with Sandra; Captain Stevens has never got over the death of his wife and infant son.
- The writer's desire to capture the essence of feeling is explored by Barclay. He finds it impossible to capture the effect, impact and sensations of love and to explore its psychological and social implications.
- The destructive effects of alcohol are seen throughout this story. Alcoholism is seen here as a disease by Miriam, something inevitable to be endured by Stevens. Alcohol both enrages and comforts Stevens as he struggles to deal with his loneliness.

Prose, Text 3: *The Trick Is To Keep Breathing* by Janice Galloway

Question 24

Reference + basic comment = 1 mark. Reference + detailed comment = 2 marks.

See Hint S2.

You may have chosen some of the examples below, although others are possible:

- Use of enjambment/line breaks (I want to be held / to be found / not to think) – suggests the disjointed, fleeting and rapid nature of her thoughts.
- Use of spacing (no going back / only further / going back) – reflects the lack of control or order she has over her own thoughts.
- Use of repetition (jesus / jesus) – suggests panic or fear.

Question 25

Reference + basic comment = 1 mark. Reference + detailed comment = 2 marks.

See Hint S2.

You may have chosen some of the examples below, although others are possible:

- 'crawl' – connotations of weakness or vulnerability due to association with toddlers.
- 'cramp makes me limp' – suggests she is weak or hurt.
- '... a junior arrives too soon' – suggests she is frightened by presence of another and does not want to be seen.
- 'He is a stranger.' – hints at fear/feeling of threat.
- 'I can't look him in the eye' – implies insecurity/vulnerability.

Question 26

Reference + basic comment = 1 mark. Reference + detailed comment = 2 marks.

See Hint S2.

You may have chosen some of the examples below, although others are possible:

- Lack of capitalisation at the start – suggests suddenness of recollection which highlights power/strength of memory over her.
- 'It felt tight and enclosed' – suggests the pressure and intimidation she felt. Connotations of 'enclosed' link her to caged animals, thus revealing the fear and threat she felt.
- Lack of punctuation – hints at her panic, lack of coherence.
- Use of repetition – reveals panic, confusion.
- Use of question – again implies confusion, uncertainty and panic.
- 'the teeth are rattling again. Chittering of the teeth …' – both 'rattling' and 'chittering' are associated with nerves, plus the lack of control over her body hints at her panic.

Question 27

Reference + basic comment = 1 mark. Reference + detailed comment = 2 marks.

See Hint S2.

You may have chosen some of the examples below, although others are possible:

- Use of line breaks appears to reflect the slowing down of Joy's thoughts. As she becomes more desperate for drugs the empty space seems to hint at the destruction of her mind.
- Lack of punctuation and ellipsis seem to reflect the disjointed nature of Joy's thoughts. We are given the impression that she is not in control of her mind/emotions due to the dependence on drugs.
- 'throwing off the sheets and searching, raking through …' – use of listing helps to convey urgency and panic while searching for pills.
- 'Pills are missing.' – use of sudden short sentence reflects panic at realisation.
- 'the drug snakes cold' – use of metaphor hints at evil, danger of drug.
- '… an arm. My arm.' – use of minor sentence helps to reflect the slow realisation and detachment she feels, as she is clearly unable to process her feelings due to the drug.

Question 28

Marks are allocated: 2 marks for commonality; 2 for comment(s) on this extract and 6 marks for comments on rest of text.

Reference + basic comment = 1 mark. Reference + detailed comment = 2 marks. Reference + insightful comment may score 3 marks.

See Hint S7.

You may have chosen some of the examples below, although others are possible:

Commonality

- These interruptions reveal Joy's struggle with depression.
- Each interruption reflects Joy's emotional state at that moment.
- These interruptions give us greater insight into Joy's personality, and factors influencing her behaviour.

Extract

- The torment of grief is made evident in this extract as it appears that Joy is suddenly consumed by recollection of her lover's death ('jesus / jesus / on a grey table'). She is evidently distressed by what she remembers.
- Use of ellipsis ('jesus / say there's nothing / say there's') helps to reveal Joy's heartbreak during the incident and the power of grief.
- The sudden breaks in her recollection ('tinged with blue / refusing to come back to / what was it?') reveal her struggle to accept his death.

Rest of text

- During Joy's first recollection of Michael's death we are given a sense of her detachment. It is evident to us that grief is making her fail to fully comprehend what happened.
- Use of flashback during first visit from David – used to reflect the detachment Joy feels. She escapes the 'now', perhaps because of lingering guilt or the wish that it was Michael who was visiting her. There is the suggestion that grief haunts us, and therefore continues to influence our actions.
- Use of scripting during visit to psychiatrist reflects Joy's failure to engage with her environment, as well as her struggle to accept help. Her grief is causing her to retreat inwardly and to fear/scorn those who she believes are failing to help her.

Prose, Text 4: *Sunset Song* by Lewis Grassic Gibbon

Question 29

Reference + basic comment = 1 mark. Reference + detailed comment = 2 marks.

See Hint S2.

You may have chosen some of the examples below, although others are possible:

- 'on Blawearie brae' – the Standing Stones are on Blawearie land; the land that Chris farms and which is central to the story.
- 'the sun just verging the coarse hills' – the sunset is appropriate as the ceremony marks the end of four lives, as well as the end of an era.
- The Standing Stones represent all that has gone, all that endures and the mystical connection the Scots have with the land.

Question 30

Reference + basic comment = 1 mark. Reference + detailed comment = 2 marks.

See Hint S2.

You may have chosen some of the examples below, although others are possible:

- 'sunset of an age and an epoch' – the deaths of the men in battle is the end of an age, reflected in the imagery of the setting sun.
- 'With them we may say there died a thing older than themselves' – the men carried with them a way of life that stretches back centuries, providing a connection with the past that was clean and true. There is a sense of identity and of history lost in the loss of these men.
- 'these were the Last of the Peasants' / 'the last of the Old Scots folk' – the men represent an ageless history, a life lived in connection with the land.
- 'A new generation comes up that will know them not' – the loss of the fathers means that there are no role models to carry on the old traditions.
- 'It was the old Scotland that perished then' – the men symbolise 'old Scotland', a past and a history that is true, is lived and has genuine meaning and connection.
- 'never again will the old speech and the old songs … but with alien effort to our lips' – future generations can never connect truly with this culture, this history. Instead, it will be revived in a search for meaning and belonging and can only be artificial as it does not represent the way that people will live in the future. Their culture is now of the past.
- 'great machines come soon to till the land' – the machines will replace man on the land. The connection the farmer has with the land is diminished as the land becomes more an asset to be worked than a livelihood.
- 'the crofter has gone' – men working the land to live off it, rather than solely for profit, have passed.
- 'For greed of place and possession and great estate those four had little heed' – the four Kinraddie men who died were not industrial-scale farmers; they worked their land to provide for their families and took pride in the toil and the repayment of their efforts.
- 'the kindness of friends and the warmth of toil and the peace of rest' – this shows what mattered to those who died; a hard life of work, well-lived, was pleasure and reward enough for these men.
- 'They died for a world that is past' – the men died to save their way of life, which was doomed anyway.

Question 31

Reference + basic comment = 1 mark. Reference + detailed comment = 2 marks.

See Hint S2.

You may have chosen some of the examples below, although others are possible:

- 'as folk stood dumbfounded' – the silence of the crowd reflects the struggle to understand the greater significance of the deaths of the men and what it means to the crowd personally.
- 'step slow round the stone circle by Blawearie Loch' –the 'slow' steps mark a processional beat around the ancient stone circle, signifying loss and renewal and the endless passage of time.
- 'slow and quiet' – to mark the ceremonial occasion and make a fitting tribute to the men. This also creates a sense of desolation and loss which connects with the bigger picture in the sermon.
- 'the dark was near' – the dark represents death and the loss of a way of life and a shared culture. The symbolism evokes the mourners feeling what has passed.

- 'it lifted your hair and was eerie and uncanny' – the narrative voice shows how the emotion produced was unsought and primitive; it cries to the heart of these people, connecting them with a past that is already half-forgotten.
- 'the Flowers of the Forest' – the ballad from centuries past which mourns the loss of the prime of Scotland's menfolk, along with the end of an age.
- 'It rose and rose and wept and cried' – escalates feeling and tension as the pipes mimic the wailing and keening of grief.
- 'that crying for the men that fell in battle' – the reality of loss and the grim starkness of the meaning of war for ordinary people is felt by the mourners.
- 'Kirsty Strachan weeping quietly and others with her' – a wife's loss of a husband is shown in front of all Kinraddie, a society which despises all softness of this sort, and yet others around her connect with her grief and feel it also in a communal sense of loss and suffering.
- 'glum, white faces' – the strain of the ploughmen shows the strain of the community. They feel the sadness of the occasion, yet can't connect with it fully.
- 'it was something that vexed and tore at them, it belonged to times they had no knowing of' – the pipes bring out a primitive feeling of grief, urging them to feel more for the loss of those who fell in battle, yet they cannot understand or fully connect with the greater meaning.

Question 32

Marks are allocated: 2 marks for commonality; 2 for comment(s) on this extract and 6 marks for comments on rest of text.

Reference + basic comment = 1 mark. Reference + detailed comment = 2 marks. Reference + insightful comment may score 3 marks.

See Hint S7.

You may have chosen some of the examples below, although others are possible:

Commonality

- Natural cycles of the seasons, and even day and night, are used to show the endless process of regeneration and decay.
- The Standing Stones are symbolic of Scotland's past where religion and nature were more closely linked.
- The novel is about the end of an era and of a culture. Modernity destroys the old 'Pictish folk'.

Extract

- 'the night waiting out by on Blawearie brae' – the darkness of night symbolises the death of a way of life, that of a culture and a connection with the past.
- 'sun just verging the coarse hills' – the ceremony takes place outside, at the Standing Stones, where the land of Kinraddie can be seen all around.
- 'ringing out over the loch' – the minister's voice is strong and forthright, reflecting a strong feeling of protectiveness over a lost heritage which produced a marginalised Scottish culture.
- 'sunset of an age and an epoch' – the death of the men is the end of an era, connected with the natural metaphor of the setting sun.

- 'It was the old Scotland that perished then' – the men symbolise an ancient Scottish way of life that will never be revived.
- 'For greed of place and possession and great estate those four had little heed' – the death of the men symbolises the domination of capitalism and with it a loss of self and history.
- 'mists that pass' – suggests that all mankind's greed, or indeed love, toil and troubles, will pass away as ethereal as mist, leaving no legacy, no marker behind them.
- 'a greater hope and a newer world' – the hope is for a more equal world in which war is a last resort and the suffering of the present is past.
- 'the Flowers of the Forest' – symbolises the death of this aspect of Scotland with its menfolk; a loss and the suffering and grief of a nation.

Rest of text

- Chris symbolises Scotland; her experience in life reflects the loss of a culture, yet she survives, adapts and moves on, as Scotland moves on.
- The structure of the novel is symbolic. The use of the cyclical structure, both in each section with the opening and conclusion being at the Standing Stones, and also in the titular metaphors of each section which connect stages of Chris' life with that of the natural cycle, symbolises the endless stages of birth, growth, death and renewal which endure.
- The Standing Stones represent a connection with a primitive history that is embedded in a deep understanding of nature.
- Chris' encounters with the past in the castles at Edzell and Dunottar, as well as in the classical languages of Latin and Greek, all symbolise the transitory nature of human ambition and existence.
- Long Rob symbolises Old Scotland. His reluctance to go to war shows his unwillingness to bring on the horror and the material changes that modernity brings. He dies, without children to survive him, symbolising the finality of the end of this way of life.
- Chae Strachan symbolises the evolution of Scotland's working man; he survives until the very dying hours of the First World War, was one of the first to enlist in the war and saw it as a means to bring about the overthrow of oppression and to create a greater equality for the working man.
- Will also symbolises a new beginning for Scotland, and shows how opportunities for Scottish people were more easily found abroad, away from the oppressive ill-nature of the native community.
- Chris' impending remarriage shows that she will survive and overcome her loss, building a new, different life.

Prose, Text 5: *The Cone-Gatherers* by Robin Jenkins

Question 33

Reference + basic comment = 1 mark. Reference + detailed comment = 2 marks.

See Hints S2 and S3.

You may have chosen some of the examples below, although others are possible:

- 'Neil did not know what to do or say' – implies a sense of helplessness in the situation.
- 'Every second of silent abjectness' – alliteration: emphasises his discomfort by highlighting how slowly time goes by; 'abjectness' has connotations of humiliation and misery.

- 'betrayal of himself' – Neil is angry at himself for not speaking up to Lady Runcie Campbell; 'betrayal' suggests inner anger at himself.
- 'All his vows' – to 'vow' is to make a solemn promise, emphasises how wrenching it is for Neil to break them.
- 'tortured' – suggests great pain.
- 'as if coals from the stolen fire had been pressed into his shoulders' – simile: emphasises burning nature of pain; use of 'stolen' implies his shame at having broken into the beach hut.
- 'he wished that the pain was twenty times greater' – Neil feels he must atone for breaking the rules of class and putting his brother in this situation, and for his own emotions when they're discovered.
- Repetition of 'could not' – emphasises the power Lady Runcie Campbell has over Neil, despite his objections to class inequality.

Question 34

See Hint S1.

- They have dared to use the beach hut to shelter from the rain. As lower class workers on her estate, she feels they should only remain in places where they have her express permission to be (1).
- Their actions meant that she and her children were exposed both to Calum's deformity and to the brothers' inferior class and poverty (1).

Question 35

You should explain that Sheila reacts like a traditional aristocrat, secure in her superiority and right to use the beach hut over the brothers, whereas Roderick is uncomfortable with his mother's expulsion of Calum and Neil, seeing them as humans in need of shelter, as they are.

For full marks both Sheila and Roderick must be referred to.

Reference + basic comment = 1 mark. Reference + detailed comment = 2 marks.

See Hints S2 and S3.

You may have chosen some of the examples below, although others are possible:

Sheila's reaction

- 'The girl giggled' – Sheila finds amusement in Calum's deformity and the fact that his child-like mind makes him reliant on the care of his brother.
- 'In the hut Sheila had run to the fire, with little groans of joy' – Sheila experiences 'joy' at the fire; she is not perturbed at all that two men have just been sent out in the storm in order to allow her to bask in the warmth without their polluting presence. She accepts that as her right.
- 'Did you see the holes in the little one's pullover' – calling Calum the 'little one' is demeaning. Sheila is also critical of the brothers' poverty.

Roderick's reaction

- 'but the boy said nothing,' – the use of 'but' contrasts Roderick's silence with Sheila's unkind giggling. He is silent as he understands he cannot question his mother's judgement in front of the brothers, but he disapproves of her decision.

- 'From the corner to which he had retreated' – Roderick tries to physically distance himself from his mother, as he wants to distance himself from her actions.
- 'his own face grave and tense' – the unhappy expression on Roderick's face highlights his objection to his mother's order.
- 'He did not move.' – single sentence paragraph, emphasising Roderick's action. He refuses to go to his mother because of what she's done.
- 'He turned and pressed his brow against the window.' – Roderick wants to hide from the cruelty he witnessed and the unfair, inhumane side to his mother that the incident revealed.

Question 36

Marks are allocated: 2 marks for commonality; 2 for comment(s) on this extract and 6 marks for comments on rest of text.

Reference + basic comment = 1 mark. Reference + detailed comment = 2 marks. Reference + insightful comment may score 3 marks.

See Hint S7.

You may have chosen some of the examples below, although others are possible:

Commonality

- Lady Runcie Campbell believes the barriers between classes must remain to preserve civilised society.
- Neil is frustrated by the unfairness of the class system but is helpless to change his position within it.
- Sheila and Laird Runcie Campbell represent the stereotypical upperclasses.
- Roderick represents the liberal, modern view – he is able to see the person rather than their class.

Extract

- Neil's (reluctant) acknowledgement of Lady Runcie Campbell's class superiority means that he is unable even to lift his face to meet her eyes when they are caught in the beach hut.
- Lady Runcie Campbell's belief that the classes must remain separate means that she cannot consider sharing the beach hut space with Calum and Neil, and so she sees no other option but to send them out into the storm.
- She is also appalled that they would be so 'presumptuous' as to use her beach hut for their own needs. She feels that the lower classes are beginning to forget their place and that she must – as a member of the aristocracy – work to retain the order and balance of society to maintain her privileged position.
- Sheila reacts as a typical aristocrat, assuming her right to the fire and shelter, and that she – as a member of the upper class – should not be expected to share it with her inferiors.
- Roderick, though a member of the aristocracy, sees Calum and Neil as people; people who are in need of shelter as much as he is.

Rest of text

- In the novel Neil rages against the class rules imposed upon him. He resents not being able to stay in the beach hut – which is empty and to be knocked down after the war.
- Sir Colin, though away at war, is portrayed as a typical Laird – he even has a family enclosure in the church to separate him from the rest of the congregation.

- Lady Runcie Campbell is torn between her Christianity and her father's teachings, which dictate compassion and justice, and her loyalty to her husband and the need to preserve her privileged way of life.
- Lady Runcie Campbell, despite her Christian leanings, shows herself loyal to her class in her decisions. At the deer drive she is horrified that Calum has ruined the drive and embarrassed her, rather than feeling pity for him in his inability to watch an animal suffer. She also cannot bring herself to allow acts of kindness such as giving the brothers a lift when she will allow dogs in her car.
- Duror, though a member of the lower class, sees himself as infinitely superior to Calum and Neil.
- Roderick is a member of the upper class, but due to his weakness he is seen as an outsider. He is unable to attend public school. This has given him a more sympathetic outlook and he is able to view the cone gatherers as people, almost as equals. He admires their skill in the trees and takes a cake to them in a gesture of friendship, although he is never able to deliver it.

Poetry, Text 1: *To A Mouse* by Robert Burns

Question 37

You need to have identified the mouse as being one of the following as the key idea in this question: fearful, small, vulnerable or alarmed.

Reference + basic comment = 1 mark. Reference + detailed comment = 2 marks.

See Hint S2.

You may have chosen some of the examples below, although others are possible:

- 'wee' – physically small, vulnerable and insignificant. This emphasises Burns' size and the power he has over the mouse.
- 'sleekit' – furtive and fearful. The mouse wishes to avoid being seen in order to escape Burns.
- 'cow'rin' – fearful and cringing. Conveys the mouse's terror of man and his power.
- 'tim'rous' – timid, fearful, nervous. Shows the mouse's extreme anxiety in this situation.
- 'beastie' – suggests that the mouse is small and insignificant. Affectionate diminutive suggests Burns' power over the mouse.
- 'panic' – suggests stress and fear of the mouse.
- 'breastie' – again the Scots diminutive emphasises the mouse's small size. It also suggests the mouse's fear by indicating that the mouse's heart is hammering.
- 'start' – literally jumping in fear.
- 'hasty' – mouse wants to make a quick getaway to escape Burns and his plough.
- 'bickering brattle' – the chattering noise conveys the mouse's fear and terror. Alliteration and onomatopoeia used here successfully to emphasise the noise and its meaning.

Question 38

1 mark per reason.

See Hint S1.

- He has just destroyed the mouse's nest.
- The mouse cannot rebuild its nest as there are no materials to build it.
- Without a nest, the mouse will most likely not survive the winter.
- The mouse is terrified of Burns as it sees him as a predator.
- The winter is coming – the weather will be cold and severe.
- The mouse took pains building its nest and now Burns has destroyed it in one swipe.

Question 39

Reference + basic comment = 1 mark. Reference + detailed comment = 2 marks.

See Hint S2.

You may have chosen some of the examples below, although others are possible:

- 'social union' – union suggests that there is a connection between the two, a balanced relationship.
- 'companion' – suggests friendship and equality, not an abuse of power.
- 'fellow-mortal' – 'fellow' suggests kinship, a connection between the two.
- 'the best-laid schemes o' mice an' men / Gang aft agley' – neither the mouse nor Burns can protect themselves against the unforeseen events of the future.
- 'us' – the use of the collective pronoun suggests a commonality between Burns and the mouse and highlights their shared powerlessness in the face of events outwith their control.

Question 40

You need to identify both tones and provide an example for each with an explanation.

Tone + example + explanation = 2 marks. More basic explanations = 1 mark each.

See Hint S6.

Up to line 37

Tone

Possible answers include: friendly/affectionate/apologetic/indulgent/pessimistic.

Examples

You may have chosen some of the examples below, although others are possible:

- Friendly/affectionate – 'I wad be laith to rin an' chase thee, / Wi' murd'ring pattle!' – 'Laith' suggests that Burns would hate to chase and kill the mouse. This conveys his affection or indulgence for the little creature.
- Apologetic – 'I'm truly sorry …' – Burns' direct address to the mouse with the heartfelt adverb 'truly' suggests that his apology is genuine and deeply felt.
- Indulgent – 'A daimen icker in a thrave / 'S a sma' request' – Burns does not see the mouse eating his crops as an issue. Burns accepts that the mouse 'maun live' and is happy to allow the mouse to live off his crops.

From line 37

Tone

Possible answers include: serious/pessimistic/wistful/anxious/self-involved/bitter.

Examples

You may have chosen some of the examples below, though others are possible:

- Pessimistic – 'An' lea'e us naught but grief an' pain, / For promis'd joy!' – Here the implication is that planning does not make one secure.
- Serious – 'But Mousie, thou art no thy lane, / In proving foresight may be vain' – the pacing of the poem here conveys the seriousness of Burns' thought. By indicating that the mouse is 'no thy lane' Burns shows the connection between the two – the mouse and himself – and makes the allegory of the mouse as the working class clearer.
- Wistful – 'Still thou are blest, compar'd wi' me.' – Burns acknowledges the difficulties the mouse faces and yet feels that the mouse has a greater advantage than him. Burns wishes that he could only concern himself with the present, like the mouse, rather than worry about the future or feel regret for the past.

Question 41

Marks are allocated: 2 marks for commonality; 2 for comment(s) on this poem and 6 marks for comments on other text(s).

Reference + basic comment = 1 mark. Reference + detailed comment = 2 marks. Reference + insightful comment may score 3 marks.

See Hint S7.

You may have chosen some of the examples below, although others are possible:

Commonality

- Burns shows that the working class is vulnerable to others' will and is not fully in control of its own fate.
- The ruling class in government and religion seeks to repress the common man in order to maintain the status quo.
- Burns suggests that traditional hierarchies and attitudes to morality are founded on hypocrisy.

To A Mouse

- Shows how vulnerable the common man is to both the inconstancies of nature and of the ruling class.
- Despite careful planning and diligence, their lives may be destroyed at the whim of another or by nature.
- Burns also suggests that the poor should be able to depend upon the rich to ensure they have the basics of food and shelter and that this is 'a sma' request'.

Man's a Man for A' That

- Shows that one's position in life is dependent on wealth, breeding and status, rather than on one's personal qualities.
- Burns stresses the commonality between rich and poor as he does the kinship with the mouse in *To A Mouse*.
- He suggests that the working man is subdued and 'obscure', in the same way as the mouse cowers, and that this is down to oppression by the established ruling classes.

Holy Willie's Prayer

- Burns shows that the repressive Protestantism of Calvinism is designed to make some people believe that they are better than others.
- By showing Willie's hypocrisy and his belief in his own predestination, Burns satirises the Calvinist church and shows that all people are equal, prey to the same sins as well as the same virtues.

A Poet's Welcome to a Love-Begotten Daughter

- Deals with the subject of illegitimacy. Burns suggests that there should be no difference in how we perceive those who are born within wedlock as without.
- Burns challenges the view that he should be ashamed of his daughter as she is a product of 'sin', or sex outwith marriage.
- He, instead, focuses on the pleasure he had with her mother and shows his great tenderness towards the resulting daughter.

Poetry, Text 2: *Valentine* by Carol Ann Duffy

Question 42

Reference + basic comment = 1 mark. Reference + detailed comment = 2 marks.

See Hint S2.

You may have chosen some of the examples below, although others are possible:

- 'Not …' – use of negative to begin poem highlights the firm rejection of traditional Valentine gifts.
- Use of minor sentence – creates a more direct, focused sentence.
- Single line verse – makes the speaker's idea very clear and determined.
- Use of simple statement ('I give you an onion.') – powerful, no sense of wavering or uncertainty.
- Parallelism in sentence opening – factual and confident.
- 'Here.' – minor sentence/imperative command on single line also implies lack of choice, determination of speaker.

Question 43

See Hints S2 and S4.

When dealing with contrasting ideas, it is essential that your evidence reveals the opposition.

1 mark for appropriate reference + comment on both aspects of love.

- 'It is a moon wrapped in brown paper.' – celestial connotations reflect the beauty and power of love, while 'brown paper' suggests the practical and purposeful nature of relationships.
- 'careful undressing of love' versus 'blind you with tears' – 'undressing' hints at sexual/intimate aspect of love and equally the closeness/bond which grows as more is revealed while 'blind' implies deception, weakness. Within this, there is a contrast between 'careful' and 'blind' which could be commented on due to the delicacy and comfort versus the pain inflicted.

- Previous positive aspects could also be compared with 'wobbling photo of grief' – reveals both the upset and the detachment that occurs when a relationship causes turmoil. The depth of emotion is revealed by 'grief', commonly associated with loss.
- 'possessive and faithful' – phrase contains both the suggestion of the intense, overbearing love which can develop and simultaneously the supportive and enduring nature of love.

Question 44

Reference + basic comment = 1 mark. Reference + detailed comment = 2 marks.

See Hint S2.

You may have chosen some of the examples below, although others are possible:

- 'It promises light / like the careful undressing of love.' – connotations of 'light' imply hope and joy, which is reinforced by the open line, not limited by punctuation. Change of line could also reflect peeling of layers.
- 'It will blind you with tears / like a lover.' – lack of punctuation after 'blind … tears' could reflect lack of sight, not being able to see the end. Shortness of second line also adds to bitterness/disappointment in lover.
- 'It will make your reflection / a wobbling photo of grief.' – break in line reflects the wobbling and thus the insecurity/upset.
- '… possessive and faithful / as we are / for as long as we are.' – line breaks help to slow pace, reflecting the length of time implied by 'faithful'. Argument could be made the breaks reflect the changes/weakness.
- 'Its scent will cling to your fingers / cling to your knife.' – line break helps to reinforce meaning of cling, suggesting the overpowering, desperate action.

Question 45

See Hint S1.

You may have chosen some of the examples below, although others are possible:

- Focuses on central concept – that love can bring pain and unhappiness as well as romance (1).
- 'Lethal.' – suggesting that love can 'kill' clearly reinforces the sense of pain/suffering hinted at earlier, especially through the image 'blind you with tears' (1).
- Final couplet strongly reflects dual nature of love – the 'scent' could be the lingering trace of love and emotion that you cannot shake, as well as perhaps giving a more literal reference to perfume. 'knife' again links to the pain and suffering caused by love (1).
- Repetition of 'cling': highlights both the desperation that love can cause, as well as its lingering impression (1).

Question 46

Marks are allocated: 2 marks for commonality; 2 for comment(s) on this poem and 6 marks for comments on other text(s).

Reference + basic comment = 1 mark. Reference + detailed comment = 2 marks. Reference + insightful comment may score 3 marks.

See Hint S7.

You may have chosen some of the examples below, although others are possible:

Commonality

- Both joy and grief/anger are revealed as significant aspects in relationships.
- Duffy reveals the power and intensity of emotion and how it influences our behaviour/attitude.
- Duffy reveals the lingering power of love, and how challenging it is to let go/forget.

Valentine

- This poem highlights the struggle to express genuine love when faced with the clichéd, superficial ideas espoused in society/industry. The speaker is very keen to reject these images ('Not a cute card …'), as they clearly believe these images are over-sentimental and misleading.
- The speaker wants to highlight the power of love. The poem appears to focus on how love can become intoxicating and overbearing, leading us to feel pain ('cling to your knife.').
- The poem also reveals that love can lead to extremes in emotions, from passionate and fulfilling to desperate and weak.

Mrs Midas

- In this poem, the hope and desire the speaker feels for her husband is challenged by his ambition and selfishness, leading to her disappointment and regret. However, despite the problems in their relationship, the lasting love for her husband is evident, reminding us that true love is very hard to forget.

Havisham

- In this poem we see the despair and suffering caused by a broken heart. It is clear that the speaker still longs for her lost love, in part because she desires revenge but also because her passion for him cannot be shaken.

Anne Hathaway

- The speaker sets out to right the false assumptions about her relationship, declaring the intensity and passion that existed between them. Through a number of images and other devices, we are given the impression that the two were very much in love, that they were almost one. It makes us consider the fact that the way a relationship appears in public may not truly reflect the intensity and desire shown in private.

Poetry, Text 3: *My Rival's House* by Liz Lochhead

Question 47

Reference + basic comment = 1 mark. Reference + detailed comment = 2 marks.

See Hint S2.

You may have chosen some of the examples below, although others are possible:

- 'peopled with many surfaces' – suggests that this home feels somewhat crowded or cramped, but as it is merely with objects this creates an unsettling feeling. These 'surfaces' may be casting her reflection, which could increase her unease/discomfort.
- '(cushions so) stiff' – suggests they are rigid and uncomfortable, perhaps purposefully so. This clearly reflects the discomfort which the speaker feels being in this house.
- 'slipper satin' – alliteration creates a 'hissing' which hints at threat or danger sensed.

- 'shuffle' – suggests they feel the need to move quietly so as not to disturb or disrupt. This appears quite unnatural, and clearly uncomfortable.
- 'tiptoe' – also suggests trepidation or uncertainty.

Question 48

See Hint S2.

1 mark will be awarded for an appropriate description of the attitude displayed:

Speaker towards mother-in-law – wary/dislike.

1 mark will be awarded for an appropriate comment on one piece of evidence.

- 'my rival thinks she means me well' – suggests speaker questions mother-in-law's intentions/attitude.
- 'But what squirms beneath her surface' – suggests that speaker believes mother-in-law is being false, masking true feelings.
- 'capped tooth, polished nail' – implies falseness, and also suggests she is unnerved by the mother-in-law's preened/fake appearance.
- 'fight, fight foul' – implies that her mother-in-law may resort to dirty tactics, revealing speaker's fear.
- 'Deferential, daughterly' – reveals the speaker is behaving out of a sense of duty, perhaps as she fears repercussions.
- 'bitter cup' – implies the animosity sensed, almost implying an attempt to poison her.

Question 49

Reference + basic comment = 1 mark. Reference + detailed comment = 2 marks.

See Hint S2.

You may have chosen some of the examples below, although others are possible:

- 'And I have much to thank her for.' – end stopped line creates force of statement. This 'fact' implies it is acceptable as truth (1) and recognised that the speaker is in her debt (1).
- 'This son she bore' – use of determiner objectifies the son, thus creating a sense of ownership.
- 'first blood to her' – conveys the strength of the connection between mother and son. 'to her' serves as a reminder that only she is connected by blood – therefore wields superiority.
- 'never, never can escape' – repetition suggests the strength of her control.
- 'Lady of the house.' – reference to title, implies power (1). Single line sentence also creates 'fact', giving greater emphasis and sense of assertiveness (1).
- 'Queen bee.' – connotations of complete control/rule over all.
- 'dangerous' – suggests threat, potential to harm.
- 'She has taken even this away from me' – use of qualifier 'even' to suggest all that has been removed/taken by mother-in-law (1) implies extreme control/invasion (1).

Question 50

See Hints S1 and S2.

Candidates should show understanding of the term 'conclusion' and show how the content of the last stanza continues — or contrasts with — ideas and/or language from the first two stanzas.

Reference + basic comment = 1 mark. Reference + detailed comment = 2 marks.

You may have chosen some of the examples below, although others are possible:

Ideas

- The speaker seems aware of the continuing control/influence/presence of her mother-in-law and recognises that this will not fade.
- Clarification of the idea that the mother-in-law's expectations are creating pressure on the relationship.
- The speaker seems to remain wary of her mother-in-law.

Language

- 'her dreams' – refers back to the sense of expectation surrounding the mother-in-law, and the pretence she wishes to create which 'must / be protected'.
- Reference to both 'breakfast' and 'dinner' reinforce maternal nature as carer and also the sense of her desire to maintain her role.
- 'her salt tears'– refers back to the animosity/ill feeling suggested in 'bitter cup'.
- 'pepper our soup' – image reinforces not only the overwhelming/large presence of the mother-in-laws but also suggests the ill-feeling created by her.
- 'She won't / give up.' – enjambment creates sense of defeat/acceptance his mother will remain a significant force in her partner's life.

Question 51

Marks are allocated: 2 marks for commonality; 2 for comment(s) on this poem and 6 marks for comments on other text(s).

Reference + basic comment = 1 mark. Reference + detailed comment = 2 marks. Reference + insightful comment may score 3 marks.

See Hint S7.

You may have chosen some of the examples below, although others are possible:

Commonality

- Lochhead exploits setting to explore romanticism and how memories augment reality.
- Lochhead's settings are crucial to our understanding of the speaker's attitude and changes which occur.

My Rival's House

- The depiction of the mother-in-law's home is central to our understanding of this strained relationship. We are given an insight into the frustration, pressure and fear a woman can experience when faced with the matriarch. Also, the setting is crucial to our understanding of the mother-in-law's desire to maintain her position/appearance, and thus gives us an insight into the fierce battle which can erupt when a mother struggles to accept her son's partner.

Some Old Photographs

- The description of setting in the poem *Some Old Photographs* is essential in conveying the romanticism of the past. This is contrasted with the glimpses of reality, which remind us that sometimes sentimentality can exaggerate our memory of times past.

View of Scotland/Love Poem

- The setting is significant as a means of exploring the sentimentality which can occur when looking at past events. Lochhead again explores the difference between 'fact' and nostalgia.

The Bargain

- The backdrop described in *The Bargain* helps to explore how love can prevent people from acknowledging their problems and ending difficult relationships. There is a bleakness to the setting which hints at the stalemate that exists between the couple, helping us to question why they are continuing with their relationship.

Poetry, Text 4: *Visiting Hour* by Norman MacCaig

Question 52

Reference + basic comment = 1 mark. Reference + detailed comment = 2 marks.

See Hint S2.

You may have chosen some of the examples below, although others are possible:

- 'smell' – word has negative connotations, unpleasant aroma.
- 'combs my nostrils' – the smell is pervasive, as if it reaches the very root of his nose hairs.
- 'as they go bobbing along' – synecdoche: the hospital smell is so potent, he has been reduced wholly to his sense of smell as he travels down the corridor.
- 'green and yellow' – connotations of sickness and disease.
- 'what seems a corpse' – MacCaig's assumption that the body is dead shows that he sees hospitals as places of disease and death rather than healing.
- 'trundled into a lift and vanishes / heavenwards' – metaphor: the lift represents the soul's journey to the afterlife, again associating the hospital with a place of death. The circumstances of his visit have prejudiced him.

Question 53

Reference + basic comment = 1 mark. Reference + detailed comment = 2 marks.

See Hint S2.

You may have chosen some of the examples below, although others are possible:

- 'I will not feel, I will not' – repetition: emphasises strength of feeling.
- 'I will not / feel' – line break highlights the word 'feel', suggesting his determination to put off his emotions.
- 'until / I have to' – enjambment: isolates the phrase 'I have to'. He knows it will be impossible to ignore what he has to face. Indicates sense of inevitability/obligation.

Question 54

Reference + basic comment = 1 mark. Reference + detailed comment = 2 marks.

See Hint S2.

You may have chosen some of the examples below, although others are possible:

- 'lightly, swiftly' – adverbs suggest an easy/carefree attitude to their movements, despite pressures of their job.
- 'here and up and down and there' – unusual syntax, emphasises the number of nurses and their constant movement as they go about their work.
- 'their slender waists miraculously / carrying their burden' – use of 'slender' makes the nurses appear small and delicate; the poet is surprised that they can withstand the emotion and responsibility associated with caring for the sick.
- 'so much pain, so / many deaths' – repetition of 'so' emphasises the amount of trauma and the number of lives lost that the nurses must witness.
- 'their eyes still clear' – they are able to cope and continue functioning in this environment despite being constantly surrounded by pain.

Question 55

Reference + basic comment = 1 mark. Reference + detailed comment = 2 marks.

See Hint S2.

You may have chosen some of the examples below, although others are possible:

- 'white cave of forgetfulness' – metaphor: the white curtains surrounding her bed create a colourless environment, lacking life. The 'cave' appears impenetrable. She is isolated, lacking sensory input.
- 'withered hand' – as if the life and health has been drained from her flesh.
- 'trembles on its stalk' – metaphor: makes the hand a dying flower, she has become brittle and frail.
- 'eyelids too heavy / to raise' – shows her lack of strength that she cannot achieve this very simple movement.
- 'arm wasted / of colour' – as with the 'white cave', her very flesh has been wasted of colour (which is associated with life and vitality).
- 'a glass fang is fixed' – metaphor: the intravenous drip becomes vampire fangs. Implies that the poet finds her poor condition frightening.

Question 56

Marks are allocated: 2 marks for commonality; 2 for comment(s) on this poem and 6 marks for comments on other text(s).

Reference + basic comment = 1 mark. Reference + detailed comment = 2 marks. Reference + insightful comment may score 3 marks.

See Hint S7.

You may have chosen some of the examples below, though others are possible:

Commonality

- Observations from experiences in MacCaig's life are used to explore ideas about the human condition.
- MacCaig uses personal experience to explore the theme of loss.
- He uses personal experience to consider ideas about death.

Visiting Hour

- In the poem MacCaig describes visiting a dying friend or relative in the hospital.
- He uses the experience to explore the idea of fear – in this case, fear of emotion. He is aware that the person he is visiting is close to death and he fears the strong emotion he knows will follow when he is forced to come face to face with their impending demise.
- The poem also explores the idea of death and its inevitability. He sees death in the body being 'trundled' down the corridor even before reaching the patient he has come to visit.
- In 'Ward 7', where the woman lies, the world has been leeched of colour as she is slowly being leeched of life.
- MacCaig reveals his frustration at the 'fruitless' prolonging of her life while he is unable to help her.

Assisi

- MacCaig, as the speaker, describes a visit to the Basilica of St Francis, where he witnesses a deformed dwarf begging while the priest ignores his suffering as he shows off the church to tourists.
- The poem's main purpose is to expose the irony that the Basilica – which was built in honour of St Francis who devoted his life to the poor – is now known for its architecture and artwork by Giotto.
- The opening stanza is dedicated to the description of the dwarf, who is described as a pathetic figure deserving of our sympathy.
- MacCaig contrasts this with a scathing portrayal of the priest who 'explained / how clever it was' and the 'clucking' tourists who lapped up his words.

Basking Shark

- MacCaig describes an encounter with a basking shark, which swam by close enough to knock his boat.
- As MacCaig is 'shoggled' by the shark, he begins to question his assumption that man is superior to all other creatures.
- Despite seeing the shark initially as a 'monster', by the end of the poem he is able to appreciate its grace and majesty.
- Furthermore, he wonders 'who's the monster?' as it is not the gentle basking shark who destroys nature for his own gain. That is the doing of humanity.

Aunt Julia

- In *Aunt Julia*, MacCaig remembers childhood visits to his aunt in the Highlands.
- He describes his aunt as being a lively, practical woman who worked the land, and the 'box bed' in her house, the only place he was able to lie in the dark and feel safe.
- His main regret is that his aunt spoke Gaelic and he 'could not understand her'. By the time he learned, she had passed away.

- This is central to the key theme of the poem: MacCaig feels frustration that he was unable to fully communicate with his aunt, but he also fears that we are losing the ability to understand and connect with the Highland heritage and culture that she represented.

Poetry, Text 5: *XIX I Gave You Immortality* by Sorley MacLean

Question 57

See Hint S1.

- The poet's creation of the poem (1)
- makes the woman immortal; she lives on, in perfect beauty, in his words. The words endure whereas the woman will age and die (1).

Question 58

See Hints S2 and S3.

Identify the attitude as: admiring/resolute to resist/powerless to resist/wistful/plaintive/inspired/grateful.

Attitude must be identified then supported by reference + comment = 2 marks. Reference + basic comment = 1 mark.

You may have chosen some of the examples below, although others are possible:

- 'oblivion of my trouble' – her lack of love for him has/had plunged him into despair.
- 'the gracious form of your beauty' – he still remembers her as beautiful.
- 'plain of the Land of Youth' – his love was a youthful one – naïve and inexperienced perhaps.
- 'I should prefer it there' – the poet wants to keep the disappointment as a past event rather than re-experience it.
- 'my weakness would return' – he would not be able to help himself; he would still be susceptible.
- 'peace of spirit / again to be wounded' – the woman has the capacity to destroy his tranquillity and cause turmoil within the speaker.
- 'O yellow-haired, lovely girl' – he still finds her beautiful. The exclamation shows his longing for her and his tenderness.
- 'you tore my strength' – connotations of ripping, rending the poet in pieces; destroying his sense of self and purpose.
- 'inclined my course / from its aim' – poet altered his ideas and ambitions to suit his lover. He was not true to himself.
- 'you are the fire of my lyric' – she inspires him; the extreme emotion he feels invigorates his writing.
- 'you made a better poet of me through sorrow' – the agony of losing her has made him a better poet.

Question 59

Poetry should be identified as being a marker that will long outlast the woman.

Reference + basic comment = 1 mark. Reference + detailed comment = 2 marks.

See Hint S2.

You may have chosen some of the examples below, although others are possible:

- 'I raised this pillar' – poetry is a lasting marker. Poet is conscious that, in writing the poem, he is trapping and memorialising his feelings for the girl forever.
- 'shifting mountain of time' – the marker remains while time moves on perpetually.
- 'memorial-stone' – the poem itself is remembering something dead, something worth celebrating and remembering – his hopeless love.
- 'heeded till the Deluge' – the poem will last until the end of time as we know it. It will be seen as of importance and note.
- 'your glory is my poetry' – the woman's beauty now becomes the beauty of the poem; it is appropriated and no longer hers.
- 'after the slow rotting of your beauty' – the beauty of the poem endures, everlasting, whereas the woman's beauty is transitory and will, inevitably, lead to decay and death.

Question 60

Marks are allocated: 2 marks for commonality; 2 for comment(s) on this poem and 6 marks for comments on other poem(s).

Reference + basic comment = 1 mark. Reference + detailed comment = 2 marks. Reference + insightful comment may score 3 marks.

See Hint S7.

You may have chosen some of the examples below, although others are possible:

Commonality

- First person highlights the immediacy of the experience and lends a depth of emotion to the poems.
- First person indicates that these are personal issues and ones which deeply concern the poet.

I Gave You Immortality

- The first person and the fact that this is a poem out of a sequence of love poems adds authenticity to the voice of the poem. The reader feels that this was MacLean's experience.
- The poet is questioning the woman he is in love with, addressing her directly ('I gave you').
- The poet is examining both his past, present and future feelings for the woman.
- The poet's pain, pride and self-conscious awareness of his weakness come through.
- The poet has pride enough to declare that his poetry is better and more lasting than the woman's beauty. He is aware of the glory of his writing.
- The poet is aware that this experience has shaped him as a poet.
- If the woman has made MacLean a better poet, he has immortalised her in his words, capturing her beauty and his pain.

Heroes

- First word is 'I'; this gives immediacy to the voice. Reader engages with it.
- This reads as a personal experience. The observations about the 'Englishman' are therefore personal observations. The judgements about him are the speaker's own.

- The visual depiction of the man in battle, as a personal experience, is more graphic and meaningful.
- The speaker's response to the man's terrified bravery in battle and the futility of his struggle is powerful in the final stanza. The speaker judges the 'poor little chap' to be a 'great warrior' – he gives credit and honour where he feels it should have been awarded.
- The inglorious manner of the man's death is clear in the tone and inference of the voice in stanza 7.

Hallaig

- The 'I' here is strongly resonant of past, place and people.
- The voice identifies his family and where they come from.
- The voice feels a connection with history and its people at these places.
- The poet feels the desolation of Hallaig keenly and imagines it repopulated with all previous generations.
- The poet aims to trap the people of the past; to preserve their memory in his poetry.
- The 'I' in this poem takes on the responsibility for reimagining and reawakening a past, a place and all its people.

Shores

- The use of the first person suggests that this unusual love poem is a 'real' experience. The speaker in the poem conveys the magnitude of his feeling; the reader is more prepared to decode and understand the speaker's feelings as it is written in first person.
- The voice of the poem is clear from the outset, addressing a new lover.
- The voice identifies place very strongly here and uses it to commune with the universe.
- Although the voice is with another, it sounds isolated – the experience of being at the shore sounds private.
- The voice in the poem uses this commune with the sea to get a sense, paradoxically, both of time passing and timelessness.
- The voice expresses the intensity of its love with the conceit of collecting the sand and the sea for the lover as testimony to his feeling.

Poetry, Text 6: *Two Trees* by Don Paterson

Question 61

Reference + basic comment = 1 mark. Reference + detailed comment = 2 marks.

See Hint S2.

You may have chosen some of the examples below, although others are possible:

- 'lay open their sides' – suggests exposing the inner core of the trees: their hearts.
- 'lash them tight' – gives the idea of ropes or tendrils holding them together, creating unbreakable bonds/a close connection.
- 'from the shame or from the fright' – personification. Suggests emotional reaction/shock at the close intimacy.
- 'two lights in the dark leaves' – contrast. 'light' equates to new life. Negative connotations of 'dark'.
- 'tangled up' – suggests intertwined/cannot be separated.
- 'double crop' – implies the trees are more fruitful together.

Question 62

In the first stanza, the tone is quite whimsical and light. The second stanza is much darker. Paterson reveals his loss through a mournful, despairing tone.

Reference + basic comment = 1 mark. Reference + detailed comment = 2 marks.

See Hint S6.

You may have chosen some of the examples below, although others are possible:

- 'had had no dream' – suggests lack of imagination/life.
- 'dark malicious' – suggests cruelty/spitefulness.
- 'whim' – thoughtlessness/spur of the moment.
- 'solitude' – loneliness/isolation.
- 'sterile' – barren/empty without each other.
- 'unhealed' – a wound that will not heal.
- 'weep' – an open wound but also implies crying.
- 'strained' – fighting to be with each other.
- 'shackled root' – metaphor. Suggests chains keeping them apart.
- 'strained on its shackled root' – alliteration.
- 'empty' – unfulfilled/lonely.

Question 63

Reference + basic comment = 1 mark. Reference + detailed comment = 2 marks.

See Hint S2.

You may have chosen some of the examples below, although others are possible:

- Rhyming couplet finishes the poem with a wry playfulness – the reader expects a deeper revelation or solemn final thought.
- Is it disingenuous? The final two lines leave the reader questioning whether the poem is simply about trees or about Paterson's relationship with a friend who passed away.
- OR he is being raw and unsentimental – commenting on the emotion/feeling that people tend to transfer to the inanimate.

Question 64

Marks are allocated: 2 marks for commonality; 2 for comment(s) on this poem and 6 marks for comments on other poem(s).

Reference + basic comment = 1 mark. Reference + detailed comment = 2 marks. Reference + insightful comment may score 3 marks.

See Hint S7.

You may have chosen some of the examples below, although others are possible:

Commonality

- Extended metaphor provides a vehicle for Paterson to develop complex ideas.

Two Trees

- The orange and lemon trees in the poem represent Don Paterson and his friend, Michael Donaghy.
- In the first stanza he describes their burgeoning friendship. This develops until they are lashed 'tight'.
- Donaghy's passing is referenced in the second stanza where a new owner viciously separates the trees. The personification of both trees as they mourn the loss of their connects reflects Paterson's feelings of loss for Donaghy.

The Thread

- In *The Thread* Paterson uses the extended metaphor of an aeroplane/flight to convey his son's birth and early life.
- A plane crash in the opening stanza represents the baby's difficult birth and fragile hold on life.
- Later in the poem, Paterson continues the aeroplane metaphor to illustrate his joy at his family, playing with his sons.

The Ferryman's Arms

- Paterson uses a pool game to represent the journey between life and death.
- A 'remote phosphorescence' draws his character, reminiscent of the light said to be seen at the moment of death.
- He put a 'coin in the tongue' of the pool table, a reference to the penny that must be paid to the ferryman.
- In the second stanza of the poem, Paterson creates a second extended metaphor in the ferry journey he undertakes.
- This is more clearly recognisable as an allegory for death, seen in the Greek myth of Charon. The ferry is the vessel that takes Paterson's soul across the water to the other world.
- The title of the poem also refers to the metaphor, as death can be seen as being taken into the embrace of 'The Ferryman's Arms'.

End of Exam C answers

For advice on the Critical essay section of the exam, see page 262.

Hints and tips

Use these hints and tips to maximise your marks when answering questions.

Reading for Understanding, Analysis and Evaluation

HINT

R1. Looking closely at the wording of this question, you will see that it is designed to **test your understanding of the writer's ideas**. Remember that the context should be read carefully as it may provide clues.

R2. You are expected to **provide relevant quotations from the passage, identify technique(s) used and comment on the effect of their use**. Marks are awarded for these comments, with insightful/detailed comments scoring up to 2 marks. 0 marks are awarded to reference alone.

R3. **Final question**

- Candidates should identify key areas of agreement and/or disagreement in the two passages by referring in detail to both passages.
- There may be some overlap among the areas of agreement. Markers will have to judge the extent to which you have covered two points or one.
- You can use bullet points in this final question, or write a number of linked statements.
- Evidence from the passage may include quotations, but these should be supported by explanations.
- The mark for this question should reflect the quality of response in two areas:
    - identification of the key areas of agreement and/or disagreement in attitude/ideas;
    - level of detail given in support.
- The following guidelines should be used:
    - **5 marks** — comprehensive identification of three or more key areas of agreement with full use of supporting evidence
    - **4 marks** — clear identification of three or more key areas of agreement with relevant use of supporting evidence
    - **3 marks** — identification of three or more key areas of agreement with supporting evidence
    - **2 marks** — identification of two key areas of agreement with supporting evidence
    - **1 mark** — identification of one key area of agreement with supporting evidence
    - **0 marks** — failure to identify any key area of agreement and/or total misunderstanding of task.

Scottish set texts

HINT

S1. This question requires you to **explain** something in the text, proving that you have ***understood*** the writer's ideas. It is best to **use your own words**.

S2. At Higher, you are not allocated marks for quoting alone. You may be allocated 2 marks for an insightful comment with reference to the text. More basic comments with reference to the text will only score 1 mark. Bullet-pointing your answers is helpful.

S3. In 4 mark questions, marks can be allocated in the following ways: 2+2, 2+1+1, 1+1+1+1.

S4. Sentence structure questions require you to **identify the technique** and then to **explain the effect** this has, **linking to the question**. Make sure you cover all three aspects in your answer.

S5. Imagery questions require you to deconstruct the image.

S6. In tone questions, you need to identify the tone, quote an example from the text to support and explain how this quotation creates the tone you have identified. To make sure you get all marks, try setting out your answer in the following way: ***TONE – EXAMPLE – EXPLANATION***.

S7. **10 mark question**

The marks are broken down as follows:

- Up to 2 marks can be awarded for identifying **commonality** between the printed text and other works/wider text.
- A further 2 marks can be achieved for **detailed reference to the extract** given. NOTE: you will not gain a mark simply for quoting here; it is the quality of your explanation that gets the marks.
- 6 additional marks can be awarded for **discussion of similar references to the other work(s)/ wider text**.
  You need to refer to evidence from the text and explain evidence with detailed, insightful explanations may achieve 3 marks; evidence with less detailed answers will achieve 2 marks. Quality comments are rewarded. Do not simply try to score marks by endlessly quoting or retelling the story.

SECTION 2 – Critical essay

Essays are marked according to the supplementary marking grid. Examiners are looking for evidence of:

- your knowledge and understanding of the text
- your ability to analyse comprehensively
- your ability to evaluate and engage with the text in a convincing way
- your ability to be understood at first reading.

When you choose which essay to do in the exam, make sure you understand the question and what your line of argument is. You must **answer the question** throughout the essay. Consistent reference must be made to relevant ideas, not just at the end.

You are not seeking to retell the story in your essay; rather you are explaining **how** the writer conveys their ideas. This is analysis and evaluation.

- **Analysis**
  This is when you deconstruct the writer's language and explain how the language creates effect. You are expected to quote and comment, referring to relevant techniques. Considering the effect of connotations *can* be helpful as can fully deconstructing imagery, particularly in poetry essays. Your analysis should always be focused on the question, otherwise it is irrelevant and will add nothing to your essay.

- **Evaluation**
  This is your engagement with the text. That means you demonstrate and validate your opinions of the text in line with the question. To do this, you need to analyse; the two are closely interrelated. By showing a clear personal response to the text and task, you will be evaluating.

Commonly asked questions

Turning point

To answer this type of question effectively you need to:

- Read the question first – some questions ask you to comment in detail about the build-up to the turning point, others ask you to begin with the turning point itself and then elaborate on the impact.
- You need to show why the turning point is significant, in terms of plot, character and theme. This means you have to bring together ideas neatly and concisely, explaining their importance as you do so.
- In drama questions, remember to consider staging and evaluate its contribution to the turning point.
- You will need to explain what impact the turning point has on the rest of the text (think about character development, relationships, plot, etc.).

Characterisation

To answer this type of question effectively you need to:

- Show an awareness of how the character is presented and how they change or develop throughout the text. This means looking at not only the character's actions and reactions, but examining other characters' reactions to them too, if applicable.
- The skill here is to analyse and show HOW you see the character changing or developing. This means detailed analysis and evaluation of specific key incidents.
- In order to show a change, you need to explain how they are presented initially, before then commenting in depth on how they develop and what factors contribute to that change.
- Often, theme is explored through characterisation. Be mindful of this; it is appropriate to comment on wider themes when discussing the impact of characterisation.

Theme

To answer this type of question effectively you need to:

- Show an awareness of how the theme is developed throughout the **whole** of the text.
- Theme can be shown through characterisation, narrative, language, setting, etc.
- You may wish to focus on **specific characters and/or key moments** in the text.

- In poetry, the writer's techniques in language and structure will be more prominent in driving the theme. Be aware of this and analyse appropriately.
- Successful responses will show thoughtful and sensitive engagement with the theme, evaluating how successfully the writer explores its ideas/concerns.

Comparative questions

To answer this type of question effectively you need to:

- Identify the key points of comparison. This can be similarities and/or differences.
- Ensure you explore the key points successfully in **both** texts. This means analysis of plot/character/language/theme or any other relevant device.
- Evaluation is a strong component in these essays; you are making a judgement about the texts and have to support your views with good, detailed textual evidence and thorough explanation.
- There must be balance in your essay – you should analyse each text equally.